STUDIES IN ENGLISH LITERATURES

Edited by Koray Melikoğlu

Taner Can

Magical Realism in Postcolonial British Fiction
History, Nation, and Narration

STUDIES IN ENGLISH LITERATURES

Edited by Koray Melikoğlu

ISSN 1614-4651

10 *Paola Baseotto*
    "Disdeining life, desiring leaue to die"
    Spenser and the Psychology of Despair
    ISBN 978-3-89821-567-1

11 *Annie Gagiano*
    Dealing with Evils
    Essays on Writing from Africa
    2nd, revised and expanded edition
    ISBN 978-3-89821-867-2

12 *Thomas F. Halloran*
    James Joyce: Developing Irish Identity
    A Study of the Development of Postcolonial Irish Identity in the Novels of James Joyce
    ISBN 978-3-89821-571-8

13 *Pablo Armellino*
    Ob-scene Spaces in Australian Narrative
    An Account of the Socio-topographic Construction of Space in Australian Literature
    ISBN 978-3-89821-873-3

14 *Lance Weldy*
    Seeking a Felicitous Space on the Frontier
    The Progression of the Modern American Woman in O. E. Rölvaag, Laura Ingalls Wilder, and Willa Cather
    ISBN 978-3-89821-535-0

15 *Rana Tekcan*
    The Biographer and the Subject
    A Study on Biographical Distance
    ISBN 978-3-89821-995-2

16 *Paola Brusasco*
    Writing Within/Without/About Sri Lanka
    Discourses of Cartography, History and Translation in Selected Works by Michael Ondaatje and Carl Muller
    ISBN 978-3-8382-0075-0

17 *Zeynep Z. Atayurt*
    Excess and Embodiment in Contemporary Women's Writing
    ISBN 978-3-89821-978-5

18 *Gianluca Delfino*
    Time, History, and Philosophy in the Works of Wilson Harris
    ISBN 978-3-8382-0265-5

19 *Taner Can*
    Magical Realism in Postcolonial British Fiction: History, Nation, and Narration
    ISBN 978-3-8382-0724-7

Taner Can

MAGICAL REALISM
IN POSTCOLONIAL BRITISH FICTION

History, Nation, and Narration

ibidem-Verlag
Stuttgart

Bibliografische Information der Deutschen Nationalbibliothek
Die Deutsche Nationalbibliothek verzeichnet diese Publikation in der Deutschen Nationalbibliografie; detaillierte bibliografische Daten sind im Internet über http://dnb.d-nb.de abrufbar.

Bibliographic information published by the Deutsche Nationalbibliothek
Die Deutsche Nationalbibliothek lists this publication in the Deutsche Nationalbibliografie; detailed bibliographic data are available in the Internet at http://dnb.d-nb.de.

Cover picture: Walter Spies' painting "Iseh im Morgenlicht".
Source: Tropenmuseum of the Royal Tropical Institute (KIT) via Wikimedia Commons.
CC BY-SA 3.0 (s. http://creativecommons.org/licenses/by-sa/3.0/deed.en).

∞

Gedruckt auf alterungsbeständigem, säurefreien Papier
Printed on acid-free paper

ISSN: 1614-4651

ISBN-13: 978-3-8382-0724-7

© *ibidem*-Verlag
Stuttgart 2015

Alle Rechte vorbehalten

Das Werk einschließlich aller seiner Teile ist urheberrechtlich geschützt. Jede Verwertung außerhalb der engen Grenzen des Urheberrechtsgesetzes ist ohne Zustimmung des Verlages unzulässig und strafbar. Dies gilt insbesondere für Vervielfältigungen, Übersetzungen, Mikroverfilmungen und elektronische Speicherformen sowie die Einspeicherung und Verarbeitung in elektronischen Systemen.

All rights reserved. No part of this publication may be reproduced, stored in or introduced into a retrieval system, or transmitted, in any form, or by any means (electronic, mechanical, photocopying, recording or otherwise) without the prior written permission of the publisher. Any person who does any unauthorized act in relation to this publication may be liable to criminal prosecution and civil claims for damages.

Printed in Germany

Table of Contents

Introduction
Novel Beginnings: The Novel and the Nation	1

Chapter 1
From Painting to Literature: A Genealogy of Magical Realism	15

Chapter 2
From Latin America to the Globe: DissemiNation of Magical Realism and the Postcolonial	51

Chapter 3
(Re)claiming Indian Past(s): Postmodern Historiography and Magical Realism in the Indian English Novel	97

Chapter 4
The Yarns of the Black Continent: Magical Realism in the African English Novel	175

Conclusion	231

Works Cited	237

Abbreviations

The following abbreviations have been used.

MC	*Midnight's Children*
GIN	*The Great Indian Novel*
FR	*The Famished Road*
LHAD	*The Last Harmattan of Alusine Dunbar*

Introduction

> What is realized in the novel is the process of coming to know one's own language as it is perceived in someone else's language, coming to know one's own belief system in someone else's system.
> - Mikhail Bakhtin, *The Dialogic Imagination: Four Essays*

Novel Beginnings: The Novel and the Nation

The early twentieth century saw the emergence of a narrative mode, namely magical realism, that seems to resist the very practice of literary categorisation as the discussions as to its origin, conceptual definition and genuine practitioners have not ceased ever since its inception. The ambiguity and confusion surrounding the term do not only stem from the literal oxymoron, magical realism, which suggests a relationship of irreconcilable realms, but also from the intricate history behind it, spanning ninety-five years with three major turning points.[1] Pictorial in origin, the term first appeared in Germany in the 1920s. It was only two years later that it crossed the Atlantic and came to be associated with an innovative literary style in Latin America. By the end of the 1960s, magical realism had already established itself as a literary style unique to Latin American literature, which found its finest expressions in the works of Alejo Carpentier, Jorge Luis Borges, Isabel Allende and Gabriel García Márquez. Starting from the 1980s, magical realism has come to enjoy a global appeal with the rise of postcolonial literatures. Today, it functions as an umbrella term, referring to the characteristics of a literary mode which makes it possible to hold together such a diverse group of writers as Gabriel García Márquez, Ben Okri, Salman Rushdie, Toni Morrison and many others. The present study focuses on

---

[1] It is a common practice among critics working on magical realism to view the evolution of the mode in three phases (Bowers 7, Reeds 175-176).

the last phase of magical realism, that is the postcolonial period, and aims at exploring the cultural work of magical realism in postcolonial Anglophone fiction by specifically pursuing answers to questions related to its widespread popularity in the former colonies. A particular focus of attention is, as the title suggests, the novelistic representations of the nation and history.

The framework of the present study is largely indebted to Mikhail Bakhtin's theory of the novel that he laid out in his famous essays, which were later collected in *The Dialogic Imagination* (1981). Particularly important and relevant to the theoretical framework of this study are Bakhtin's ideas concerning the resolute contemporaneity of the novel, and his emphasis on the necessity to deploy a contextual approach for the study of the novel. Bakhtin states that he decided to formulate his own theory of the novel because of the inadequacy of the existing literary theories to elucidate the profound originality of the genre. For Bakhtin, much of the difficulty of providing a theory of the novel rises from the fact that it is a genre of a new and changing world, and it is "yet uncompleted" and "continues to develop," as he notes in "Epic and Novel" (3). It is precisely this ceaseless process of development that does not allow the novel a fixed generic definition. Bakhtin takes this quality of the novel not as a problem to be overcome, but as its defining characteristic. For Bakhtin, the novel is, above all, "a genre-in-the-making," one in "a living contact with unfinished, still-evolving contemporary reality (the openended present)" (7). Unlike the novel, other genres, such as epic and tragedy, have already lost their literariness and become obsolete. These dead genres "preserve their rigidity and canonic quality in all classical eras of their development; variations from era to era, from trend to trend, or school to school are peripheral and do not affect their ossified generic skeleton" (8).

Bakhtin offers three characteristics to help distinguish the novel in principle from the epic and other obsolete genres,

(1) its stylistic three-dimensionality, which is linked with the multi-languaged consciousness realized in the novel; (2) the radical change it effects in the temporal coordinates of the literary image; (3) the new zone opened by the novel for structuring literary images, namely, the zone of maximal contact with the present (with contemporary reality) in all its openendedness. (11)

These three characteristics are all organically interrelated since they came into being as a result of a significant event in European history: capitalist expansion. For Bakhtin, the rise of the novel coincides with European countries' coming into contact with other cultures and widening their linguistic repertoire. The novel is, as Bakthin puts it, "powerfully affected by a very specific rupture in the history of European civilization: Its emergence from a socially isolated and culturally deaf semi-patriarchal society, and its entrance into international and interlingual contacts and relationships" (11). As a literary outcome of this multitude of different languages, cultures and times, the novel is in a constant flux, "ever questing, ever examining itself and subjecting its established forms to review" (39). The aptness for self-criticism is the source of the novel's immense capacity for change and experimentation, which Bakhtin calls "stylistic three-dimensionality" (39).

Temporality is the central concept in Bakhtin's distinction between the novel and completed genres, including the epic. "In general," Bakhtin notes, "the world of high literature in the classical era was a world projected into the past, on the distanced plane of memory, but not into a real, relative past tied to the present by uninterrupted temporal transitions; it was projected rather into a valorized past of beginnings and peak times" (19). The epic is, by definition, a poem about an absolute past, shared by the collective national memory. However, Bakhtin alerts us to the fact that "'absolute past' is not to be confused with time in our exact and limited sense of the word; it is rather a temporally valorized hierarchical category" (18). Bakhtin believes that the epic depicts a fixed idealised image of the national past, which demands a pious attitude as it is hierarchically above the reader. It is, as he puts it, the world of "firsts" and "bests." (15). It follows that the epic is monochromic since it does not have any organic connections with the present. Although the author and his/her audience share the same temporal plane, the present, "the represented world of the heroes stands on an utterly different and inaccessible time-and-value plane, separated by epic distance" (14). It is, therefore, impossible to rethink and re-evaluate the present in the zone of an absolute distant image created by the epic. It does not serve the future but "the future memory of a past" and therefore the epic creates "a world that is always opposed in principle to any *merely transitory* past" (19 emphasis original).

For Bakhtin, the novel marks the shift of the temporal centre of artistic orientation from the absolute past to living contemporaneity with all its multiplicity. The creative impulse behind the novel is not the memory, but "experience, knowledge and practice (the future)" (15). It is contemporary reality that forms the novel's point of view. Anchored in evolving contemporary reality rather than the distant past, the novel "reflects more deeply, more essentially, more sensitively and rapidly, reality itself in the process of unfolding" (7).[2] According to Bakhtin, it is laughter that destroys the hierarchical epic distance and thus the closed

---

[2] Of course, Bakhtin is not the only critic to draw attention the novel's capacity for change and experimentation. In his *The Sense of an Ending*, Frank Kermode makes a distinction between myth and fiction in a similar fashion to Bakhtin's original argument. For Kermode, both fiction and myth can be seen as explanatory agents of human imagination; however, they differ in their capacity to reflect the changing nature of social reality. According to Kermode, myth is based on "ritual, which presupposes total and adequate explorations of things as they are and were" while fictions serve the purpose of "finding things out, and they change as the needs of sense-making change" (39). Like Bakhtin, Kermode views the novel as an evolving literary genre: "myths are the agents of stability, fictions agents of change. Myths call for absolute, fictions for conditional assent. Myths make sense in terms of a lost order of time […] fictions, if successful, make sense of the here and now […]" (39).

world of the epic: "[t]he 'absolute past' of gods, demigods and heroes is here, in parodies and even more so in travesties, 'contemporized': it is brought low, represented on a plane equal with contemporary life, in an everyday environment, in the low language of contemporaneity" (21). In this narrative plane opened by the novel, different voices, styles, and languages come into play, giving rise to what Bakhtin terms as 'dialogism.' As Bakhtin explains in his *Problems of Dostoyevsky's Poetics*, the term dialogism refers to "a plurality of independent and unmerged voices and consciousnesses, a genuine polyphony of fully valid voices" (6). In stark contrast with the monologism of traditional authorial discourse as in the epic tradition, in dialogic texts characters speak for themselves, representing different social strata and ideological concerns. However, it should be noted that in Bakhtinian theory 'dialogue' does not mean a mere exchange of words or ideas as the everyday use of the word suggests. On the contrary, it entails "a struggle among sociolinguistic points of view" ("Discourse" 273). As an example of dialogic imagination, Bakhtin points to Dostoevsky's ability to create textual spaces in which several voices maintain equal dominance where the contestation among socio-linguistic points of view results in resistance to discursive unities.

In addition to contesting worldviews, the novel also incorporates in its body different types of texts, or in Bakhtin's own words, "extraliterary genres," "the genres of everyday life" and "ideological genres" ("Epic" 33). That is to say, different texts and discourses come into play within the textual plane of the novel, providing a meaningful context for the analysis of the socio-cultural changes taking place in a given society. Bakhtin writes,

> The novel makes wide and substantial use of letters, diaries, confessions, the forms and methods of rhetoric associated with recently established courts and so forth. Since it is constructed in a zone of contact with the incomplete events of a particular

present, the novel often crosses the boundary of what we strictly call fictional literature – making use first of a moral confession, then of a political tract, then of manifestos that are openly political, then degenerating into the raw spirituality of a confession a "cry of the soul" that has not yet found its formal contours [...] *After all, the boundaries between fiction and nonfiction, between literature and nonliterature and so forth are not laid up in heaven. Every specific situation is historical. And the growth of literature is not merely development and change within the fixed boundaries of any given definition; the boundaries themselves are constantly changing.* ("Epic" 33; emphasis added)

Here, Bakhtin anticipates one of the fundamental postulates of poststructuralist theories, such as New Historicism and Cultural Materialism: all texts, literary or non-literary, are part of the same sign system and they are inevitably embedded in a given historical context. This equal weighting between history and literature that rejects any hierarchical separation between the two is succinctly put forward by Louis Montrose in his famous assertion of "the historicity of texts and the textuality of history" (23).[3]

The above excerpt is also important in that it underscores the condition of interdependency among texts, literary or otherwise. It was Julia Kristeva who reformulated the Bakhtinian notion of the dialogic through her semiotic study of text, textuality and their relation to wider ideological structures. According to Kristeva, Bakhtinian theory is characterised

---

[3] Montrose explains that "[b]y the textuality of history, I mean to suggest, firstly, that we can have no access to a full and authentic past, a lived material existence, unmediated by the surviving textual traces of the society in question – traces whose survival we cannot assume to be merely contingent but must rather presume to be at least partially consequent upon complex and subtle social processes of preservation and effacement. Secondly, that those textual traces are themselves subject to subsequent textual mediations when they are construed as the 'documents' upon which historians ground their own text, called 'histories'" (20).

by his conception of "'literary word' as an *intersection of textual surfaces* rather than a point (a fixed meaning), as a dialogue among several writings: that of the writer, the addressee (or the character), and the contemporary or earlier cultural context" (65). In her interpretation of Bakhtin, Kristeva substitutes the concept of literary word with that of text. For Kristeva, the act of writing means interweaving of already existing texts. In other words, the author does not create anything new, but rewrites existing contemporary or earlier texts into his or her own text. Thus, Kristeva concludes that "any text is constructed as a mosaic of quotations; any text is the absorption and transformation of another" (66). In the Bakhtinian theory of dialogism and its extension in Kristeva's intertextuality, the novel with its ability to incorporate different texts and discourses in its textual body stands as a quintessential register of humankind's social and political existence and its attendant problems.

It is difficult to subscribe to some of Bakhtin's ideas concerning the novel, for instance his proposition that the novel is the sole genre that continues to develop, or that the novel does not have a generic canon of its own. However, his proposition of the novel as a critical cultural medium for tracing social and cultural changes in history is still relevant and widely influential today. In keeping with Bakhtinian theory, the novel in this study is taken to mean a historically engaged explanatory genre, which in its attempt to describe an evolving contemporary reality challenges and subverts the established paradigms of knowledge and perception.

Described by Mikhail Bakhtin as a literary genre most sensible to social and historical changes, the novel came to the fore in the emerging postcolonial literatures in the second half of the twentieth century. The 1950s and the 1960s witnessed a period of rapid decolonisation as colonial countries one after another gained independence through a process of anti-colonial resistance that ranged from legal and diplomatic manoeuvres to wars of independence (Mishra and Hodge 282). In the early phases of decolonisation, postcolonial writers saw literature as yet another means of national self-assertion through which they could reclaim their past overshadowed by European interpretation. To this end, writers, poets and playwrights alike turned to their pre-colonial cultural heritage and endeavoured to help reconstruct themselves as the subjects of their own histories. The novel became a major agent in the process of forging national consciousness in the wake of new nation states. In "The National Longing for Form," Timothy Brennan notes,

> Nations [...] are imaginary constructs that depend for their existence on an apparatus of cultural fictions in which imaginative literature plays a decisive role. And the rise of European nationalism coincides especially with one form of literature – the novel.
>
> It was the *novel* that historically accompanied the rise of nations by objectifying the 'one, yet many' of national life, and by mimicking the structures of the nation, a clearly bordered jumble of languages and styles. Socially, the novel joined the newspaper as the major vehicle of the national print media, helping to standardize language, encourage literacy, and remove mutual incomprehensibility. But it did more than that. Its manner of presentation allowed people to imagine the special community that was the nation. (173; emphasis original)

Brennan proceeds to argue that "it is especially in Third World countries after the Second World War that the fictional uses of 'nation' and 'nationalism' are most pronounced" (170).[4] As such, the postcolonial novel with its rich thematic concerns and strong historical rootedness has

---

[4] Brennan's argument as to the nation as a fabrication is indebted to Benedict Anderson's seminal study *Imagined Communities: Reflections on the Origin and Spread of Nationalism*. For further discussion on the nation as an imagined community as well as the relationship between the novel and the nation, see Benedict Anderson.

brought literary studies an exciting dynamism in the last forty years or so, serving as one of its central mobilising tropes.

The novelistic representation of national identity has changed along with the question of what constituted that identity. In the early independence period, the nationalist ideologies in former colonies adopted an essentialist outlook, rejecting the influence of the colonial culture to a great extent. However, as people have become more attuned to a multicultural postcolonial perspective, an awareness of cultures and identities as heterogeneous hybrids, inseparable from the influence of the colonising culture, has grown stronger. The transformation in the novelistic representations of the nation followed a similar course. Nineteenth-century realism dominated the early period of the postcolonial novel, giving rise to a large body of works that tend to promote the pre-colonial indigenous culture as authentic. Concomitant with the advent of postcolonial theories that see postcolonial cultural identity essentially as a combination of the indigenous people and the coloniser's cultural practices, magical realism replaced conventional realism as the dominant mode of literary representation (Ashcroft *at al., Key* 21-22). As Maggie Anne Bowers points out, many postcolonial critics have come to see magical realism as "a highly appropriate and significant concept for cultural production created in the context of increasing heterogeneity and cross-culturalism at the end of the twentieth century and into the twenty-first" (6).[5]

The mode's capacity to represent hybrid identities seems to lie in the definition of the term itself. A basic definition of magical realism, Christopher Warnes notes, "sees it as a mode of narration that naturalizes or normalizes the supernatural; that is to say, a mode in which real and fantastic, natural and supernatural, are coherently represented in a state of rigorous equivalence – neither has a greater claim to truth or referentiali-

---

[5] Similarly, both Jean-Pierre Durix and Steven Slemon see magical realism as one of the most appropriate literary modes for the representation of "hybrid" postcolonial culture (Durix *Mimesis* 152; Slemon, "Magic" 411).

ty" (2). The two opposing narrative elements, the realistic and the fantastic, are presented in a harmonious integrity so that the supernatural in the text seems to grow out of everyday reality. As a fusion of traditionally incompatible fictional worlds, magical realism is thought to reflect the situation of peoples from former colonies living in an essentially hybrid cultural environment where the elements of indigenous cultural heritage such as myths, legends and folk tales and those of the coloniser's exist side by side. Critics like Brenda Cooper, Elleke Boehmer and Stephen Slemon, among others, consider magical realism as a decolonising agent that gives voice to the suppressed or silenced communities. They maintain that there is a natural correlation between the formal characteristics of the mode and its cultural work. For instance, Elleke Boehmer succinctly summarises the relationship between magical realism and postcolonialism as follows:

> Drawing on the special effects of magic realism, postcolonial writers in English are able to express their view of a world fissured, distorted, and made incredible by cultural displacement. […] [T]hey combine the supernatural with local legend and imagery derived from colonialist cultures to represent societies which have been repeatedly unsettled by invasion, occupation, and political corruption. Magic effects, therefore, are used to indict the follies of both empire and its aftermath. (*Colonial* 235)

In more recent scholarship, however, it has been acknowledged that magical realism should be regarded as a global literary phenomenon whose roots can be found in different cultural and literary traditions. For instance, Anne C. Hegerfeldt claims that "[t]o disconnect magic realism from postcolonial literatures is not to say that the mode is not essentially a postcolonial one. In challenging the rational-empirical world-view's claim to hegemony and revaluing alternative modes of thought, magic realism pursues decidedly postcolonial aims" (303). In keeping with this view, the scope of the present study is not restricted to postcolonial literatures and extends to a discussion of magical realism as a global literary mode. In other words, magical realism, in this exegesis, is not treated as a strictly postcolonial literary narrative mode, and its relation to postcolonial literatures, particularly its cultural work as a decolonising agent, is investigated in a longer historical perspective and a broader literary context.

Accordingly, the aim of this study is twofold: (i) to survey the historical evolution of magical realism from its pictorial origins to the present in order to identify the characteristics of the mode that make its wide dissemination and appropriation in different cultural contexts possible, (ii) to delineate the place of magical realism in postcolonial Anglophone fiction through analyses of four novels selected from the two major postcolonial locations, India and Africa: Salman Rushdie's *Midnight's Children* (1981), Shashi Tharoor's *The Great Indian Novel* (1989) from postcolonial Indian literature; Ben Okri's *The Famished Road* (1991) and Syl Cheney-Coker's *The Last Harmattan of Alusine Dunbar* (1990) from postcolonial African literature. Given the impossibility of comprehensive coverage of magical realist writing, the present study is necessarily and unavoidably selective in its attempt to discuss the mode in relation to postcolonial literature. The above-mentioned four novels are not, of course, the only texts that could be chosen, and they should not be treated as paradigmatic of postcolonialism. Nor do they represent the wide-ranging magical realist writing in an exhaustive fashion. Rather, it is their shared thematic concerns and technical experimentation with magical realism that bind these novels together as a meaningful group of texts to be studied in a single framework. In sum, the selected novels technically reflect the generic characteristics of magical realism as a literary mode, and thematically they are endowed with postcolonial issues of culture, identity and nationality and therefore present a compelling context for a study of this highly problematic literary mode.

Magical realism, like other literary modes, such as allegory and satire, has been adopted and modified by writers and critics in order to articulate a wide range of political, social and cultural realities. The cultural work of magical realism has also evolved and diversified along with its historical development, turning it into one of the most complicated and disputed literary terms. The present study does not seek to settle the ongoing debates around magical realist literature by offering a restrictive definition for the term. Such a project is doomed to failure given the intricate history and theoretical background of the mode. It is therefore necessary to turn to the history of the term in order to understand how and why it has taken on its current meanings and implications. To this end, chapter 1, "From Painting to Literature: A Genealogy of Magical Realism," surveys the development of magical realism from its origin in European painting to its appropriation into literature by European and Latin American writers and critics. The contested definitions of magical realism and critical questions surrounding these are also explored here. In an attempt to conclude the survey commenced in chapter 1, the remainder of the study focuses on the last phase in the development of magical realism, namely the postcolonial period, and aims at studying the relationship between magical realism and representations of postcolonial identity in Anglophone Indian and African novels. Chapter 2, "From Latin America to the Globe: DissemiNation of Magical Realism," provides historical contextualisation for the discussion of the selected novels, outlining the generic and thematic preoccupations in postcolonial literatures in Africa and India immediately before and after independence. Then, it proceeds to analyse the relation between the paradigmatic transformation in postcolonial studies and the concomitant rise of magical realism as the literary expression of Third World countries. This chapter also provides a brief history of postcolonial studies and specifies terminology related to the field of study with particular attention to the difference among such terms as "commonwealth," "postcolonial" and "neo-colonial." Chapters 3 and 4 are devoted to a thorough analysis of the selected novels. The main focus of attention in these chapters will be the ways in which the novelists in question have exploited magical realism to represent their national identities and history. The conclusion brings together debates conducted in the course of the research work and attempts to provide some insights that may help to understand the cultural work of magical realism in postcolonial Anglophone fiction.

Chapter 1
From Painting to Literature: A Genealogy of Magical Realism

> Reality is not always probable, or likely.
> - Jorge Luis Borges

It seems that the term magical realism, as Frederick Jameson puts it, has "a strange seductiveness" (302), for despite all the terminological and conceptual problems, it has survived as one of the key literary concepts. It can now be found in university curricula, theses, dissertations and academic articles. It has also received significant attention in popular culture, particularly in children's literature and cinema. As the theoretical attempts to pin down the concept have proved to be inconclusive, critics have subsequently come to acknowledge the fact that the usefulness and popularity of the term is due in large measure to its elusive conceptual definition and complex history. The task of defining magical realism, therefore, entails tracing the genealogy of the term first in the context of European art and then in Latin American and postcolonial literatures respectively. Such a survey with special emphasis on the nuances between the applications of the term in different contexts as well as its development through history will allow the fundamental nature of magical realist literature to be revealed.

One of the main sources of confusion surrounding the term seems to be taxonomy. Different labels have been offered to define the works of art and literature that have come to be classified under the rubric of magical realism: "magic realism," "new objectivity," and "*lo real maravilloso americano*" (the American marvellous real). While some critics make subtle distinctions between these terms in order to eschew obfuscation, others use them indiscriminately to refer to both works of art and literature. Maggie Ann Bowers, for example, employs "magic realism" and "magical realism" in different contexts: the former refers to paintings and the latter to literary works, particularly fiction. Bowers offers the catch-all term "magic(al) realism" to refer to works of art and literature where they have common features (3). However, most of the scholars and critics whose works were consulted in the course of the present study tend to use the two terms interchangeably, which indicates the fact that the terms "magic realism" and "magical realism" have conflated in theoretical use. It is interesting to note that the use of the term can vary within the same critical work. For instance, although Lois P. Zamora and Wendy B. Faris, the editors of *Magical Realism: Theory, History, Community,* favoured "magical realism" for the title of their study of the mode, the contributors to the compendium employed both terms, "magic realism" and "magical realism," interchangeably in their analysis of literary works. In the present study, the mode, as indicated in the title, shall be referred to as "magical realism" in the context of literature except when other sources are quoted verbatim. The term "magic realism" shall be used specifically in art-historical context in keeping with Wendy B. Faris" translation of the term from German *Magischer Realismus* into English as "magic," not "magical" realism. The other related terms, such as "new objectivity," and *"lo real maravilloso americano"* shall be examined within their specific historical contexts.

    The changes the term underwent were not limited to taxonomy. Although certain traits of its pictorial origin have stayed with the term along the way, magical realism has gained new connotations as it has been (re)located geographically and (re)defined theoretically. Each variation of the term, despite certain common features, has its own history and conceptual definition, making it almost impossible to scribe a unified history for such an immense artistic phenomenon. There have been numerous attempts to unravel the complexity of the term. Perhaps the most interesting of such attempts was the International Congress of Latin American Literature (*Congreso Internacional de Literatura Iberoamericana*) held at Michigan University in 1974. The declared objective of the congress was to reach a standard definition of the term, thereby resolving the discrepancies in its theoretical use and application.

The participants' efforts were, however, inconclusive. In the course of the congress it became clear that such a scheme was not applicable to magical realism, an international artistic phenomenon with several different locations, theoretical models and a vast number of practitioners. Nine years after the congress, Seymour Menton writes in recollection, "many papers were read, heated discussions ensued, and some scholars even argued that, because of the lack of agreement, the term should be eliminated completely" (*Magic* 9).[6]

There is also a disparity of views among scholars and critics with regard to the classification of magical realism whether as a genre or as a mode. This seemingly trivial disagreement is, in fact, of great significance since the literary classification of magical realism should account for its capacities for adaptation to various generic, cultural and other conditions of expression. In her seminal study, *Magical Realism and the Fantastic*, Amaryll Chanady contends that magical realism should be classified as a literary mode rather than a genre, making a distinction between the two based on their ability to articulate the characteristics of literary categories that transcend historical and national boundaries. Chanady argues that a genre is "a well-defined and historically identifiable form," whereas a mode is a "particular quality of a fictitious world that can characterize works belonging to several genres, periods or national literatures" (*Magical* 1-2). Similarly, Maggie Anne Bowers points out that "[t]he flexibility of the mode resides in the fact that it is not a genre belonging to one particular era, and therefore is not related to a particular critical approach" (63). This distinction also provides the

---

[6] Critics almost customarily begin their studies of the mode by stating that magical realism is a notoriously difficult concept to define mainly because of its complex history. For instance, Roberto González Echevarría finds it difficult to validate a "true history" of the concept (112). Irene Guenther notes, "the fluidity of boundaries, the ambiguity of definitions, and the sometimes untraceable transformation of concepts, conjecture and fact have intertwined in the history of Magical Realism and its eventual dissemination. In effect, Roh's artistic child of the 1920s has become a present-day historian's nightmare" (34). For an extended discussion of the definition problem, see Kenneth Reeds.

grounds for understanding the appearance of magical realism in different forms of art, such as painting, cinema and literature, its global appeal and above all, the critical tendency to trace its origins back in the oral literature.[7] In view of its ability to transcend genres, schools, movements and national boundaries, magical realism shall be referred to as a literary and when appropriate, as an artistic mode in the present study.

The term "magic realism" entered the cultural lexicon in 1925 with the publication of the German art historian Franz Roh's (1890-1965) seminal study entitled *Nach-Expressionismus, Magischer Realismus: Probleme der neuesten europäischen Malerei (Post-expressionism, Magic Realism: Problems of the Most Recent European Painting)*.[8] Roh coined the term to describe a new tendency flourishing in European painting after Expressionism, which he labelled *Magischer Realismus* (magic realism). Roh was not the only intellectual interested in the changes European painting was undergoing. In 1923, two years before the publication of Roh's book, Gustav Hartlaub (1884-1963), the director of the Mannheim museum, recognised the significance of the emerging artistic trend and offered the name "Neue Sachlichkeit" (New Objectivity) for it. He also organised an exhibition with the same name that would travel Germany to introduce and popularise the representative works of the new art. Hartlaub's new objectivity overshadowed Roh's magic realism as the more popularly recognised name for the art form until around the 1960s. Ultimately, it has been Roh and not Hartlaub, who is predominantly remembered as the initial theoretician of magical

---

[7] In their introduction to *Magical Realism: Theory, History, Community*, Lois P. Zamora and Wendy B. Faris consider magical realism as "an international commodity" that has a long tradition, "beginning with the masterful interweavings of magical and real in the epic and chivalric traditions and continuing in the precursors of modern prose fiction – *the Decameron, The Thousand and One Nights, Don Quixote*" (2).

[8] In 1798 the German Romantic poet and philosopher, Novalis, used the term 'magical realist' to describe "a 'true prophet' or an 'isolated being' who would not be bound by the limits that govern the lives of ordinary humans" (qtd. in Walter 2). Since Novalis' definition is related to philosophy rather than art, his ideas are not given any space or not generally discussed at length in the studies of magical realism as a literary mode.

realism, for his ideas played a crucial role in the conceptualisation of magical realism first in the sphere of art and then in literature.[9]

Magic realism was not an art movement in the sense that it was pronounced by a cohesive group of artists with a manifesto; it was rather the predominant artistic style of the early 1920s that appeared under different labels in several countries, including Austria, Holland, Italy, France and Russia (Guenther 44-45; Bowers 11). The common denominator that held this large of group artists together was their repudiation of Expressionism. Hence, Roh did not attempt to formulate a strict conceptual definition for the term. Instead, he tried to identify the new art's points of departure from the tenets of Expressionism. As Lois P. Zamora and Wendy B. Faris point out in their note to the excerpt from Franz Roh's theoretical writing, for Roh magic realism, above all, signified "a return to Realism after Expressionism's more abstract style" (15). Contrary to Expressionism that "shows an exaggerated preference for fantastic, extraterrestrial, remote objects [… and] resorts to the everyday and the commonplace for the purpose of distancing it, investing it with a shocking exoticism," magic realism is more sober in subject matter and representational in style (Roh 16). The abandonment of the religious and transcendental themes in favour of the familiar and the mundane has become the hallmark of magic realist art; a fact also evident in Roh's own study. "Our real world re-emerges before our eyes," Roh rejoices as he writes after a decade of Expressionist interval (17).

Interested in the aesthetic qualities of the new art more than its historical background, Roh dispenses with the context in which magic realism developed in only a few lines. When explaining the difference between magic realism and Expressionism, Roh writes, "instead of the remote horrors of hell, the inextinguishable horrors of our own time" were drawn onto the canvas (17). What Roh referred to as "the inextinguisha-

---

[9] There is a clear consensus among the majority of contemporary critics, such as Amaryll Chanady, Seymour Menton, Maggie Ann Bowers, Lois P. Zamora and Wendy B. Faris about the inception of magic realism and its application in an art-historical context.

ble horrors of our time" was the realities of post-war Germany. Unlike Roh, the later critics have become increasingly interested in the historical context of magic realism, for they tend to view the artists' departure from abstract aesthetic forms as a response to the unprecedented destruction caused by the First World War. Maggie Anne Bowers, for example, argues that "democratically distanced from the rest of Europe and caught between the demolition of their old world and the uncertainty of the future, a desire for *"Sachlichkeit"* [Objectivity] was the growing focus of the nation" (8). This desire found its expression in art in the form of magic realist paintings, which Franz Roh describes as "the mirror of palpable exteriority" (18). Magic realists concentrated on urban themes and used them to offer social and political criticism of the difficult situation in which Germany found herself during the period between the World Wars (Bowers 43-44).

The works of art produced by the magic realists were found "degenerate" by the Nazi standards. Several painters such as Max Beckmann, Max Ernst, Otto Dix and George Grosz, whose works Roh included in his book, were accused of being Bolshevists by the Nazi Chamber of Culture and prohibited from exhibiting their paintings. Hartlaub was removed from his position as museum director and Roh, denounced as a cultural Bolshevist, was taken to the Dachau concentration camp in 1933 only to be released with the intercession of a respected friend (Guenther 55). Certainly, the Nazi reaction to magic realist artists cannot be interpreted as a typical reception of the mode in other countries. It, nevertheless, pinpoints an important fact: magical realism is from the outset associated with socio-political agendas. The ability of magic realism to provide political criticism and social commentary would proliferate after its appropriation into literature. Lois P. Zamora and Wendy B. Faris, for example, define magical realism as a literary mode "suited to exploring – and transgressing boundaries – whether the boundaries are ontological, political, geographical, or generic" (Zamora and Faris 5). Similarly, Brenda Cooper notes, "[m]agical realism at its best opposes fundamentalism and purity; it is at odds with racism, ethnicity and the quest for tap roots, origins and homogeneity" (22). Its resistance to and refusal of monologic political and cultural structures offers a possible explanation for the widespread popularity of the mode in postcolonial countries and Latin America.

Another aspect of the pictorial origin of the term that has proved its relevance to literary studies is its innovative spirit. Notwithstanding its return to a more representational style, magic realism was, as Roh notes, "still alien to the current idea of Realism," and it was to the admirers of nineteenth-century Realism "as inappropriate as Expressionism itself" (Roh 17). The artists whom Roh listed in his book as magic realists produced paintings anchored in the objective world, but they did not reproduce nature like photography. Instead, they reconstructed the external reality through spiritual phenomenon. "For the new art," Roh asserts, "it is a question of representing before our eyes, in an intuitive way, *the fact, the interior figure, of the exterior world*" (24; emphasis original). Whilst using real objects and familiar scenes as their starting point, the artists tried to show the hidden behind the surface of things and offered "a magical gaze opening onto a piece of mildly transfigured reality" (Roh 20). The "magic" of the binominal denotes the innovative characteristics of this new artistic mode that shows a significant deviation from the mimetic tradition with its intuitive recreation of objects.

As an art historian, Roh regards the innovative strand of magic realist painting as an endeavour to overcome the limitations of "simple external imitation" produced by then-new art forms, which he refers to as "marvellous machines (photography and film) that imitate reality so incomparably well" (25). Following Roh's lead, it can be argued that the innovative spirit of magic realism is an attempt to revitalise realistic conventions, made *impasse* by the new art forms, through technical experimentation. Magic realists, according to the art historian Irene Guenther, set out to reach a new definition of the object through "clinically dissected, coldly accentuated, microscopically delineated" painting (36). Exposing objects down to their minute details, this intensified realism, in turn, paradoxically gives the picture a sense of unreality. In other words, unlike Expressionism that completely rejects art's traditional figurative concepts, experimentalism inherent in magic realism works from within the conventions of realism. This also holds true for magical realist literature. "Magical realism," Wendy B. Faris asserts, "radically modifies and replenishes the dominant mode of realism in the West, challenging its basis of representation from within" (*Ordinary* 1).[10]

The concept of "magic" in magic realism, then, does not denote the fantastic or supernatural; on the contrary, it belongs to the phenomenal world and is captured in the course of artistic creation. It is for this reason that Roh does not describe "magic" in metaphysical terms. "With the word "magic,"" Roh urges, "as opposed to "mystic," I wished to indicate that the mystery does not descend to the represented world, but rather hides and palpitates behind it" (16). Roh's definition provides another important link between magic realist painting and magical realist literature. With this definition, Roh, as Zamora and Faris note, "anticipates the practice of contemporary magical realists" who treat the supernatural as part of everyday life in their novels (15). In magical realist narratives, the improbable or the fantastic events are presented as an integral part of everyday life and narrated in a matter-of-fact style.

The magic realist artists, as noted above, did not have a coherent style. It was their search for a new kind of realism rather than an easily recognisable uniform style that identified them as the representatives of the same artistic phenomenon. The major reason for this stylistic varia-

---

[10] This tendency to subvert the conventional realism leads critics to align technical aspects of magical realist literary works with modernism and postmodernism. In *Ordinary Enchantments: Magical Realism and the Remystification of Narrative,* Wendy B. Faris locates magical realism at the intersection of modernism and postmodernism: "the epistemological concerns, along with the mythic elements, the primitivism, the psychological interiors and depths, align magical realism with much of modernism; the ontological questions raised by the presence of magical events, and the confrontations between different worlds and discourses, together with the collective spirit and political pointedness of the writing, align it with postmodernism" (32-33).

tion seems to be the fact that magic realism began as a hybrid style, embodying the characteristics of both realism and the experimental art movements before it. Kenneth Reeds maintains, "magical realism was a return to reality, but not simply going back to the realism which existed before Expressionism – a homecoming which carried with it the baggage from the trip through Expressionism's existential voyage – a mix of wild flights anchored in reality" (178). Like their predecessors in art, magical realist writers vary in their stylistic inclinations. Magical realism, which Wendy Faris refers to as "[p]erhaps the most important contemporary trend in international fiction," found expression in diverse cultures in different fashions (*Ordinary* 1). It is, therefore, almost impossible to formulate a standard definition of magical realism to include all its stylistic variations; a fact that both enriches and complicates the mode.

In the light of what has been said so far, it can be argued that the pictorial origin of magic realism is crucial to the term's contemporary relevance in literary context not only because it marks the inception of the term historically, but also because the early denotation of the term in the context of art provides a solid theoretical ground for literary studies. There seem to be three major characteristics of magic realism in its art-historical context that anticipate the application of the term in literature. Firstly, magic realism began as a socially and historically conscious, if not overtly political, form of art. Turning away from the fantastic dreamscape of Expressionism, the artists produced paintings with social contents. Secondly, magic realism is an innovative artistic mode that works from within the conventions of realism in order to revitalise its exhausted artistic potential through experimentation. Last but not least, as a result of its hybrid theoretical foundation and stylistic variations among its practitioners, magic realism, from its inception, has strongly defied easy categorisation. The remaining portion of this chapter shall focus on the ways in which the two essential strands of magic realism, its cultural work of providing socio-political criticism and innovative spirit, have evolved after its appropriation into literature with special emphasis placed on the contested theoretical attempts aimed at defining the ever broadening margins of the concept.

The initial influence of Roh's art-historical argument on literary studies was seen in Italy. Massimo Bontempelli (1878-1960), a prominent critic of the time and the editor of the literary review *900 (Novecento)*, forged a theory and practice of *realismo magico* (magical realism). Writing essays on the new art almost simultaneously as Roh, Bontempelli is generally credited as the first critic to use the term in the context of literature (Faris, *Ordinary* 39; Bowers 12; Warnes 4; Guenther 60, Walter 13). It should, however, be noted in passing that the transposition of the concept into literature was not completely realised until its introduction to Latin America, where several acknowledged masterpieces of the mode were written. Bontempelli's formulation of magical realism echoes that of Roh's with his emphasis on the necessity of discovering the magic quality of everyday life. According to Seymour Menton, Bontempelli viewed magical realism as a narrative mode that "rejects both reality for the sake of reality and fantasy for the sake of fantasy, and lives with the sense of magic discovered in the daily life of human beings and things" (*Magic* 131). In spite of their similar theoretical views, Bontempelli and Roh differ in their artistic methods. While Roh, as mentioned before, endeavours to reveal the magic in everyday life through estrangement of the familiar, Bontempelli seeks the same effect in the reconciliation of the real and the miraculous (Walter 13).

The Fascist ideals had a central place in Bontempelli's theory of magical realism. "Fascist Italy," as Keala Jewell notes, "became the model in [Bontempelli's] view for a new European collectivity rooted in Latin and Mediterranean culture (Italy being the link)" (288). He believed that myths were instrumental in creating a collective identity. In keeping with this view, Bontempelli defined the writer's task in modern society as "the invention of new myths" (Jewell 288) and the prime function of a properly modern literature as "[acting] on the collective consciousness by opening new mythical and magical perspectives on reality" (Dombroski 522). His call for creating new myths was more like an expansion of his Fascist historical vision than a purely literary exercise. According to Bontempelli, there were three epochs of history: classical (from Homer to Christ), romantic (from Christ to World War I) and Fascist (starting from World War I). In the Fascist epoch, the creation of modern myths was imperative to help humankind rise out of its ashes after the First World War. The new myths, reflecting the renovating power of Fascism, would mark this rebirth and herald the new era. Therefore, Bontempelli urged the writers not to imitate old myths and naïve imaginings, but to create a new, self-conscious idea of primitivism (Witt 109-110).

Bontempelli's ideas concerning the promotion of a collective European cultural identity and his critique of twentieth-century literary practices consolidated into an influential critical voice in Italy between the First and Second World Wars (Jewell 286). However, contemporary critics attribute varying significance to Bontempelli's place in the history of magical realism. Some critics, for example, point out his pivotal role in spreading Roh's ideas in Europe with his bilingual magazine, relegating him to a position of secondary importance (Guenther 60, Hegerfeldt 15). For other critics like Erik Camayd-Freixas, however, "Bontempelli is a more relevant figure than Roh to magical realism's genealogy in terms of both concept (the reconciliation of the everyday and the miraculous; but also "conscious primitivism") and terminology (the specific use of the phrase itself)" (qtd. in Warnes 4). Both arguments are equally valid in their own right, but for the scope of this study, the most significant contribution of Bontempelli's work to the history of magical realism is his intention to employ the mode to create a collective cultural identity which would become the central tenet of Latin American magical realist writers in the second half of the twentieth century.

As Anne C. Hegerfeldt notes, "[a]fter its brief flourishing in the 1920s, the term seems to have languished in comparative disuse" (15).

Magical realism resurfaced in the 1940s in Latin America with the publication of numerous magical realist works of literature, which, according to most critics, marks the second phase in the genealogy of term (Echevarría 109, Reeds 179, Bowers 7). In fact, Franz Roh's ideas had been introduced to Latin America two decades earlier, in 1927, with the partial translation and publication of his book in José Ortega y Gasset's *Revista de Occidente*. With this translation, the term did not only cross the Atlantic, but it was also transferred from the domain of art to that of literature. In the years to follow, the term was applied in variations to describe works of literature, particularly fiction, rather than paintings.

Although based in Madrid, *Revista de Occidente* helped the term's dissemination in Latin America as it was circulated widely among Latin American writers as the primary source for texts translated from European languages (Bowers 12, Reeds 179-180). That the term magical realism started to be used in the literary circles of Buenos Aires as early as 1928 to describe certain European novels is a clear indication of the sphere of influence of Gasset's magazine (Spindler 76-77, Reeds 180).[11] In the ensuing years, however, the application of the term changed completely with the influence of the theoretical works written by Arturo Uslar Pietri, Alejo Carpentier and Ángel Flores, and it started to be employed in a strictly national context to define and label the works of literature produced by Latin American writers. It is, therefore, pertinent to draw an outline of the cultural atmosphere in which Franz Roh's magic realism was transposed into its new context prior to the discussion of theories produced by Latin American writers and critics.

Historically, the introduction of magical realism into Latin American literature coincided with the early stages of the post-colonial experience of Latin American nations when writers and intellectuals were in search

---

[11] Here, Kenneth Reeds bases his argument on an anecdote where "Enrique Anderson Imbert recalled having heard of a friend tell him as early as 1928 in one of the literary cafes that Jean Cocteau's novel *Les Enfantes Terribles* was completely magical-realist" (180). The same anecdote is also cited in Imbert's book titled *El Realismo mágico Y Otros Ensayos*.

of ways of constructing an autonomous cultural identity. As European countries, particularly Spain, were losing their colonial power, several Latin American countries started to demand their political and cultural independence. The literary critic Jean Franco points to three vast and momentous historical events in the early twentieth century that raised national consciousness among Latin American countries: the First World War (1914-1918) and the socialist revolutions in Mexico (1910-1917) and Russia (1917). Politically, these events "marked the end of European hegemony," inspiring a new faith among Latin Americans (Franco 193). Culturally, they posed the fact that "the era of imitating Europe ended," and Spanish Americans "stood on their own feet" (Franco 193-194). Dominated by the efforts of formation and consolidation of modern nation states, this era in Latin American history is generally referred to as the national period.[12] Franco lists five key notions influential in the national period, two of which are particularly important in explaining the underlying motivations behind the promotion of magical realism as a distinctly national literary style:

> (1) The belief that literature was an agent of national integration and that through it, divergent areas and peoples could be brought into the stream of national culture, (2) The recognition that American racial mixtures and landscapes were totally different from those of Europe and a new approach was needed if literature was to be an expression of this experience (193-194).

Magical realism with its ability to juxtapose alternative perceptions of reality and history and more particularly with its affiliation to myths,

---

[12] José Carlos Mariátegui summarises the stages in the development of Spanish American literature as: "a colonial period, a cosmopolitan period, and a national period. During the first, a people are in terms of their literature nothing but a colony, a dependency of another. During the second, they assimilate simultaneously elements of diverse foreign literatures. In the third, their own personality and their own feelings achieve a well-modulated expression" (qtd. in González 239).

folklore and legends provided Latin American writers the cultural catalyst they were seeking. As such, magical realism became the dominant narrative style among Latin American writers from 1940 to 1970, giving rise to the production of an unprecedented number of novels.

This immensely creative and prolific period in Latin American literature was given the self-explanatory name *el boom* (the Boom).[13] The most significant achievement of the Boom writers was the internationalisation of Latin American literature. Up until the 1960s, Latin American literature did not have a wide recognition; it was not highly publicised or taught in the academia. "The Boom," Stephen M. Hart notes, "centring on writers such as Gabriel García Márquez, Julio Cortázar, Carlos Fuentes and Mario Vargas Llosa – signalled the definitive birth of Spanish American literature, thrusting it to the centre of the world's literary stage" (121). The common traits of the Boom texts were questioning of the linear concept of time, acceptance of magic as part of everyday life and extensive use of myths, folklores and legends (Ching *et al.* 59). Like Bontempelli, they recognised the ability of magical realism to create a collective cultural identity through myths and legends, and claimed it to be an authentic product of Latin America. Although numerous writers and critics have made contributions to the appropriation of the term into an exclusively Latin American context, there are three major figures that need to be discussed at length here, for their arguments have also had a decisive impact on the evolution of magical realism as an internationally recognised literary mode: Alejo Carpentier, Ángel Flores and Luis Leal.

While Arturo Uslar Pietri is generally credited as the first critic to apply the term to Latin American literature in his 1948 book *Letras y hombres de Venezuela* (*Letters and People of Venezuela*)[14], it is his con-

---

[13] In the critical works on Latin American literature, magical realism and the Boom are generally treated as synonyms (Ching *et al*, 270).

[14] Pietri's definition of magical realism is rather vague: "What became prominent in the short story and left an indelible mark there was the consideration of man as a mystery surrounded by realistic facts. A poetic prediction or denial of reality. What for lack of another name could be called a magical realism!" (qtd. in Leal 120).

temporary Alejo Carpentier, who is acknowledged as the most influential figure in the formation of a Latin American understanding of magical realism. Both writers lived in Paris in the 1920s and 1930s, and they returned to their countries, having been influenced by European artistic movements of the time, namely magical realism and surrealism. However, they used the knowledge and experience they acquired in their ten-year residence in Europe to devise a new form of magical realism unique to Latin America. At the foundation of their theories, as later explained by Uslar Pietri, was "the notion of a particular condition of the American world that could not be reduced to any European model" (qtd. in Reeds 182).[15] By claiming the sole right of a distinctly Latin American magical realism, they shifted the emphasis Roh placed on the aesthetic and stylistic features of the mode to political and cultural issues, which would dominate much of the discussion on the mode in its second phase.

Indeed, looking at the theoretical work produced by Carpentier, it can be argued that he worked almost as a cultural archaeologist as he did not endeavour to create a genuine literary theory, but to discover what, he believed, had always been there since the beginning of Latin American history: *lo real maravilloso americano* (the American marvellous real). With this term, Carpentier referred to the unique historical and cultural heritage of Latin America, in which he saw the possibility of establishing a national literary tradition. As a culturally specific term, it also helped Carpentier to mark the decisive rupture with the European models that had dominated Latin American literary studies until that time. The term appeared for the first time in an essay published in the Caracas newspaper *El Nacional* on 8 April 1948, which was reprinted as a prologue to his novel *El Reino de Este Mundo* (*The Kingdom of This World*) in 1949 (Hegerfeldt 17). Paradoxically, the prologue that Carpentier proposed as the manifesto of the distinctively Latin American narrative

---

[15] Reeds cited the sentence verbatim: "la noción de una condición peculiar del mundo americano que no era posible reducir a ningún modelo europeo" (translation mine).

style became a fundamental document of the internationally celebrated phenomenon of magical realism, recurrently cited in the bibliographies and anthologies of the mode. Similarly, his marvellous real came to be used as a synonym for magical realism.

Carpentier's prologue reads like a travelogue where he relates his observations in several Asian and European countries and employs these to establish points of contrast with Latin American culture. Carpentier claims that he started to see his own country under a new light upon his return from his extensive travels: "The Latin American returns to his own world and begins to understand many things" ("Marvelous" 83). His trip to Haiti in 1943, in particular, helped Carpentier to realise the potentials of Latin America's cultural and historical heritage. The following excerpt from the prologue provides insights into both Carpentier's theory of marvellous realism as an indigenous and endogenous cultural expression of Latin America and his stern attitude towards European artistic movements.

> After having felt the undeniable spell of the lands of Haiti, after having found magical warnings along the roads of the Central Meseta, after having heard the drums of the Petro and the Rada, I was moved to set this recently experienced marvelous reality beside the tiresome pretensions of creating the marvelous that has characterized certain European literatures for the last thirty years [...] ("Marvelous" 84)

> Furthermore, I thought, the presence and vitality of this marvelous real was not the unique privilege of Haiti but the heritage of all America, where we have not yet begun to establish an inventory of our cosmogonies. ("Marvelous" 87)

Carpentier strongly believed that this new aspiration could be an answer to Latin American writers' yearnings for an autonomous national identity, but he was also well aware of the fact that his proposition of the marvellous real as a literary correlative to Latin America's "extraordinary reality" would further complicate the on-going theoretical debate about the mode. Perhaps that is why he devoted much of his critical studies to justify his argument by evoking the catalogue of cultural peculiarities of Latin America that distinguish it as a marvellous place. For instance, in what might well be seen as a response to the question why Latin America is the chosen territory of the marvellous real, Carpentier writes,

> Because of the virginity of the land, our upbringing, our ontology, the Faustian presence of the Indian and the black man, the revelation constituted by its recent discovery, its fecund racial mixing [*mestizaje*], America is far from using up its wealth of mythologies. After all, what is the entire history of America if not a chronicle of the marvelous real? ("Marvelous" 88)

Carpentier aggressively attacks European Surrealism by labelling it unfavourably as "cliché," "arranged," "calculated," and "manufactured" in his key theoretical works: his prologue to *The Kingdom of This World* and his 1975 article "The Baroque and the Marvelous Real."[16] Behind this derogatory view of European literature lies Carpentier's belief that in contrast to the marvellous that manifests itself as an ontological reality in the mythology, history, geography and architecture of Latin America, the idea of the marvellous in the Western world is a learned practice,

---

[16] Carpentier finds Franz Roh's theory completely irrelevant to the discussion of the mode although he acknowledges the fact that it was Roh, who first coined the term: "The term magical realism was coined around 1924 or 1925 by a German art critic called Franz Roh in a book entitled *Realismo mágico*, published by the *Revista Occidente*. In fact, what he [Franz Roh] called magical was simply painting where real forms are combined in a way which does not conform to daily reality" ("Baroque" 102). Carpentier does not talk about the literary works classified as magical realist in European literature. Nor does he explain his ideas concerning Massimo Bontempelli's magical realism. It seems that for Carpentier, the Surrealist fantastic epitomises the literary traditions and modes in European literature.

pursued "through books and through prefabricated objects" ("Baroque" 104). In his final analysis, Carpentier thus boldly avers, "the phenomenon of the marvelous presupposes faith" on this side of the Atlantic ("Marvelous" 86). Latin Americans do not have to learn how to create the marvellous in their literary works because unlike the artificial mystery of European literature, the marvelous real is "encountered in its raw state, latent and omnipresent, in all that is Latin American" ("Baroque" 104). Obviously, Carpentier draws a theoretical framework in which the marvellous is presented as an integral part of reality in Latin America. It seems to emerge out of Latin American lifestyle, culture, history and its flora and fauna. It is preserved in the collective memory, transmitted from one generation to another through myths, legends and rituals. Perhaps, it is thus not surprising that Carpentier firmly asserts, "[a]s far as the marvelous real is concerned, we [Latin Americans] have only to reach out with our hands to grasp it" ("Baroque" 107).

At this point it is worthwhile to compare the theories of magical realism developed in Europe with Carpentier's marvellous real in order to demonstrate the conceptual change the term underwent in almost two decades after its inception. Carpentier's novel *The Kingdom of This World* is particularly telling in this respect, for it illustrates the two key elements of his theory of the marvellous real: the promotion of cultural nationalism and the insistence on faith as an essential feature of the mode. To begin with, in contrast to Roh and Bontempelli's emphasis on the urban and the modern and particularly the latter's aspiration to create modern myths, Carpentier makes use of stories drawn from the Latin American history. In Carpentier's imagination, Latin America with its multicultural and multiracial identity provides a fertile ground for producing myths out of common reality. Thus, in *The Kingdom of This World*, Carpentier recounts the story of the Haitian slave leader François Mackandal during the transition of Haiti from slavery to emancipation and from colony to republic. In other words, Carpentier, following his own precept, looks to Latin American history as a source of inspiration instead of creating a genuinely original story.[17]

In the prologue, Carpentier probes into a comparison of Le Comte de Lautréamont's *Les Chants de Maldoror* (*The Songs of Maldoror*, 1868), which would later become a canonical work of surrealist literature and his own novel in order to illustrate the fundamental place of faith in his theory of the marvellous real. A prose poem of six cantos, *Les Chants de Maldoror* tells the story of an imaginary misanthropic character named Maldoror. Centred on the lives of eccentric characters, the two works have certain thematic similarities and abound with fantastic happenings. Carpentier focuses on a particular scene present in both works: Maldoror's escape from an army of agents and spies and Mackandal's escape from a burning stake at his public execution. Maldoror escapes from his enemies by adopting the shapes of certain animals and by transporting himself to different cities like Madrid, Peking and Saint Petersburg. Carpentier calls the fantastic in Lautréamont's prose poem "marvelous literature in full force" since all of the supernatural events in the book are the product of the writer's imagination ("Marvelous" 87). The hero of Carpentier's novel, Mackandal, was believed to have the same powers, but they were not imposed on him by the author. It was the Haitian blacks' collective faith in Mackandal's magical powers that "produced a miracle on the day of his execution" ("Marvelous" 87). Thus, the passages where Mackandal's escape is narrated have the centrepiece in the novel:

> The fire began to rise toward the Mandingue, licking his legs. At that moment Mackandal moved the stump of his arm, which they had been unable to tie up, in a threatening gesture which was none the less terrible for being partial, howling unknown

---

[17] Carpentier's other major works, such as *The Lost Steps* (1953), *The Chase* (1956), *Explosion in a Cathedral* (1962) and *The Harp and the Shadow* (1978) are set in Latin American countries and have historical themes.

spells and violently thrusting his torso forward. The bonds fell off and the body of the Negro rose in the air flying overhead, until it plunged into the black waves of the sea of slaves. A single cry filled the square: "Mackandal saved!"

Pandemonium followed. The guards fell with rifle butts on the howling blacks, who now seemed to overflow the streets, climbing toward the windows. And the noise and screaming and uproar were such that very few saw that Mackandal, held by ten soldiers, had been thrust head first into the fire, and that a flame fed by his burning hair had drowned his last cry. (*The Kingdom* 51-52)

The double-vision in the scene illustrates Mestizaje's ability to generate myths out of everyday reality. While the slaves believe that Mackandal has escaped by slipping his binding to fly away as a mosquito, the French soldiers witness his being thrown into the fire and burning to death. Carpentier's ideas with regard to Lautréamont's *The Songs of Maldoror* bear implications on his likely view of magical realism as developed by Franz Roh and Massimo Bontempelli since the element of faith is not present in their theories of the mode. Last but not least, Carpentier compares the two novels in terms of the impact that they had on cultural history. He notes that "Maldoror left behind only an ephemeral literary school. The American Mackandal, on the contrary, leaves an entire mythology, preserved by an entire people and accompanied by magic hymns still sung today during voodoo ceremonies" ("Marvelous" 87-88). That is to say, Carpentier's marvellous real does not correspond to the aesthetic values of a single artist or a small group of artists as the fantastic does in European literature; it is part of everyday life collectively experienced by Latin American people. It is apparent that Carpentier developed his theory of the marvellous real to seek cultural emancipation from the West by promoting magical realism as an authentic expression of Latin American literature and also by repudiating similar practices in European literature.[18]

While it is arguable whether Carpentier can be considered to be the first proponent of magical realism as a genuine postcolonial literary style, it is certain that his ideas had a decisive impact on the theoretical discussion of the mode by other Latin American critics. As Kenneth Reeds notes, in the successive works written by Emir Rodríguez Monegal, Juan Barroso and Irlemar Chiampi in the late 1970s "a common theme was developing in separating magical realism from 'lo real maravilloso' along the difference in the first representing reality and the second being reality" (187). In spite of the fact that their categorisation was not based on geographical boundaries or cultural peculiarities, their arguments, in effect, read like a reformulation of Carpentier's original distinction in which the marvellous in Latin American literature is regarded as an ontological reality of a particular cultural context, whereas the similar narrative elements in the Western literature are treated as the product of a single writer's imagination. In more recent scholarship, however, the two paradigms are not treated as subtle distinctions, but as the two formal features of magical realist fiction. William Spindler, for instance, argues that the two approaches should be seen as "two sides of the same coin" since neither approach is "sufficient to account for all different examples of magical realist works" (76-77). By the same token, Christopher Warnes draws attention to the fact that the techniques to naturalise the supernatural vary in accordance with literary influence, cultural context and political agenda, and that different narrative techniques can be present in the same work of literature (9).

Carpentier's ideas, particularly his thesis that magical realism is a narrative mode that springs from indigenous people's mythological be-

---

[18] Amaryll Chanady considers Carpentier's ideas as part of an anti-colonial discourse where indigenous writers claim equality or even superiority to the literature of the coloniser by promoting magical realism as an authentic cultural expression of Latin America. Chanady has critically called this appropriation of magical realism into a strictly Latin America context "a territorialization of the imaginary" (*Territorialization* 131).

liefs, their turbulent history and impressive geography of their native lands, also carried much weight among magical realist writers both inside and outside of the Latin America. In Latin American context, Gabriel García Márquez and Isabel Allende uphold a culturalist view of magical realism that strongly recalls Carpentier's theory of the marvellous real. In an interview, for example, Márquez asserts that magical realism constitutes a truly Latin American realism:

> Everyday life in Latin America proves that reality is full of the most extraordinary things. [...]. In Comodoro Rivadavia, in the extreme south of Argentina, winds from the South Pole swept a whole circus away and the next day fishermen caught the bodies of lions and giraffes in their nets. [...] You only have to open the newspapers to see that extraordinary things happen to us every day. ("Conversation")

For Márquez, the reception of his works by Latin American readership also proves the fact that the marvellous in his novels is only a reflection of Latin American cultural heritage:

> After I'd written *One Hundred Years of Solitude*, a boy turned up in Barranquilla claiming to have a pig's tail. [...] I know very ordinary people who've read *One Hundred Years of Solitude* carefully and with a lot of pleasure, but with no surprise at all because, when all is said and done, I'm telling them nothing that hasn't happened in their own lives. [...] *There's not a single line in my novels which is not based on reality.* ("Conversation"; emphasis added)

The same patterns of thought can also be seen in the public speeches of Isabel Allende, the author of the best-selling magical realist novel *The House of Spirits* (1982). Allende tries to correct the widely accepted western view of magical realism as a subgenre of the fantastic. "Critics in Europe and the United States," she protests, "often stare in disbelief at Latin American books, asking how the authors dare to invent those incredible lies" (45). As a response to such critical attacks, Allende contends,

> we can register the most extravagant, evil, obscene, incredible or magnificent facts – which in Latin America, are not hyperbole, because that is the dimension of our reality. [...] It is very hard to explain to critics that these things are not a product of our pathological imaginations. They are written in our history; we can find them every day in our newspapers. (45-46)

As the above quotations suggest, both writers see themselves as the rightful inheritors of the Latin American marvellous real. The firm tone in their arguments and their constant reference to true news stories and their personal experiences of unusual happenings indicate that they believe in Carpentier's precept: Latin Americans have only to reach out with their hands to grasp the marvellous.

With the internationalisation of the mode, Carpentier's ideas were adopted by magical realist writers from different countries, such as Ben Okri and Salman Rushdie, who started their literary careers in the peripheries of the Western canon. Ben Okri, the Nigerian author of the Booker prize winning magical realist novel *The Famished Road* (1991), claims that magical realism bespeaks nothing but a putative African reality: "This is just the way the world is seen: the dead are not really dead, the ancestors are still part of the living community [...]. It's quite simple and straightforward. I'm treating it naturally. It's a kind of realism, but a realism with many more dimensions" (qtd. in Lim 115). Salman Rushdie took the discussion a step further when he defined magical realism as the expression of "a genuinely third world consciousness" ("Gabriel" 301). For Rushdie, the supernatural presented in these works of literature is part of the ontological reality of the third world countries. He points to Márquez's *One Hundred Years of Solitude* as an example of the third world consciousness and thereby combines the magical realist tradition of Latin American literature with that of postcolonial countries:

> In the works of Márquez, as in the world he describes, impossible things happen constantly, and quite plausibly, out in the open under the midday sun. It would be a mistake to think of Márquez's literary universe as an invented, self-referential, closed system. He is not writing about Middle-earth, but about the one we all inhabit. Macondo exists. That is its magic. ("Gabriel" 302)

The various reformulations of Carpentier's initial theory by the renowned authors of the mode helped establish magical realism as an authentic expression of postcolonial countries. However, as the following chapters hope to illustrate, their assumptions were challenged and refuted to a great extent by postcolonial critics who claimed that magical realism's growing popularity in postcolonial countries is indebted in large degree to its ability to register the cultural heterogeneity and multiplicity of these countries rather than their uniqueness and distinction.

Ángel Flores was another influential figure in the theoretical discussions of magical realism in Latin American literature. Although he shared with Carpentier and Pietri the notion that with magical realism Latin America found an authentic expression, and that its literature was booming by virtue of it, he differed from them in certain aspects. For one thing, Flores, assuming the role of the literary historian, tried to be more precise in his argument and offered specific names and dates important to the rise of magical realist literature in Latin America. For another, he adopted a more inclusive approach in identifying the sources of magical realism. It is for this reason that he used the term *realismo magico* (magical realism) instead of Carpentier's culturally specific *lo real maravilloso* in his studies. In his speech, "Magical Realism in Spanish American Literature," at the Congress of the Modern Language Association in 1954, Flores proposed the year 1935 as the beginning of this new era of Latin American Literature and Jorge Luis Borges as its initiator. He believed that it was after Borges' 1935 collection of short stories entitled *Historia universal de la infamia* (*A Universal History of Infamy*) that there appeared a new generation of magical realist writers from Latin American countries, including Cuba, Mexico, Ecuador, Chile, Uruguay and Argentina (114). These writers broadened the aesthetic and thematic perspectives of Latin American literature with their experimental works.

In addition to his substitution of magical realism for Carpentier's marvellous real, Flores also disputed his assumption that the marvellous is an integral part of Latin American reality by offering a new conceptual definition for the term based on aesthetic and stylistic features. Flores believed that the sensation of the marvellous present in magical realist texts was an aesthetic effect generated through narrative techniques rather than an amplification of Latin American cultural heritage. Defining magical realism as "the amalgamation of realism and fantasy," Flores stressed the role of the writer in combining the opposing elements in the narrative process (115). According to his definition, all texts, regardless of their cultural and historical origin, can be included in the category of magical realism provided that they achieve a "transformation of the common and everyday into the awesome and unreal" and that they have a narrative frame where "time exists in a kind of timeless fluidity and the unreal happens as a part of reality" (114). As such, for Flores, the sources of magical realism cannot be confined to Latin America, and therefore, he provided an inclusive list of precursors of the mode, including Cervantes, Gogol, Dostoevsky, E.T.A. Hoffmann, the Grimm Brothers, Poe and Melville.

Flores regards Franz Kafka and Marcel Proust as the prominent practitioners of the mode in the twentieth century, singling out the former as the major influence in Latin American context. His contention seems to rest on the fact that Jorge Luis Borges translated Kafka's 1915 novella *Metamorphosis* into Spanish, assisting the dissemination of the style in Latin America. Flores claims that Kafka's literary practice of "mingling his drab reality with the phantasmal world of his nightmare" in *Metamorphosis* epitomises the quintessence of magical realist literature (112). *Metamorphosis* is the story of a young travelling salesman called Gregor Samsa, who awakes one morning to find that he has been transformed into a giant cockroach. This fantastic phenomenon is, however, treated as part of everyday reality and narrated in a matter-of-fact tone, starting from the opening sentence of the novella:

> As Gregor Samsa awoke one morning from uneasy dreams he found himself transformed in his bed into a gigantic insect. He was lying on his hard, as it were armour-plated, back and when he lifted his head a little he could see his domelike brown belly divided into stiff arched segments on top of which the bed quilt could hardly keep in position and was about to slide off completely. (89)

This matter-of-fact tone is reinforced firstly by the protagonist's confirmation of the fact that it is not a dream and secondly by a precise description of the setting as an ordinary room: "What has happened to me? he thought. It was no dream. His room, a regular human bedroom, only rather too small, lay quiet between the four familiar walls" (89). The opening passage is then followed by a detailed depiction of Gregor's room in nineteenth-century realistic fashion with the catalogue of the numerous items in the room. The interplay between Gregor's calm, factual tone and the references to his terrible physical situation continues for several pages, merging the two opposing narrative planes, the fantastic and the realist, into one. In other words, Kafka employs the matter-of-fact style to naturalise the supernatural elements present in the text, allowing the reader to accept these as part of everyday reality.

The opening section of Kafka's novella is also important in terms of the presentation of the concept of time in magical realist novels. In true examples of the mode, Flores notes, "[f]rom the very first line the reader is thrown into a timeless flux and/or the unconceivable, freighted with dramatic suspense" (190). Flores draws attention to the fact that there is no specific time reference in the text. The modifier "one day" in the opening sentence of the novella, as Flores points out, situates the narrative in "an infinite, timeless perspective," allowing the writer combine the elements of fantasy and reality (115). Although Flores' ideas concerning the concept of time in magical realist fiction did not become a definitive characteristic of the mode, similar patterns can also be seen in other canonical examples. Ben Okri's *The Famished Road*, for example, opens with a mythical depiction of the unnamed suburban ghetto of an African metropolis: "In the beginning there was a river. The river became a road and the road branched out to the whole world. And because the road was once a river it was always hungry. In that land of beginnings spirits mingled with the unborn" (1). Márquez's description of the fictional town of Macondo in *One Hundred Years of Solitude* recalls the biblical tale of Adam naming the animals: "The world was so recent that many things lacked names, and in order to indicate them it was necessary to point" (3). In these magical realist novels, the concept of time is presented in such a way as to confirm our primitive sense of reality, blurring the distinction between the natural and the supernatural.

Later critics largely discredited Ángel Flores' arguments. Seymour Menton, for example, criticises Flores for his "overly broad use of the term" ("Magical" 145). For Menton, Flores has "lumped together under Magic Realism all manifestations of experimental, cosmopolitan literature as opposed to the social protest, proletarian and telluric prose fiction which had dominated the 1920s and 1930s, and most of the 1940s"

("Magical" 145). By the same token, Jean-Pierre Durix attacks Flores, arguing that his "definition is very wide in its application and suggests a reference to phenomena more currently described as 'the fantastic'" (*Mimesis* 104). Amaryll Chanady, on the other hand, draws attention to a serious inconsistency in Flores' theory of magical realism, where he argues: "[...] Latin America is no longer in search of its expression [...] – we may claim that Latin America now possesses an authentic expression, one that is uniquely civilized, exciting and, let us hope, perennial" (*Territorialization* 116). In response to Flores, Chanady argues, "if magical realism is described as imaginative and innovative fiction that has assimilated the most modern narrative and stylistic techniques, and can be found in Kafka as well as Borges, it cannot be 'genuinely Latin American' or the 'authentic expression' of the continent" (*Territorialization* 130). In spite of these counter-arguments, Flores' essay has acquired a status of seminal importance in the history of magical realist literature. As Kenneth Reeds notes, Flores' essay "provided the institutionalized confirmation of Arturo Uslar Pietri's separation of magical realism from Roh" and "institutionalized the idea that magical realism was the proper nomenclature for referring to the new Latin American literature" (183).[19]

It was this line of thought that gave rise to a number of articles and theses in the 1950s and the 1960s which regarded magical realism as a strictly Latin American phenomenon: J. E. Irby's "La influencia de William Faulkner en cuatro narradores hispanoamericanos" (1957), Ray Verzasconi's doctoral thesis "Magical Realism and the Literary World of Miguel Ángel Asturias" (1965) and E. Dale Carter's thesis titled "Magical Realism in Contemporary Argentine Fiction" (1966) (Reeds 183). Though most of these studies are not used as reference sources today, the fact that they were written during a period when magical real-

---

[19] Likewise, William Spindler notes, "Flores' lecture contributed to popularize the term Magical Realism among critics to the extent that it came to overshadow *lo real maravilloso*" (76).

ism was seen as a Latin American phenomenon is indicative of Alejo Carpentier and his followers' success in appropriating of the term in its new context.[20]

Nonetheless, there were some dissenting voices in Latin American academy to confront the paradigm developed by Pietri, Carpentier and Flores. The most notable of these was the Mexican critic Luis Leal, who wrote an article in 1967 as a response to Ángel Flores' 1954 essay and raised objections with regard to Flores' proposition that magical realism started in 1935, his definition of magical realism as the amalgamation of realism and fantasy and the group of authors he conceived as magical realists. First and foremost, Leal disputes Flores' proposition that magical realism originated in Borges's 1935 short story collection, tracing the term "magical realism" back to its origins in Franz Roh's study. His definition of magical realism thus echoes Roh's initial formulation with the exception that Expressionism is replaced by literary narrative modes, namely science fiction and fantasy. "[M]agical realism," Leal notes, "does not use dream motifs; neither does it distort reality or create imagined worlds, as writers of fantastic literature or science fiction do […] In magical realism the writer confronts reality and tries to untangle it, to discover what is mysterious in things, in life, in human acts" (121).

Leal knew that by re-establishing the link between Roh's original formulation and Latin American literature, he did not only free the term from its strict cultural context, but also paved the way for a reconsideration of the mode in a broader perspective. Thus, he devoted a greater part of his relatively short article to a comparative discussion of magical

---

[20] Patently, the separation of magical realism from its European roots further complicated the issues related to the origin and definition of the term. The theories claiming magical realism to be uniquely Latin American, along with the international achievements of Latin American writers, perpetuated the misconception that magical realism began in Latin America. The online researches conducted in the course of this study showed that in most of the popular Internet sources, magical realism is promoted as a Latin American literary mode, partially or completely ignoring the theories developed by Franz Roh and Massimo Bontempelli.

realism and its neighbouring modes, the fantastic and science fiction, based on their aesthetic and stylistic features. Leal considered the fantastic and science fiction as examples of escapist literature since they create futuristic settings or imaginary worlds where the reader loses touch with reality. The magical realist writer "doesn't create imaginary worlds in which we can hide from everyday reality" (121). As the supernatural in magical realism is presented as an integral part of everyday reality, "the author does not need to justify the mystery of events, as the fantastic writer has to" (Leal 123). The revelation of the marvellous can be captured in a myriad of ways. Thus, Leal argues that the narrative techniques of magical realist writers cannot be categorised in standard divisions: "magical realism is, more than anything else, an attitude toward reality that can be expressed in popular or cultured forms, in elaborate or rustic styles, in closed or open structures" (121). Leal's study, although not exhaustive, presents a preliminary assessment of magical realism as a literary mode that cannot be limited to one particular period of history or a specific cultural location.

The practice of defining magical realism through a comparative discussion with its neighbouring narrative modes, particularly the fantastic, has become a common tendency in more recent scholarship. For instance, in *Magical Realism and the Fantastic: Resolved Versus Unresolved Antinomy*, Amaryll Chanady reaches a definition of magical realism through a discussion of Tzvetan Todorov's theory of the fantastic. Todorov's ideas on the reader's "hesitation" when confronted with a supernatural event in the narrative offer a useful means for defining magical realism. According to Todorov, the fantastic requires the fulfilment of three conditions:

> First, the text must oblige the reader to consider the world of the characters as a world of living persons and to hesitate between a natural or supernatural explanation of the events described. Second, this hesitation may also be experienced by a character;

thus the reader's role is so to speak entrusted to a character, and at the same time the hesitation is represented, it becomes one of the themes of the work. [...] Third, the reader must adopt a certain attitude with regard to the text: he will reject allegorical as well as "poetic" interpretations. (33)

In Todorov's view, then, the fantastic springs from the moments of uncertainty; a liminal state that leaves the reader with a sense of confusion and leads him or her to question the reality of the phenomenon presented in the text: "Does it transcend the laws of Nature as we know them?" (Todorov 28). The reader's answer to this question determines the fundamental characteristic of the mode. "Once we choose one answer or the other," Todorov notes, "we leave the fantastic for a neighbouring genre, the uncanny or the marvellous" since the fantastic essentially relies on the unresolved hesitation created in the course of the narrative (25). Accordingly, the fantastic can be described as a literary mode where the reader's hesitation is prolonged for the duration of the narrative.

Amaryll Chanady substitutes Todorov's concept of "hesitation" with "antinomy," which is indication of her attempt to discuss the two modes primarily on the textual level through the concept of the implied reader rather than the actual reader. Chanady argues,

A far more satisfactory term than hesitation, which is a reaction on the part of the reader to textual indications, is antinomy, or the simultaneous presence of two conflicting codes in the text. Since neither can be accepted in the presence of the other, the apparently supernatural phenomenon remains inexplicable. (*Magical* 12)

While the antinomy in the fantastic is maintained so as to provoke hesitation in the reader, it is resolved in magical realism in the course of the narrative. Chanady goes on to introduce three criteria to define magical realism that correspond to those proposed by Todorov. According to Chanady magical realism is first of all characterised "by two conflicting, but autonomously coherent, perspectives, one based on an 'enlightened' and rational view of reality, and the other on the acceptance of the supernatural as part of everyday reality" (*Magical* 21-22). In other words, in magical realism, as in the fantastic, the reader is confronted with a world where the natural and the supernatural coexist. The distinction between the two narrative modes stems from the presentation of the supernatural: "Whereas the simultaneous presence of the natural and the supernatural in the fantastic creates a[n] ambiguous and disturbing fictitious world, it is the essential characteristic of a harmonious and coherent world in magical realism" (*Magical* 23). Thus, Chanady defines the second characteristic of the mode as "the resolution of logical antinomy in the description of events and situations" (*Magical* 26). In the fantastic, the reader is drawn into the tension created between the conflicting narrative codes through identification with the characters, whereas in magical realism "the supernatural appears as normal as the daily events of ordinary life," and thus it does not disconcert the reader (*Magical* 24).

Finally, Chanady points out the author's role in the resolution of the logical antinomy. Informed by the reader-response theory, Chanady claims that "the real reader's response varies according to his cultural background, that of the implied reader is based on the text. […] The real reader cannot be radically different from the construct of the implied reader if he is to understand the text" (*Magical* 33).[21] The attitude of the author, the narrator and the characters is equally important and function-

---

[21] Wolfgang Iser outlines his theory of the implied reader as follows, "[t]he implied reader as a concept has his roots firmly planted in the structure of the text; he is a construct and in no way to be identified with any real reader. The concept of the implied reader is therefore a textual structure anticipating the presence of a recipient, without necessarily defining him: this concept prestructures the role to be assumed by each recipient, and this holds true even when texts deliberately appear to ignore their possible recipient or actively exclude him. Thus the concept of the implied reader designates a network of response-inviting structures, which impel the reader to grasp the text" (145).

al in naturalising the supernatural in the text. They either preserve their reticence with regard to the supernatural circumstances or accept them as part of everyday reality, thereby constructing a magical realist worldview where the natural and the supernatural coexist harmoniously. As a result, the reader adopts the same attitude and does not question the reality construed in the text on the level of fictional representation. "If the narrator," Chanady urges, "stressed the exclusive validity of his rational world view, he would relegate the supernatural to a secondary mode of being (the unreliable imagination of a character) and thus the juxtaposition of two mutually exclusive logical codes, which is essential to magical realism, would become a hierarchy" (*Magical* 29-30). In other words, the logical antinomy rising from the simultaneous presence of the natural and supernatural is resolved through "authorial reticence, or absence of judgments about the veracity of the events and the authenticity of the worldview expressed by characters in the text" (*Magical* 29). The authorial reticence that serves to naturalise the supernatural in magical realism emerges as the third characteristic of magical realism in Chanady's theoretical work.

It is not surprising that Chanady does not give a generic definition of magical realism despite her lengthy discussion of the mode. Most of the scholars and critics of magical realism avoid pretending to have reached an all-inclusive definition of the term. Instead, they offer a working definition appropriate for the context of their own study generally through a survey of the historical evolution of the mode as presented in this chapter. Chanady's subtle discussion with its emphasis on the structural and stylistic features of the mode and the historical view of magical realism as an innovative artistic expression with strong socio-political themes provide the theoretical framework for the analyses of the four novels in the following chapters.

Franz Roh's 1925 coinage has thus become an internationally recognised literary term. The ideological agenda of Roh's magic realism, which manifested itself first in German painting with socio-political themes, has evolved with its transposition into the domain of literature. While Massimo Bontempelli saw magical realism as a literary instrument that serves his Fascist ideals to create a collective cultural identity for Europe, Latin Americans, as the citizens of newly established nation states, sought for emancipation from Europe by promoting magical realism as an authentic cultural product. Wendy B. Faris makes an astute observation with regard to the critical moments in history when magical realism made its appearance. She notes that "[…] a sense of cultural loss and recovery often generates magical realist fiction, whether or not the social situation is postcolonial […]" and quotes Günter Grass' retrospective comment about his magical realist novel, *The Tin Drum,* to support her argument "[b]y losing the war I lost my home town, Danzig,... and I tried to bring something back to write about, to win it again by writing (*Ordinary* 134). In the light of the survey presented in this chapter, it is possible to revise Faris' observation so as to include the pictorial origin of the mode, which she seems to ignore, into the discussion. It is true that magical realism is generated by a sense of cultural loss. Both Franz Roh and Massimo Bontempelli developed their theories of magical realism in the aftermath of the Great War. Likewise, the inception of magical realism in Latin America, as in many other postcolonial countries coincided with the end of colonial hegemony. Magical realism can also be seen as the harbinger of a new era following a cultural demise. The magic realist artists and magical realist writers alike attempted to heal the wounds caused by the Great War or a trauma experienced immediately after the collapse of institutionalised colonial power through their works by employing the formal and thematic possibilities offered by magical realism. This could be expressed as an individual response as in the example of Günter Grass, or a collective one as in the cases of Bontempelli, Carpentier and the postcolonial writers like Salman Rushdie. In the following chapters, the cultural work of magical realism in postcolonial literatures shall be studied through the analyses of four magical realist novels. However, there is yet one final question to be addressed: how could magical realism so aggressively and persistently claimed by Latin Americans make its way into the postcolonial world? Chapter 2 will address this and some other related questions, providing a preliminary insight into postcolonial studies as well as the perception of magical realism in the postcolonial world.

Chapter 2
From Latin America to the Globe: DissemiNation of Magical Realism and the Postcolonial

> Never again will a single story be told as though it were the only one.
> - John Berger

If any date could be taken to mark the pivotal point in the history of magical realism, signalling its transformation into a complex, global literary phenomenon, it might be 1967. It was in that year that the Guatemalan magical realist writer Miguel Ángel Asturias was awarded the Nobel Prize for Literature "for his vivid literary achievement, deep-rooted in the national traits and traditions of Indian peoples of Latin America" ("Nobel Prize"). Gabriel García Márquez's *A Hundred Years of Solitude*, the novel, which, to quote Wendy B. Faris, "put the term *magical realism* on the international literary map," was also published in the same year (*Ordinary* 29). While earning themselves worldwide fame and popularity, these writers also helped introduce magical realism to an international readership. The success magical realist writers achieved in the subcontinent misled some critics to associate the mode with Latin American literature, ignoring its origins in European painting and literature to a great extent. For instance, Phil McCluskey asserts that "[a]ny discussion of magic realism outside a Latin American context must inevitably begin by using the literature of the Latin American 'boom' and its immediate precursors as a site of origin, drawing parallels between the two conditions in order to lend authority to the 'translation' of the form" (qtd. in Schroeder 19). It is true that Latin American writers' success helped magical realist novels become part of the established literary canon; however, it would be misleading to suggest that Latin American literature is magical realism's fulfilment and its norm. Rather, the legacy of magical realism in Latin America should be considered as an important phase in the history of the mode which has travelled across continents and cultures, and perhaps more significantly across genres – fiction, film and arts. In an attempt to illustrate the widespread dissemination of the mode in literature, Wen-chin Ouyang offers an incomplete list of the languages in which magical realist novels are written: "Arabic, Chinese, English, German, Italian, Japanese, Persian, Portuguese, Spanish, Tibetan and Turkish" (15).

In line with its globalisation, there was a significant change in the theoretical works devoted to the study of magical realism. Stephen M. Hart notes that "[c]ritical theorizations of magical realism during this period [after Márquez's won the Nobel Prize for literature in 1982] also began to reflect its gradually broadening parameters" (5). Hart summarises the change in the critical perception of magical realism in three stages. The initial critical works, such as Ángel Flores' essay published in 1955 and Luis Leal's conference speech in 1967, mainly concentrated on the formal characteristics of the mode. With the advent of postcolonial studies in the 1980s, critics began to shift the focus of critical attention to social and ideological issues associated with the mode, as epitomised in Stephen Slemon's 1988 essay, "Magic Realism as Post-Colonial Discourse." In the 1990s, a new paradigm came into being with Lois P. Zamora and Wendy B. Faris' compendium *Magical Realism: Theory, History, Community* (1995), which discerns magical realism as a global literary phenomenon and attempts to study the mode in its historical context through contemporary literary theories (Hart 5-6). Informed by the scope and parameters delineated by the contemporary critics, this and the following chapters shall mainly focus on the appropriation of the mode in postcolonial literatures with particular attention to the ways in which postcolonial writers have exploited the narrative possibilities of the mode. The discussion presented in the following pages unfolds in two sections. In the first section, a brief survey of the national liberation movements in Africa and India and their repercussions on the rise of national literatures are presented. This section also provides some insights into the critical reception of literary works from former colonies in the Western academia. The second section of this chapter focuses on the perception of magical realism in postcolonial countries, seeking answers to questions like how and why the mode has become popular in the postcolonial world. Prior to these discussions, however, it is necessary to draw an outline of the rise and development of postcolonial studies in the Western academia.

The conception and exact denotation of the term "postcolonialism" have proved to be as problematic as magical realism itself. It has been the subject of an inconclusive debate mainly centred on the meaning that critics have attributed to the prefix "post."[22] Different spellings of the term designate different areas of interest. Therefore, the distinction between "post-colonialism" with a hyphen and "postcolonialism" without needs to be made from the outset. In their introduction to *Colonial Discourse and Postcolonial Theory*, Barker, Hulme and Iversen use the former as a "temporal marker" and the latter "to indicate the analytical concept of greater range and ambition, as in postcolonial theory" (4).[23] The hyphenated form of the term was first used by historians, economists and political scientists basically to denote the period after the demise of colonialism. In other words, the terms "post-colonialism" and "post-colonial" focus on the temporal linearity of historical events. The unhyphenated version is the name of a critical theory initiated by literary critics in the late 1970s to discuss wide-ranging cultural effects of colonisation. In this sense, postcolonialism begins with the birth of colonialism itself. It is already and always present in every colonial situation where there is a resistance and challenge against the codes of colonial discourse (Ashcroft *et al.*, *Key Concepts*: 186-192). That is to say, post-

---

[22] For a detailed discussion on the meaning of the prefix 'post-' in postcolonial theory, see J. E. Elliott, "What's 'Post' in Post-Colonial Theory?"

[23] Some critics attempted to steer clear of discussions by offering a new term. For instance, Bruce King argues that "[d]uring the second half of the twentieth century the literature of England went through a major change [...]. This [change] was often termed Postcolonial, although, as England has not been a colony for a long time, Post-imperial might be better, and I think Internationalization is best" (1).

colonial discourse, whether political or artistic, is never completely exempt from colonial culture as it is at work within that culture regardless of the fact that the imperial power has officially ended or not. For instance, Chinua Achebe's *Things Fall Apart* (1958), often studied as one of the key postcolonial texts, was written while the nation in question, Nigeria, was still a colony.

Peter Childs and Patrick Williams explain the meaning the prefix "post" attains when it is spelled as part of a compound noun and thereby summarise the central tenets of the critical theory emerging in the late 1970s as follows,

> The other meaning of post- is one which is shared with those sets of theories which use the compound term, especially post-structuralism, where the emphasis may not be so much on the chronologically subsequent – i.e. coming after structuralism, modernism or feminism but on conceptually transcending or superseding the parameters of the other term. In this perspective, texts which are anti-colonial, which reject the premises of colonialist intervention (the civilising mission, the rejuvenation of stagnant cultures) might be regarded as post-colonial insofar as they have 'got beyond' colonialism and its ideologies, broken free of its lures to a point from which to mount a critique or counter-attack. (3-4)

In the same vein, Steven Slemon notes that "[d]efinitions of the post-colonial, of course, vary widely, but [...] the concept proves most useful not when it is used synonymously with a post-independence historical period in once-colonised nations, but rather when it locates a specifically anti- or *post*-colonial *discursive* purchase in culture" ("Modernism's"; 3 emphasis original).[24] In this context, postcolonialism, first and foremost,

---

[24] Similarly, In his *The Location of Culture*, Hommi K. Bhabha states that he understands the prefix "post-" as going beyond: "At the century's edge, we are less exercised by an-

is a critique of colonialism characterised by a disengagement from and resistance to its practices in various cultural forms. It involves the discussion of different kinds of colonial experience, such as those of slavery, resistance, migration, diaspora, and their repercussions on the issues of gender, nationality and identity. In this light, the unhyphenated form of the term shall be used in the present study both to distinguish it from its historically categorised derivative and to designate writing in opposition to colonialism, resisting its power politics both during and particularly subsequent to the end of colonial period.

To consider postcolonialism as a discursive cultural practice, however, does not mean that it is exempt from a historical context. Postcolonialism, particularly as it is understood in European context, does have a history. The second half of the twentieth century saw the decline and dissolution of European colonial empires (British, French, Italian, Dutch, German, Belgian, Spanish and Portuguese) that had been dominant since the sixteenth century. However, the sense of ending of one period of history and the emergence of another, as suggested by the historically designated term "post-colonialism," is hard to maintain (Childs and Williams 2). Several reasons account for this difficulty to mark the end of colonisation. For one, colonies gained their independence asynchronously: India and Pakistan gained their independence in 1947, Ghana in 1949, Nigeria in 1960 and Jamaica, Trinidad and Tobago in 1962 (McLeod 9). For another, although it is relatively easier to talk about political independence in terms of power transfer between the coloniser and the colonised, it is almost impossible to pinpoint the end of colonial hegemony. In the period following decolonisation, it became apparent that the effects of colonialism did not end with the independence of former colonies. The newly established nations found it difficult to create

---

nihilation – death of the author – or epiphany – the birth of the 'subject.' Our existence today is marked by a tenebrous sense of survival, living on the borderlines of the 'present,' for which there seems to be no proper name other than the current and controversial shiftiness of the prefix 'post': postmodernism, postcolonialim, postfeminism" (1).

independent economies in a radically globalising world, and thus they remained dependent on colonial powers to a large extent. In other words, the political and economic equation between the coloniser and the colonised remained more or less what it was in the days of colonial rule. Subsequently, a growing number of critics have come to view postcolonialism as a phase within an undisrupted imperial history, rather than as a completely new and liberating era. Peter Childs and Patrick Williams note that "although colonial armies and bureaucracies might have withdrawn, Western powers were still intent on maintaining maximum indirect control over erstwhile colonies, via political, cultural and above all economic channels, a phenomenon which became known as neocolonialism" (5). In view of this primary fact, another critic, Anne McClintock, considers the term postcolonialism anachronistic in that it registers "a premature celebration of the pastness of colonialism" (qtd. in Gorra 6). That is, "postcolonialism" cannot be regarded as a fully achieved state. Nor can it denote a completely new historical epoch free of the ills of colonialism.

The diversity of colonial experience further complicates the term. Resistance to colonialism was never a homogenous act. That is to say, just as there has not been one idea of colonialism, there also has been no one idea of postcolonialism that can be readily applied to all postcolonial experiences in the world. This fact makes it impossible to formulate one critical procedure appropriate to address the social, cultural and political repercussions colonial experience had in former colonies. For instance, although Canada and Nigeria can be referred to as postcolonial, mainly because they both underwent a process of colonisation, it is hardly possible to claim that they were postcolonial in the same way. Thus, much of the criticism mounted against postcolonial theory is about its simplistic view of the diversity of postcolonial experience. Anne McClintock, for instance, argues that "[t]he term [postcolonialism] signals a reluctance to surrender the privilege of seeing the world in terms of a singular and ahistorical abstraction" (qtd. in Parry 57). Hence, postcolonialism should not be seen as a single structure that repeats itself in the same way regardless of cultural, political, and social differences among countries.

Why do critics continue to employ a term inflicted with so many problems? One possible answer might be the usefulness of the term. However arbitrary and complicated it might be, the term still enables critics to talk about a vast historical and cultural phenomenon under a single rubric. Perhaps, a more satisfactory answer to this question of validity can be found in the theoretical works of postcolonial scholars and critics. In formulating a working definition of the term, critics tend to concentrate on the promising potentialities of the term whilst acknowledging its shortcomings. For instance, Childs and Williams view postcolonialism as an anticipatory discourse in recognition of the fact that "the condition which it names does not yet exist, but working nevertheless to bring that about" (7). They take their cue from the Marxist critic Frederick Jameson's view that there is a utopian dimension to theories, ideologies and other forms of intellectual practices. In a dialectical movement, they, even unsavoury ideologies like Fascism, project a utopian model (7). For Childs and Williams, it is this utopian project set by postcolonialism that makes it both a useful critical term and productive field of study. By the same token, another critic, John McLeod, argues that a working definition of the term needs to recognise a sense of historical continuity and affirm a commitment to change:

> On the one hand it acknowledges that the material realities and modes of representation common to colonialism are still very much with us today, even if the political map of the world has changed through decolonisation. But on the other hand, it asserts the promise, the possibility, and the continuing necessity to change, while also recognising that the important challenges and changes have already been achieved. (33)

Both of these arguments are powerfully liberating. Despite all of its ambiguities and hazards, the concept of postcolonialism bespeaks possibility, vitality and challenge. It is this movement forward; this desire to alter and transform that inspires the postcolonial writers and critics alike to continue using the term not as a sign of a completed project, but as a sign of persistent resistance.

Literature has been an integral part of colonial history both as an agent of colonisation and anti-colonial resistance. In *Colonial and Postcolonial Literature* Elleke Boehmer argues that "[t]o assume control over a territory or a nation was not only to exert political or economic power; it was also to have imaginative command" (5). Thus, Britain started to disseminate colonial, or more precisely, colonialist texts, such as romances, memoirs, adventure tales or the later poetry of Tennyson, in the second half of the nineteenth century in order to consolidate the view that the world was directed from the colonial metropolis (*Colonial* 15). Once the colonised peoples mastered the coloniser's language and its forms of literary expression, they started to write back, to speak perhaps for the first time on their own behalf. The colonial strategy of self-representation, thus, created its antagonist double. It is perhaps for this reason that postcolonial literature is generally regarded as a response to colonial power structure as suggested by the title of the renowned postcolonial study, *The Empire Writes Back*. Boehmer argues, "resistance to imperial domination – especially on the part of those who lacked guns or money – frequently assumed textual form. […] in the written word, in histories and epic re-creations of the past early nationalists found a compelling medium to counter colonialism's self-representations, to write a self-defining story" (*Colonial* 15). Given the international achievements of magical realist writers, it is not difficult to recognise the role the mode has played in the proliferation of postcolonial literatures. This was not, however, an easy, straightforward process. At the time when magical realism made its appearance on the literary stage of the world, the Western academia was dominated by a prejudice against literatures from former colonies. The possibility that indigenous people could produce sophisticated literary works comparable to those of the West was something that was rarely entertained by Western critics. Literary works written in former colonies were either seen as exotic objects or social documents to be studied (Durix, *Mimesis* 6; McLeod 15-17). Postcolonial literature, as understood today, is the story of the transition of works of literature from being perceived as exotic artefacts into being accepted as serious works of art. In academia, it was a transition from the hegemonic category of Commonwealth literature to postcolonial studies.

2.1. The Rise of National Literatures and Commonwealth Criticism

As Edward Said noted in his seminal study *Orientalism*, writing about the other started long before "the actual act of colonisation itself."[25] However, it was not until the 1960s that the interest in literary

---

[25] According to Edward Said, Orientalism is "a *distribution* of geopolitical awareness into aesthetic, scholarly, economic, sociological, historical, and philological texts; it is an *elaboration* not only of a basic geographical distinction (the world is made up of two unequal halves, Orient and Occident) but also of a whole series of 'interests' which, by such means as scholarly discovery, philological reconstruction, psychological analysis, landscape and sociological description, it not only creates but also maintains; it *is*, rather than expresses, a certain *will* or *intention* to understand, in some cases to control, manipulate, even to incorporate, what is a manifestly different (or alternative and novel) world; it is, above all, a discourse that is by no means in direct, corresponding relationship with political power in the raw, but rather is produced and exists in an uneven exchange with various kinds of power, shaped to a degree by the exchange with power political (as with a colonial or imperial establishment), power intellectual (as with reigning sciences like comparative linguistic or anatomy, or any of the modern policy sciences), power cultural (as with orthodoxies and canons of taste, texts, values), power moral (as with ideas about what 'we' do and what 'they' cannot do or understand as 'we' do)" (12; emphasis original). Said further argues that a Westerner experiences the Orient initially as a representative of Western society, and only secondarily as an individual. This particular tendency of involvement and experience was largely shaped by the colonial policies of the nineteenth century, but its roots, according to Said, lie farther back in time. He traces it back to Shakespeare, Chaucer and Dante, and even to the Homeric era in the ancient Greek civilisation. Therefore, Orientalism, as a pattern of knowledge of the Other, precedes the actual act of colonialism. It should nevertheless be noted that its most prominent advocators were among the political leaders of the Western empires.

works written in the peripheries of the empire established itself as an academic discipline. The dismantling of British colonies after the Second World War encouraged a vast body of new literatures in which the Western literary modes, particularly the novel, were aptly adapted to represent the distinctive regional sensibilities of the former colonies. In the mid-1960s, literary critics began to study this large body of literature written in English, thereby giving rise to an emergent field in literary studies with the name of "Commonwealth literature." Proposed to group together writing from former colonies, Commonwealth literature officially began at British universities with a conference held at Leeds University in 1964 (King 26). Commonwealth literature can be seen as an antecedent of postcolonialism mainly because the two terms presuppose characteristics shared by countries which, at some point in their history, underwent a process of colonisation; however, as shall be shown in due course, they signify different theoretical preoccupations.

The rise and development of national literatures in the former colonies were tied to the emergent politics of nationalism. The early postcolonial writers worked rigorously to appropriate Western literary forms to the political and cultural realities of the time. For instance, Jean-Pierre Durix points out that while the early postcolonial writers showed a strong tendency to write historical novels enriched with myths and oral traditions, they generally avoided utopias as they "belong to triumphant societies sure of their power and confident in the ideology of 'progress'" (*Mimesis* 30). In the early postcolonial novels, the birth of the new nation is idealised in quasi-epic forms in which the protagonist becomes an allegorical figure. "The fate of the protagonist," Durix points out, "frequently serves as an allegory of the major problems of the young nations […] the novels frequently trace the growth of a young hero whose progression from innocence to experience follows the passage of his/her country from colonial dependence to self-government" (*Mimesis* 24). There is no way this comparatively brief study can do justice to nationalist ideologies born in the postcolonial world. However, it is necessary to touch upon the rise of independence movements in Africa and India, two postcolonial locations to be studied in this exegesis, and their contributions to the development of national literatures.

2.1.1. The Awakening of African Nationalism

The question of self-determination in Africa, that is, how African peoples can achieve political and economic independence without compromising their national identities, has a significant place in modern African thought. Scholars working on the colonial period in Africa generally maintain that the first stirrings of nationalist ideas were provoked by the African military experience in the First World War. "African nationalism was," as Adebayo Williams puts it, "an ironic product of the ruins of European nationalism, delivered on its death bed" because after the Great War, it became almost impossible "to justify the civilizing trope of colonization or the notion of a superior race on a God-ordained mission to rescue savages from their historic *cul-de-sac*" (495). It was not only the demystification of the Western ideals that triggered the nationalistic sentiments in Africa. In the course of the war, African peoples came to the belated realisation that they could fight for their own freedom instead of helping European countries to retain their colonial domination over the less powerful. In discussing the effect of the First World War on African national consciousness, Bethwell Ogot states, "[t]he Africans became more aware of themselves as a distinct racial group; they discovered the weakness and the heterogeneity of the white men; and even more crucial, they learned the importance of organized resistance" (265). Consequently, the end of the Great War marked the beginning of a new era for African nations, accompanied by an indigenous renaissance in art, literature and culture.

Out of this atmosphere of optimism and hope were born new ideological and literary movements aimed at furthering the cause of nationalism by promoting the notions of Africanism and Black Pride. The most influential wave of this rising tide of nationalism surfaced in Paris in the late 1920s, where a group of African intellectuals and poets, including Aimé Césaire, Birago Diop and Léopold Sédar Senghor united in a revolutionary action to seek the liberation of the Blacks from colonial power. They developed an essentialist and nativist theory of negro people called Négritude "that sought to extend the perception of a unified negro 'race' to a concept of specifically 'African personality'" (Ashcroft *et al., Key Concepts* 161). The word "Négritude" was coined by Aimé Césaire in his 1939 poetry book *Cahier d'un retour au pays natal* (*Notebook of a Return to the Native Land*) (Reiss 507). Négritude means in Césaire's own words, "the simple recognition of the fact that one is black, the acceptance of this fact and of our destiny as blacks, of our history and culture" (qtd. in Nichols 157).

Césaire's *Notebook* reveals the essence of the cultural politics of Négritude. The poem is a quest for identity. A French-educated black man returns to his homeland, Martinique. First, he feels like an outsider, for he thinks himself superior to the Creole speakers. However, he soon realises that there is a quest that he has to embark on in order to find reconciliation with his black African heritage. The poem, thus, recounts the story of the persona's gradual realisation that his people are not inferior or subordinate to any other nations, but simply the victims of colonisation. Upon this painful realisation, he transforms into a spokesperson for all the oppressed people of Africa: "My mouth shall be the mouth of those calamities that have no mouth,/my voice the freedom of those who break down/in the prison holes of despair" (45). It is towards the end of the poem that the persona achieves reconciliation with black collective identity and defines what it means to be a black in a short list of affirmations and negations:

> oh friendly source of light
> oh fresh source of light
> those who have invented neither powder nor compass
> those who could harness neither steam nor electricity

> those who exploited neither the seas nor the sky but those
> without whom the earth would not be earth
> [...]
> my negritude is not a stone, its deafness hurled against the clamor of the day
> my negritude is not a leukoma of dead liquid over the earth's dead eye
> my negritude is neither tower nor cathedral
> it takes root in the red flesh of the soil
> it takes root in the ardent flesh of the sky
> it breaks through the opaque prostration with
> its upright patience. (67-69)

Just like the persona in the poem, Négritudinists proudly affirmed their African racial and cultural heritage and celebrated the beauties of the continent and its indigenous people so that that they could establish a stable identity in the face of the instability of displacement caused by colonialism. However, their philosophy was not a mere attempt to encourage African communities to take pride in their native culture. Rather, it was a kind of cultural and social rehabilitation aimed at imposing self-confidence to peoples of a continent that became synonymous with slavery and savagery. To this end, they endeavoured to rewrite the Black history falsified by the West (Ashcroft *et al., Empire* 166). They turned to their native land to discover the features of African culture and life before colonial "contamination" in order to reveal, what they believed, the true authentic nature of African communities and their cultural production. Therefore, Négritude is generally regarded as "a backward movement" which promoted "a glorification of African past and a nostalgia for the imaginary beauty and harmony of traditional African society" (Irele 40-41).

The Négritudinists asserted distinctive features of Black culture and identity in a similar fashion to the Western philosophical tradition, essentially based on binary oppositions. They advocated that Black culture was "emotional rather than rational; it stressed integration and wholeness over analysis and dissection; it operated by distinctive rhythmic and temporal principles, and so forth" (Ashcroft *et al., Empire* 21). As a pertinent example of the distinctive features that separated Black culture from European values, Sédar Senghor, a major theorist of the Négritude movement, maintains that there is not a rigid distinction between reason and emotion in the African understanding of reality in a Western empirical sense. It is endowed with emotion and feeling as well as reason. Senghor notes,

> The African is, as it were, shut up in his black skin. He lives in primordial night. He does not begin by distinguishing himself from the object of study, the tree or stone, the man or the animal or social event. He does not keep it at a distance. He does not analyse it. Once he has come under its influence, he takes it like a blind man, still living, into his hands. He does not fix or kill it. He turns it over and over in his supple hands, he fingers it, he feels it. The African is one of the worms created on the Third Day [...] a pure sensory field. (qtd. in McLeod 78)

There were fierce critics of the Négritude movement among African intellectuals. For instance, the Nigerian playwright Wole Soyinka argued that Négritude propelled African people into self-absorption ironically by affirming one of the central Eurocentric prejudices against Africans, namely the dichotomy between European rationalism and African emotionalism. He therefore called Négritude "a narcissistic cult of the African world" (98). Soyinka also found Négritudinists' emphasis on black identity superfluous, pointing out that "a tiger does not proclaim his tigritude, he pounces" (101). The South African writer and academic, Ezekiel Mphahlele, on the other hand, complained about the idealised image of Africa promoted in Négritude poetry: "[t]he poetry of négritude origin may also falsify the image of Africa by representing it as a symbol of innocence, purity, naked beauty, human decency [...] Some négritude verse leaves one rather worried by its elusiveness" (137). It is clear that Soyinka and Mphahlele, among others, expressed their dismay that Négritude would extend the already established gap between Africa and Europe by promoting an image of Africa isolated from the influences of other cultures.

A more systematic critique of the Négritude movement was offered by Franz Fanon, the Martinican psychiatrist, political theorist, literary critic and revolutionary activist who would become one of the most influential figures of African liberation movement. Fanon developed his theories regarding Black identity and the independence of Black communities in his *Peau noire, masques blancs* (*Black Skin, White Masks*, 1952) and *Les damnés de la terre* (*The Wretched of the Earth*, 1961). He drew on a range of disciplines, such as existentialism, psychoanalysis and anthropology to analyse the psychological and sociological consequences of colonisation (Ashcroft *et al., Empire* 124). As a colonial subject, Fanon himself suffered from colonial policies of the West. He claimed that much of what he valued in his indigenous culture had been undermined in the period of French colonialism. Hence, he describes colonised people as those "in whose soul an inferiority complex has been created by the death and burial of its local cultural originality" (*Black Skin* 9). Fanon was profoundly interested in national consciousness and culture, and the fact of "blackness" became one of the central tenets of his theory of colonial resistance. For Fanon, the desire to define a national culture is a direct result of the process of colonialism since colonised intellectuals attempted to defy the colonial ideology by exalting their national and cultural heritage. He argues,

> Colonialism is not satisfied merely with holding a people in its grip and emptying the native's brain of all form and content. By a kind of perverted logic, it turns to the past of the oppressed

people, and distorts, disfigures and destroys it [...] To fight for national culture means in the first place to fight for the liberation of the nation, that material keystone which makes the building of a culture possible. (*Wretched* 169)

Just like Négritudinists, Fanon also finds the efforts of reclaiming the national past legitimate. He writes,

> this passionate search for a national culture which existed before the colonial era, finds its legitimate reason in the anxiety shared by native intellectuals to shrink away from that Western culture in which they all risked being swamped. Because they realize that they are in danger of losing their lives and thus becoming lost to their people, these men, hot-headed and with anger in their hearts, relentlessly determine to renew contact once more with the oldest and most pre-colonial springs of life of their people. (*Wretched* 168-169)

However, Fanon, as a psychiatrist, was more interested in the positive effects of the cultural revival on the individual psyche of the colonised subject, for he believed that Black subjects can only achieve their independence through political action not by subverting the Western tropes of binary oppositions. Hence, the national culture, Fanon cautions, should be supported, inasmuch as it helps to provide a cure for the inferiority complex that the colonial subject has suffered from for centuries: "[t]he claim to a national culture in the past does not only rehabilitate that nation and serve as a justification for the hope of a future national culture. In the sphere of psycho-affective equilibrium it is responsible for an important change in the native" (*Wretched* 169).

Contrary to the Négritudinists, who placed absolute faith in Black cultural identity, Fanon was aware of the pitfalls of such a unifying view of national identity. As the writers of *The Empire Writes Back* point out,

Fanon recognised the essential fictionality of racial identities and perhaps more importantly "the readiness with which the assimilated Black colonized could be persuaded to don a white mask of culture and privilege" (123). He was therefore highly critical of Négritudinists since they "simply confirmed racism by turning 'negative' stereotypical racial identities into 'positive' racial values" (Richards 15). It was nothing but a reversed colonial racism, and thus it was destined to fail. Fanon further argues that Négritude would only help enlarge the distance between African and European countries. He argues,

> White civilisation and European culture have forced an existential deviation on the Negro. I shall demonstrate elsewhere that what is often called the black soul is a white man's artefact. The educated Negro, slave of the spontaneous and cosmic Negro myth, feels at a given stage that his race no longer understands him [...] Then he [the Negro] congratulates himself on this, and enlarging the difference, the incomprehension, the disharmony, he finds in them the meaning of his real humanity. Or more rarely he wants to belong to his people. And it is with rage in his mouth and abandon in his heart that he buries himself in the vast black abyss. We shall see that this attitude, so heroically absolute, renounces the present and the future in the name of a mystical past. (*Black Skin* 6-7)

It is particularly in a chapter titled "The Pitfalls of National Consciousness" in his *Wretched of the Earth* that Fanon delineates the failure of national consciousness in eliminating the dominance of colonial institutions in the emerging African states. For Fanon, it is vital for postcolonial nations to establish new forms of social democracy instead of utilising the institutions inherited from the colonial rule by simply filling the administrative positions with native people. Fanon cautions that if national intelligentsia falls into the trap of reproducing the concepts and beliefs of the colonisers in the period of postcolonial rebuilding, their policies will inevitably lead to a new form of colonisation rather than help create an independent country. He maintains that "[n]ational consciousness, instead of being the all-embracing crystallization of the innermost hopes of the whole people, instead of being the immediate and most obvious result of the mobilization of the people will be an empty shell, a crude and fragile travesty of what it might have been" (*Wretched* 119).

It is interesting to note the similarities between the ideological and aesthetic concerns of Négritude and the ideas defended by Latin American magical realist writers. The Négritudinists' quest for an authentic African identity is, like that of Carpentier's, tinted with a culturalist view. Instead of promoting a genuine national identity, both Latin American writers and Négritude thinkers endeavoured to rescue a lost original culture from the destruction caused by European imperial powers. They believed that it was only around this original, irreducible identity that a national culture and literature could healthily root and develop. Given this close association between the two, one may surmise that postcolonial countries provided a suitable atmosphere for the rise of magical realist fiction in the early days of independence.[26] Nevertheless, the dominant narrative mode in the early postcolonial period was social realism. An important reason for this tendency is that the early postcolonial writers saw literature as a practical means of contributing to the liberation of their country by raising national consciousness in the reading public.

The Nigerian novelist Chinua Achebe's creative and theoretical writing, in particular, bears witness to this idea. His theoretical writing is based on a sense of communal responsibility to teach the indigenous people about their history and culture. In his 1965 essay "The Novelist as Teacher," Achebe maintains that the novel offers an opportunity for

---

[26] Bruce King notes that the most influential magical realist writer of the time was Wilson Harris who "examines the divisions of Guyana by trying to reimagine history not as one continuous story but as a continual revisioning of characters and events" (50).

education, but it is not the same as the moralising type of education that European theorists from Plato to I. A. Richards exhorted. For Achebe, the African writer is more concerned with the importance of challenging and combating African peoples' acceptance of "racial inferiority" and "the disaster brought upon the African psyche in the period of subjection to alien races" ("Novelist" 43). His essay reads like a plea to African novelists to assume the role of a teacher and take up the responsibility of "re-education and regeneration" of their society (45). In doing so, they may help the society "regain its belief in itself and put away complexes of the years of denigration and self-abasement" inflicted upon it during the period of colonisation (44). Achebe does not excuse himself from the task of educating the masses. He states that "I would be quite satisfied if my novels (particularly the ones I set in the past) did no more than teach my readers their past – with all its imperfections – was not one long night of savagery from which the first Europeans acting on God's behalf delivered them" (45).

Achebe was also aware of the fact that the novel might turn into a dangerous ideological tool in the hands of Western writers. In a lecture at the University of Massachusetts in 1975, he made a remarkable and often-quoted anti-colonial statement, mainly focusing on Joseph Conrad's 1899 novella *Heart of Darkness*. He criticised the Westerners' stereotyping of African culture and the ignorance of the so-called intellectuals who claimed that Africa had no history. For Achebe, it is not a trivial tendency, but an expression of a deep-rooted desire in "Western psychology to set Africa up as a foil to Europe" ("Image" 3). He regards Joseph Conrad's novella *Heart of Darkness* as an embodiment of European prejudice against African communities. For Achebe, the narrator of the story, Marlow, is the mouthpiece of Conrad himself. Marlow, a representative of the English liberal tradition, manages to shock his fellowmen by describing atrocities in the African Congo. He utters touching sentiments about the Black man's condition, but he never sees him as his equal. Achebe writes,

> The kind of liberalism espoused by Marlow/Conrad touched all the best minds of the age in England, Europe and America. It took different forms in the minds of different people but almost always managed to sidestep the ultimate question of equality between white people and black people, [...] [Conrad] would not use the word 'brother' however qualified; the farthest he would go was "kinship." ("Image" 10-11)

Achebe presents several lengthy excerpts so as to demonstrate how Conrad carefully weaves Africa and Europe as cultural antagonists through his binary parings. Achebe contends that African people are either underrepresented or silenced in the narrative, which, in turn, creates an image of Africa "as a metaphysical battlefield devoid of all recognizable humanity, into which the wandering European enters at his peril" ("Image" 12). For Achebe, Conrad's novella is just another piece of narrative that confirms the Western underestimation of the East, as once voiced by Rudyard Kipling in his famous lines, "East is East, and West is West and ne'er the twain shall meet" and thus condemns Conrad as a "thoroughgoing racist" ("Image" 11).[27]

How could postcolonial writers use literary forms borrowed from the West if the modes of cultural expression associated with the powers of colonialism were regarded as contaminated and therefore anti-national? Writers made a concerted effort to invent new strategies to free their works from the colonial influences. These include, as has been shown, the revitalisation of indigenous myths as a form of cultural counter-assertion and the appropriation of indigenous social and cultural features as a subversive force against the established colonial norm. The authors of *The Empire Writes Back* argue that "the seizing of the means of communication and the liberation of post-colonial writing by the appro-

---

[27] In his first version of this article as published by the *Massachusetts Review*, Achebe used the word "bloody" to describe Conrad's attitude towards African people. In the subsequent versions he changed this to "thoroughgoing."

priation of the written word become crucial features of the process of self-assertion and of the ability to reconstruct the world as an unfolding historical process" (Ashcroft et al., Empire 82).

Achebe's novels also epitomise the strategies that postcolonial writers employed to adopt Western literary forms to their own needs. Like his contemporaries, Achebe integrated vernacular vocabulary and dialect into his narratives. However, his strategies of appropriation were not limited to linguistic features, but also involved cultural strategies. For instance, he included in his works indigenous customs, traditions as well as discourses ranging from folk tales to myths. In his 1958 debut novel *Things Fall Apart,* Achebe employed most of these strategies, paving the way for the emergence of a sub-genre called "the village novel" in African literature (Durix, *Mimesis* 25-26). Set in the 1890s, *Things Fall Apart* depicts the conflicts between Nigeria's white colonial government and the traditional culture of the indigenous Igbo people. Achebe's novel is a response to the stereotypical European portraits of native Africans as primitive others. He meticulously portrays the complex, sophisticated social institutions as well as artistic traditions of Igbo culture in the pre-colonial period so as to give voice to the repressed colonial subject. "Achebe," as Durix notes, "strives hard to put words onto Conrad's dark continent of Africa [...] and manages to bring to life a village in pre-European times with its assets and weaknesses" (*Mimesis* 26). The dialogue between Obierika and Okonkwo, two clansmen, in chapter 20 is particularly telling with respect to the indigenous people's view of the colonial enterprise. Okonkwo, who has been on exile for seven years for killing a clansman accidentally, returns to his village only to find that it has dramatically changed under the colonial rule. The white men now subject the villagers to their judicial and governmental systems. Obierika narrates all the changes that their clan underwent since the arrival of the colonialists. Then, the two men get into a heated discussion about a clansman, Aneto, who has been hanged by the white government for killing a man with whom he has had a dispute. Aneto has rejected the court's arbitration on the dispute, claiming that the white men undermine the Igbo sense of justice. Obierika condemns the colonialists for their cunning plans to capture their land and their disrespect toward Igbo customs. His criticism also extends to some clan members who have converted to Christianity, betraying their own brothers. Obierika comes to the conclusion that it is impossible for the white men to comprehend Igbo people without learning to speak their language.

> "Does the white man understand our custom about land?" "How can he when he does not even speak our tongue? But he says that our customs are bad; and our own brothers who have taken up his religion also say that our customs are bad. How do you think we can fight when our own brothers have turned against us? The white man is very clever. He came quietly and peaceably with his religion. We were amused at his foolishness and allowed him to stay. Now he has won our brothers, and our clan can no longer act like one. He has put a knife on the things that held us together and we have fallen apart." (*Things* 124-125)

Obierika seems to voice Achebe's own thoughts on colonialism. African customs and traditions are not savage or primitive; they are simply the reflection of a different worldview. This incompetence to understand "the other" is not, however, confined to Europeans only. African people fail to understand the coloniser, too. In chapter 15, the villagers kill a white man who arrives at their village on an iron horse, a bicycle, only because they cannot understand his language. Achebe seems to communicate the message that the cultural distinction between Africa and Europe is not a matter of superiority or inferiority, but a problem of communication that can be resolved if both parties give up their prejudices about "the other."

Towards the end of the 1960s, the atmosphere of optimism and euphoria that accompanied independence gave way to one of disappointment and frustration as "the political space which was opened up by the struggle for independence and the decolonization of the continent swiftly contracted as indigenous tyrants stepped into the shoes of the departing colonial masters" (Williams 499). African writers responded to this tragic development instantaneously by writing novels about the disillusionment of the public with the indigenous politicians. In this phase, much of the literary output was indebted to the theoretical views of Franz Fanon, who foresaw many of the problems new nation-states would face in the post-independence period. In discussing the influence of Fanon in African literatures, James Ogude notes,

> Fanon's prophetic study of the transition from colonialism to neocolonialism in Africa touched the imaginations of many writers and intellectuals, and in the next two decades (the 1970s and 1980s) the concerns of the writers would focus on the failure of independence to make a decisive break with colonialism, and the centrality of national culture in shaping the African revolution that was faltering. This radicalized vision of literature was to continue well into the 1990s. (223)

Simon Gikandi, claims that the novels written in Africa in the 1970s and 1980s can be categorised in two groups in keeping with their reflection of Fanonian themes. The first group includes Ngugi wa Thiong'o's *A Grain of Wheat* (1966), Ousmane Sembéne's *God's Bits of Wood (Les bouts de bois de Dieu)* (1960), Ahmadou Kourouma's *Suns of Independence (Les soleils des indépendances)* (1968), and Ayi Kwei Armah's *The Beautyful Ones Are Not Yet Born* (1968). The novels in this group are centred on the motif that nationalism was a narrative and experience caught between its promise and betrayal (Gikandi, "Colonialism" 174). In the second group, there are Ngugi's *Petals of Blood* (1977), Sembéne's *Xala* (1973), *The Last of the Empire (Le dernier de l'empire)* (1981), and Ama Ata Aidoo's *Our Sister Killjoy* (1979). The novels included in the second group were "driven by the need to provide a critique of neocolonial economic relations, the persistence of imperialism in the fields of economics, and to imagine an alternative political economy based on the ideology of African socialism" (Gikandi, "Colonialism" 174). From the survey conducted thus far, it can be concluded that before magical realism started to reshape novelists' imagination in the 1980s, the African novel in English was mainly dominated by themes aimed at both acknowledging and questioning the political and cultural policies of anti-colonial nationalisms.

2.1.2. The Awakening of Indian Nationalism

Like other former colonies, India also gained her independence as a consequence of indigenous anti-colonial nationalism; however, the process of national liberation in India took longer than in other former colonies. As Peter Childs and Patrick Williams point out, India is a singular example of the achievement of independence as a result of sixty years of cumulative efforts at all levels of society (29-30). The first steps towards liberation were taken in the form of a series of rebellions with different political motives, ranging from religious to secular, from reformist to revolutionist. The last of this series of rebellions, known as the Mutiny of 1857, marked a turning point in Indian history. Barbara and Thomas Metcalf state that "the revolt of 1857-1858, which swept across much of north India in opposition to British rule, has conventionally been taken as the dividing point that marks the beginning of modern India" (92). The most important outcome of these earlier claims for independence was the establishment of the Indian National Congress in 1885. As a result, the colonial resistance could be operated from a single centre at national level (Childs and Williams 28-29).

There were numerous figures that took part in India's independence movement; however, none of them was as influential as Mahatma Gandhi, who is known as the father of modern India. Gandhi spent most of his life in diaspora, leaving India at the age of eighteen only to return to resettle there when he was forty-six. After completing his legal education in law in Britain, he spent twenty-one years of his life in South Africa, where he came to an understanding of his own culture and formed the basis of his anti-colonial politics (Young 317). Mahatma Gandhi's appearance on the political scene in 1920 brought rays of hope in a century of colonial violence and bloody acts of resistance. Like his African counterparts, Gandhi also considered the mobilisation of national culture as an essential anti-colonial strategy. Thus, the notion of a return to "pure" indigenous traditions became a vital aspect of Gandhi's political struggle for independence. He revitalised the ideal of establishing *Ram Raj*, a society built on humane values and spiritual principles, drawn from the memories of a long lost Golden Age. He claimed that such an ideal could not be realised through a violent resistance against the coloniser. Therefore, when Gandhi became the leader of national liberation movement in 1920, he demanded *Swaraj* (self-government) and *Satyagraha* (nonviolent resistance) (Young 318-20). He also organised a number of hunger strikes, boycotts and events of civil disobedience and campaigned for social reform. As a result of Gandhi's powerful campaigns, the English had to introduce a further constitutional reform, known as the Government of India Act, in 1935. The Congress Party, demanding basic rights and social reforms, became the strongest party in the 1936 general elections. Despite numerous arrests of notable figures of resistance by the English, the struggle for liberation continued until 1947, when India was granted her independence (Metcalf and Metcalf 190-196).

There were two main reasons that forced the British Government to grant independence to India. The first was that the strength of the national movement under the leadership of Mahatma Gandhi. The other reason was that Great Britain, greatly weakened by the Second World War, found herself unable to keep India under control. It was announced in February 1947 that the government was to hand over power in India by June 1948. The planned independence was drawn back to 15 August

1947 because of political riots. Lord Mountbatten, the last English Viceroy, announced his scheme for the transfer of power in India, which was agreed both by the Congress and the League. On 15 August 1947 it was proclaimed and enshrined in the India Independence Act. The Act of 1935 was the base for the new constitution of an independent India. In 1950 India became a republic with Dr. Rajendra Prasad as its first President and Nehru as its Prime Minister (Metcalf and Metcalf 217-220).

The rise of Indian literature in English was conterminous with the institutionalisation of English education in the early nineteenth century with two legislative regulations: the Charter Act of 1813 and Lord Bentinck's English Education Act of 1835. However, as Aparna and Vinay Dharwadker note in their survey of Indian literature in English, the early men of letters who preferred to write in English rather than vernacular Indian languages, such as Rammohun Roy (1772-1833) and Henry Derozio (1809-1831), had already completed their literary careers before the introduction of these legislative acts (89). The hope of discarding the coloniser's language after the independence of the country in 1947 also proved to be futile as poems, plays, novels and polemical writings in English continued to flow, making the English language an important part of Indian literary production. This is not, of course, to claim that English has always been accepted as an integral part of Indian culture. Like postcolonial African literatures, Indian literature in English has been vexed by the question of authenticity and of indignity right from its beginnings. Aparna and Vinay Dharwadker view the development of Indian literature in English in three specific historical stages. Within two decades following the independence there appeared a heated discussion among the prominent literary figures, such as Latika Basu, Purushottama Lal and Jyotirmoy Datta over the place of the English language in the contemporary Indian literary and cultural scene. While Basu and Datta rejected writing in English on nationalistic grounds, Lal saw the English language as the only medium that could communicate the cosmopolitan nature of India. In the mid-1970s, a symbiotic relation between the two groups started to develop. Successive translations of Indian literary works produced in about a dozen of Indian vernaculars helped to rehabilitate the English language "as a culturally necessary and historically inescapable component of the national literary system, and to 'domesticate' it in a network of linguistic interdependencies" (Aparna and Vinay Dharwadker 93-94). In the late 1970s and the early 1980s Indian literature in English achieved a global readership with the publication of ten collections of Indian English poetry and Salman Rushdie's epochal novel *Midnight's Children*. These remarkable contributions secured the English language as an unquestionable facet of Indian literature, ending the debates in the preceding decades over its linguistic, literary and cultural relevancy in India (Aparna and Vinay Dharwadker 94).

Like their African counterparts, the early Indian novelists largely drew their subject matters and themes from their native culture and history. In *The Indian English Novel: Nation, History, and Narration*, Priyamvada Gopal observes that "the novel emerged in nineteenth-century India with a profound interest in the writing of history and, relatedly, in articulating a sense of nationhood" (20). Regarded as the earliest known attempts at producing Indian fiction in English, Kylas Chunder Dutt's *A Journal of Forty-Eight Hours of the Year 1945* (1835) and Soshee Chunder Dutt's *The Republic of Orissa: A Page from the Annals of the 20th Century* (1845) epitomise this interest in history (Gopal 20-22, Mukherjee 94-95, Mehrotra 7). Both are imaginary histories projected into distant future of the twentieth century, describing battles of liberation and uprisings against the British rule. In a similar, but perhaps a more radical fashion to the role that Achebe would assign to the African writer a century later, both writers encouraged Indian people to seek freedom from imperial oppression, drawing attention to organising and consolidating the collective power of indigenous people in the liberation movement.

Shoshee Chunder Dutt's *The Republic of Orissa* describes the anti-colonial war of an imaginary country. The people of Orissa rebel against the British imperial government subsequent to the legalisation of slavery in the country in 1916. After eighty-five years of constant struggle with the British, Orissa declares itself a republic on 15 October 2001. Gopal rightly argues that in Chunder Dutt's *The Republic of Orissa*, "India ('Hindustan') is exhorted to follow the example of Orissa, which has joined the order of world nations by laying claim to the idea of freedom over tyranny" (21). In *A Journal of Forty-Eight Hours of the Year 1945* Kylas Chunder Dutt tells a similar story of an armed rebellion against the British rule, yet with a different resolution. The introductory paragraph of Chunder Dutt's novel should suffice to demonstrate the colonial writer's subtlety in representing historical events, which is only comparable to that of a historian:

> The people of India and particularly those of the metropolis had been subject of the last fifty years to every species of subaltern oppression. The dagger and the bowl were dealt out with a merciless hand, and neither, age, sex nor condition could repress the rage of the British barbarians. Those events, together with the recollection of the grievances suffered by their ancestors, roused the dormant spirit of the generally considered timid Indians. (149)

Having thus lost their tolerance, an Indian army of patriots led by a charismatic leader Bhoobun Mohan starts to fight against the British forces, commanded by Lord Fell Butcher and Colonel John Blood Thirsty. Although the Indians are the victorious party in the first battle, they have to concede defeat when their leader is killed by the British.

In a similar fashion to the Négritudinists, Anglophone Indian writers also aimed at showing that they were by no means inferior to the coloniser by narrating stories from pre-colonial India. As Meenakshi

Mukherjee points, these novelists took a fierce cultural pride and asserted "the antiquity and superiority of Indian civilisation in relation to Europe" (96). Mukherjee points to two works of fiction written from a nationalist perspective: Sarath Kumar Ghosh's *The Prince of Destiny: The New Krishna* (1909) and K. K. Sinha's *Sanjogita* (1903). The propensity to write about nationalist themes and subject matters continued to exist in the Indian novel in English in the twentieth century. The legacy of the founder of the nation, Mahatma Gandhi, had a central place in the fictions written immediately after the independence of India. As Priyamvada Gopal maintains,

> Gandhi's influence on literature generally and the Anglophone novel more particularly is best understood in terms of the pivotal role he played in decisively bringing together diverse communities under the rubric of the 'India' possessed, according to him, of a civilizational and spiritual unity that long preceded 'English' rule. (44)

Thus, novelists from different political backgrounds engaged prolifically with Gandhi and his ideas during the 1940s and the 1950s when the new nation was coming into being. The group, as Gopal points out, included writers with different political and philosophical inclination, such as R. K. Narayan, Mulk Raj Anand, Raja Rao, Bhabani Bhattacharya, K. Nagarajan, and K. S. Venkataramani. Although these writers differed in style, the image of the father of the nation was writ large in their works. Gopal notes "[e]ven where Gandhi or Gandhism were not the explicit subject matter, there was a noticeable shift to village settings and agrarian life, in keeping with Gandhi's repeated reminder that India was a fundamentally agrarian society based in villages" (46). The glorification of the past, along with the portrayal of Gandhi as the father of the nation, provided a cultural hub to help maintain and strengthen the national integrity in the early days of its independence.[28]

These early examples of fiction, which are not read today except by those with a specialist's interest in colonial history, started a tradition that would help forge national identity in postcolonial countries. Commonwealth critics did not fail to recognise the role literature played in the development of new nations. For instance, in the introductory essay to a collection of papers, *The Commonwealth Pen: An Introduction to the Literature of the British Commonwealth*, the editor, A. L. McLeod, underscores the fact that commonwealth literatures are the direct result of the formation of new nation states, and that if a nation fails to establish its literature, this is because it lacks a national identity. McLeod proposes,

> The genesis of a local literature in the Commonwealth countries has almost always been contemporaneous with the development of a truly nationalist sentiment: the larger British colonies, such as Fiji, Hong Kong and Malta, where there are relatively large English-speaking populations, have produced no literature, even in the broadest sense of the term. The reason probably lies in the fact that they have, as yet, no sense of national identity, no cause to follow, no common goal. (qtd. in McLeod 12-13)

However, as McLeod warns, Commonwealth literature was never fully free from the imperious connotation of the term. Commonwealth critics emphasised the importance of themes associated with universality and timelessness and thus, "the attention to the alleged nationalist purpose of much Commonwealth literature often played second fiddle to more abstract concerns which distracted attention from specific national concerns" (McLeod 13). Of course, English literature with its supposedly

---

[28] For a comprehensive list of nationalist novels written immediately before and after India gained her independence in 1947, see Kunjo Singh.

universal messages became the measure of value in determining "good writing." In his *After Empire: Scott, Naipaul, Rushdie*, Michael Edward Gorra states that "the first books on what we then called 'Commonwealth' literature often opposed British novels to works from India or Africa – E.M. Forster with R.K. Narayan, Joyce Cary with Chinua Achebe" (4). This led later critics to shun the term. For example, in *The Empire Writes Back*, Ashcroft, Griffiths, and Tiffin reject the term "Commonwealth" on the grounds that it rests "purely on the fact of a shared history and the resulting political grouping" (23). Nevertheless, the achievements of Commonwealth criticism cannot be ignored altogether as McLeod notes "[t]he patient, detailed and enthusiastic readings of Commonwealth literature laid the foundation for the various postcolonial criticisms that were to follow, and to which much postcolonial critical activity remains indebted" (16). It was instrumental in bringing about new and creative directions in contemporary literary and cultural studies, thereby paving the way for postcolonial studies.

2.2. Toward an Aesthetics of Hybridity: Postcolonial Studies

The growing dissatisfaction with the theoretical framework offered by Commonwealth criticism became more apparent in the 1970s and 1980s. During this period, postcolonial writers and critics wrote numerous essays to draw attention to the darker side of colonialism, obscured by the liberal humanist principles of Commonwealth literature. Written in this period, Salman Rushdie's 1983 essay, entitled "'Commonwealth Literature' does not exist," stands out with its different approach to the experience of colonialism. In this relatively short essay Rushdie is more interested in the cultural condition created by the interaction between the coloniser and the colonised than the suffering and pain that it caused. His remarks are characteristically incisive and go some way towards indicating the need for a new critical paradigm for the study of emergent postcolonial literatures. In the course of his essay, Rushdie raises a number of objections to Commonwealth literature. To begin with, for

Rushdie, the term Commonwealth is "unhelpful and even a little distasteful" since it helped establish an exclusive literary "ghetto" whose effect is to change the meaning of English literature "into something far narrower, something topographical, nationalistic, possibly even racially segregationist" ("Commonwealth" 61, 63). Having said this, Rushdie goes on to stress the fact that "Commonwealth" is a misnomer in that it counts within its purview only those writers who write in English, excluding literary works written in vernacular languages to a large extent. As a result of this biased practice, it has become uncertain whether the citizens of Commonwealth countries writing in languages other than English or those who have ceased to write in English can be categorised as Commonwealth writers. In other words, the term "Commonwealth" has come to denote a group of privileged writers who write in the acquired colonial language rather than a literary categorisation with certain shared cultural and literary traits as its name suggests.

The categorisation of the emergent postcolonial literatures under the rubric of Commonwealth has also led the English language to retain its privileged position in academia. "At best, what is called 'Commonwealth Literature,'" Rushdie points out, "is positioned *below* English literature 'proper' – or [...] it places Eng. Lit. at the centre and the rest of the world at the periphery" ("Commonwealth" 66). Rushdie alerts us to the fact that the central position of English literature is undergoing a radical crisis as the literary map of the world has started to change. English has become an integral part of the culture of the countries Britain once colonised, turning it into the *lingua franca* of world literature. "The English language," in Rushdie's own words, "has ceased to be the sole possession of the English some time ago" ("Commonwealth" 70). Rushdie argues that people who were once colonized by the English "are now rapidly remaking and domesticating it [the English language] [...] carving out large territories for themselves within its frontiers" ("Commonwealth" 64). It is clear that Rushdie perceives the cultural repercussions of the decolonisation process, particularly in literature, as a blowback, or a reverse movement from the periphery to the centre in which people from former colonies took over the imperial centre. The stylistic, linguistic and thematic variations among this new wave of writers changed the conception of English literature in an unprecedented way. This revolutionary expansion of postcolonial literatures is, of course, in stark contrast with the scope provided by Commonwealth literature, which attempts to place English culture and language at the centre of literary studies. Rushdie writes,

> I think that if *all* English literatures could be studied together, a shape would emerge which would truly reflect the new shape of the language in the world, and we could see that Eng. Lit. has never been in better shape, because the world language now also possesses a world literature, which is proliferating in every conceivable direction. [...] Perhaps "Commonwealth literature" was invented to delay the day when we rough beasts actually slouch into Bethlehem. In which case, it is time to admit that the centre cannot hold. ("Commonwealth" 70)

There is an overriding assumption in Rushdie's position that the national literatures of the former colonies should be freed from the constraints of imperial powers and hegemonic categories like Commonwealth.

However, for Rushdie, the necessity to denounce the Commonwealth as a literary categorisation does not result from the protests from the former colonies, but from the effects of colonialism itself. Instead of focusing on negatives, he proposes that it is more useful to identify the strengths of the postcolonial condition. He is celebrant of the new dimensions of linguistic heterogeneity offered to English literature by the writers emerging from the postcolonial world. The remaking of the English language outside institutional channels has unsettled the borders between countries, bringing cultures into a new relationship by means of translation and dialogue. It is for this reason that Rushdie identifies a multilingual and multicultural state of consciousness as the driving force behind the transformation taking place in English literature. He believes that postcolonial literatures are a result of cross-cultural interaction, exchange and transformation, which Rushdie calls a "transnational, cross-lingual process of pollination" ("Commonwealth" 69). Rushdie asserts that this global phenomenon, thus far obscured by the hegemonic categorisations like the Commonwealth, opens a new horizon for literary studies:

> [...] if we were to forget about "Commonwealth Literature," we might see that there is a kind of commonality about much literature, in many languages, emerging from those parts of the world which one could loosely term the less powerful, or the powerless. The magical realism of the Latin Americans influences Indian-language writers in India today. The rich, folk-tale quality of a novel like *Sandro of Chegem*, by the Muslim Russian Fazil Iskander, finds its parallels in the work – for instance – of the Nigerian, Amos Tutuola, or even Cervantes. It is possible, I think, to begin to theorize common factors between writers from these societies – poor countries, or deprived minorities in powerful countries – and to say that much of what is new in world literature comes from this group. This seems to me to be a "real" theory, bounded by frontiers which are neither political nor linguistic but imaginative. ("Commonwealth" 68-69)

Here, Rushdie does not only articulate many of the preoccupations postcolonial critics would deal with in the years to come, but also identifies the major trends in postcolonial literatures around the world. His formulation recalls the Russian theorist Mikhail Bakhtin's concept of "polyglossia," which means the interaction of two or more national languages within a given culture, for instance, that of English and French in medieval England. For Bakhtin, a true dialogue between cultures is only possible through polyglossia:

> Language is transformed from an absolute dogma it had been within the narrow framework of a sealed-off and impermeable monoglossia into a working hypothesis for comprehending and expressing reality. But such a full and complete transformation can occur only under certain conditions, namely, under the condition of thoroughgoing polyglossia. Only polyglossia fully frees consciousness from the tyranny of its own language and its own myth of language. ("Prehistory" 61)

Bakhtin envisions a polyglot world where different cultures and languages coexist, interacting with each other. In this actively polyglot world, Bakhtin argues, a new cultural and creative consciousness comes into being, setting "into motion a process of active, mutual cause-and-effect and interillumination" ("Epic" 12). Bakhtin proposes this multilingual cultural diversity as the ideal precondition for the rise of the novel: "the novel emerged and matured precisely when intense activization of external and internal polyglossia was at the peak of its activity; this is its native element" ("Epic" 12). Given the Bakhtinian prerequisite of polyglossia, or dialogue between cultures and languages, it can be argued that the novel has entered a new, exciting phase with the rise of postcolonial literatures, where linguistic and political borders are eliminated to a great extent through cross-cultural interaction.

It is not a coincidence that this strong objection to Commonwealth literature was pronounced by a world-renowned magical realist writer. Nor is it that Rushdie acknowledges magical realism as one of the key literary practices complicit in the proliferation of postcolonial literatures as well as the change in their reception in the West. Just like Rushdie, later critics also point to a growing tendency among postcolonial novelists towards writing magical realist fiction. Jean-Pierre Durix observes that novels written in colonial/postcolonial countries followed a course from social realism "as an articulation of a local idiom" to magical realism in which writers "use metafictional devices to debunk the realistic illusion, while continuing to believe that fiction should have a firm base in reality" (*Mimesis* 23-24). Similarly, discussing the development of Anglophone fiction in India, Priyamvada Gopal remarks, "[r]epressed elements – wonder, fantasy, poetry – would emerge through the gaps in even many stolidly realist works and, of course, over time, 'magical realism' or the bringing together of the fabulous and real, would come to be one of the most celebrated achievements of the tradition" (20). Why has magical realism become a championed literary mode among postcolonial writers? What does magical realism offer in the context of postcolonial writing? In fact, these questions have been briefly addressed in chapter 1 with regard to the prominence of magical realism in Latin American literature in the post-independence period. Nonetheless, it is worthwhile to reconsider these questions in connection with the narrative possibilities of magical realist writing and the cultural and linguistic heterogeneity of the postcolonial world.

As put forth by the discussion in chapter 1, magical realism is essentially an experimental narrative mode, challenging and modifying the preceding tendencies in art and literature. At the centre of its innovative style lies a preoccupation with the notion of reality and a search for alternative ways of representing it. As its very name suggests, magical realism has an ambivalent relationship with the concept of reality because it "works both within and against the aesthetics of realism" (Chamberlain 17). It works within the aesthetics of realism since no matter that fantastic or supernatural elements are incorporated in the narrative, magical realist writing is always anchored in empirical reality. "In the magical realist texts […]," as Lois P. Zamora and Wendy B. Faris observe, "the supernatural is not a simple or obvious matter, but it *is* an ordinary matter, an everyday occurrence - admitted, accepted and integrated into the rationality and materiality of literary realism" (3). Magical realism also works against the aesthetics of realism, for magical realist writers search for new ways of defamiliarisation to reconstruct and redefine nineteenth-century realism. The experimentalism inherent in magical realism particularly became evident in the Boom novels, generally referred to as prototypical magical realist writing. In outlining the common characteristics of the Boom novels, Doris Sommer states that they are marked with "a demotion, or diffusion of authorial control and tireless formal experimentation, all, it seems, directed towards demolishing the straight line of traditional narratives" (71). Contemporary critics, too, tend to foreground the experimental features of magical realism as a literary mode, indicating the fact that magical realist writers from postcolonial countries have continued to employ many of the experimental writing techniques that they have inherited from their Latin predecessors. For instance, in their entry to a glossary of literary terms, M. H. Abrams and Geoffrey Galt Harpham describe magical realist novels as those that

> [...] violate, in various ways, standard novelistic expectations by drastic – and sometimes highly effective – experiments with subject matter, form, style, temporal sequence, and fusions of the everyday, the fantastic, the mythical, and the nightmarish, in renderings that blur traditional distinctions between what is serious or trivial, horrible or ludicrous, tragic or comic. (196)

Its preoccupation with the concept of reality and the ways in which it attempts to surpass conventional literary narrative techniques have led critics to associate magical realism with postmodernism. As a result, magical realist texts have been examined under a variety of headings, such as "historiographic metafiction," "postmodern gothic" and "postmodern realism" (Hedgerfelt 40). The discussion whether or not magical realism can be or should be classified under postmodernism falls outside the scope of the present examination. However, it is necessary to dwell a little on the advantages experimentalism permeating magical realist writing. The close affinities between magical realism and postmodernist writing techniques made it easier for postcolonial writers to reach an international readership. Jean-Pierre Durix notes that the international success of magical realist writers has eliminated the persistent stereotyping in the West that postcolonial literatures "lack in post-structuralist and deconstructionist subtleties" and are "ignorant of the most sophisticated *avant-garde*" (*Mimesis* 7). In other words, magical realist novels help change the perception of postcolonial literatures in the Western academia, establishing that writers from former colonies are capable of producing serious works of literature, worthy of including in the canon and university curricula.

As the survey presented in the foregoing chapter makes clear, experimentalism inherent in magical realism does not relate to the idea of art for art's sake, or suggest a compromise of social and political function of art for the sake of aesthetic autonomy as in some forms of modernist art and literature. On the contrary, as evident in Franz Roh's initial study of the mode, magical realism started as a reaction to abstract experimentalism of expressionist art and drew attention to social and political tensions in the Weimar Republic. In the context of postcolonial literature, magical realism continued to retain its function of providing sociopolitical commentary. The emergence of magical realism in Latin America coincided with its peoples' struggle for cultural independence from Europe and the United States. The same relationship between magical realism and liberationist ideals also holds true for postcolonial countries. Magical realist writers employed experimental writing techniques to present alternative versions of the stories, or more precisely histories told by the coloniser. In an attempt to explain the role of magical realist fiction in postcolonial countries, Anne Hegerfeldt notes,

> Critics have repeatedly diagnosed in magic realism an obsession with history and its concomitant Western mode of produc-

tion, historiography. [...] These works undertake rewritings of official versions of history, playfully offering alternative accounts. By telling the story from a different, usually oppressed perspective, they reveal the extent to which history never consists of purely factual and impartial accounts, but serves the interests of those who write it. (63)

Jean-Pierre Durix draws much the same conclusion about magical realism. He regards magical realist writing as "a literal rendering of the impression felt by many Third-World people whose reality is imposed from the outside and who thus need to invert or deconstruct it in order to substitute their own vision" (*Mimesis* 134). Enriched by myths, legends, folklore and oral tradition, magical realist novels provide postcolonial nations a means of resistance against the dominant political or social hegemony.

At this point one might question the differences between magical realism and other forms of realist narratives, particularly social realism, the dominant narrative style in the early postcolonial era. As has been noted, one of the principal motivations in the early phases of postcolonial experience was to (re)activate a past that most would prefer to forget because of centuries of colonial suppression and cultural denigration. In a parallel fashion to nationalist ideologies, the early postcolonial writers generally reclaimed pre-colonial forms of history and culture in order to help the process of nation building. They idealised the national past in its pristine form based on local histories and endeavoured to prove that their societies do have a civilisation, equal or even superior to that of the West. Despite the fact that it is intended as a positive postcolonial strategy, this obsession with the past might prove to be counterproductive. In his *The Location of Culture* Homi Bhabha, a prominent postcolonial theorist, maintains that this unquestioning adherence to tradition imposes a straitjacket upon the present, for it does not take the changing nature of nationality into account (9).[29] The early postcolonial writers then fell into the same trap of culturalism as their Western counterparts, for they continued to advocate a discourse based on a crude understanding of the relationship between the coloniser and the colonised as "us" versus "them." However, it has become clear in time that the construction of national identity in postcolonial countries is far more complex than it was understood in the early days of independence. Bill Ashcroft, Gareth Griffiths and Helen Tiffin delineate this paradigmatic change in the perception of the postcolonial identity as follows,

> [...] the idea of the nation is often based on naturalised myths of racial or cultural origin. That the need to assert such myths of origin was an important feature of much early post-colonial theory and writing, and that it was a vital part of the collective political resistance which focused on issues of separate identity and cultural distinctiveness is made clear [...]. But what is also made clear is how problematic such construction is and how it has come under question in more recent accounts. [...] Such writing [Most post-colonial writing] focuses on the fact that the transaction of the post-colonial world is not a one-way process in which oppression obliterates the oppressed or the coloniser silences the colonised in absolute terms. (*Post-colonial* 183)

The idea of "authenticity" entertained by most of the thinkers and writers in the early stages of independence has become a myth within the contact zone produced by colonisation. In this context, Homi Bhabha's concept of hybridity has become a major theoretical reference point and

---

[29] Here Bhabha refers to Fanon's critique of Négritudinists' nativist ideology: "Fanon recognizes the crucial importance, for subordinated peoples, of asserting their indigenous cultural traditions and retrieving their repressed histories. But he is far too aware of the dangers of the fixity of fetishism of identities within the calcification of colonial cultures to recommend that 'roots' be stuck in the celebratory romance of the past or by homogenizing the history of the present" (9).

a useful theoretical framework in describing postcolonial identity. Instead of directly opposing colonial discourses, Bhabha redefines the postcolonial positively as the space with multiple cultural borders, namely the Third Space, characterised by hybridity, ambivalence and liminality. His concept of hybridity basically suggests that coexistence of different cultures opens up a third space in which opportunities for interaction and change for both cultures are created. Bhabha concedes that "it is significant that the productive capacities of this Third Space have a colonial or postcolonial provenance" (38). Open to the influence of the indigenous cultural practices as well as those of the colonising culture, colonial and/or postcolonial space is essentially a site of hybridisation, for the emergent identity embodies the traits of both the imposing colonial structures and indigenous cultural practices. The cultural hybridity, which in Bhabha's words, "entertains difference without an assumed or imposed hierarchy" and thereby dispels the nostalgic notion of uncontaminated "authenticity" underlying many of the claims to absolute cultural otherness (5).

It is this paradigmatic change in the perception of postcolonial identity that lies behind the growing interest in magical realist writing. Postcolonial critics and writers have begun to pay considerable attention to representations of hybrid identities, particularly the symbolism associated with passages through the fissured spaces between ostensibly fixed identifications. The immediate artistic imperative was to discover a mode of expression appropriate to representing this liminal cultural space. It was in this period that magical realism ensured its wide dissemination and popularity among postcolonial writers. In recognition of its potentialities to represent this in-betweeness, magical realism has been designated as the poetics of the postcolonial world by prominent postcolonial critics. For instance, Homi Bhabha asserts that "'[m]agical realism' after the Latin American Boom, becomes the literary language of the emergent post-colonial world" (3). Likewise, Maggie Anne Bowers argues that "combination of realistic and fantastical narrative, together with the inclusion of different cultural traditions, means that magical realism reflects, in both its narrative mode and its cultural environment, the hybrid nature of much postcolonial society" (1).[30]

On the face of it, it may seem that the generation of critics who began to work on the mode in the 1980s concurred with their Latin American counterparts in designating magical realism as an essentially postcolonial mode of expression born from the unique cultural endowments of former colonies. However, these critics focus on the textual and formal characteristics of magical realism as the primary factor that enables it to reflect the multiplicity of postcolonial cultures. In an attempt to explain the reason why magical realism can reflect the postcolonial cultural identity more subtly than conventional realism, Lois P. Zamora and Wendy B. Faris argue,

> An essential difference, then, between realism and magical realism involves the intentionality implicit in the conventions of the two modes. [...] realism intends its version of the world as a singular version, as an objective (hence universal) representation of natural and social realities – in short, that realism functions ideologically and hegemonically. Magical realism also functions ideologically but [...] less hegemonically, for its program is not centralizing but eccentric: it creates space for interactions of diversity. In magical realist texts, ontological disruption serves the purpose of political and cultural disruption: magic is often given as a cultural corrective, requiring readers to scrutinize accepted realistic conventions of causality, materiality, motivation. (3)

---

[30] Suzan Baker makes a similar point when she argues that magical realist texts offer "two systems of possibility" within the limits of a single text; one that "aligns with European rationality and another which is incompatible with a conventional Western worldview" (84).

The above excerpt reveals an essential trait of magical realist writing. Magical realism does not only reject nineteenth century realism on the grounds of artistic concerns, but also opposes its proposition of empirical realism as an objective and absolute way of knowing and representing the world. In this respect, magical realism's disruption of the two fixed categories, the real and the fantastic, holds immense artistic possibilities in resisting monologic political and cultural structures. Just like hybrid identities, magical realist texts entertain the possibilities of occupying two different, and often conflicting, plains without subscribing to either of them completely. In other words, they open up a textual space necessary for the representation of hybrid cultural identities. As Suzanne Baker argues, "[m]agic realism does not create imaginary worlds. What it does create, through its 'dual spatiality,' is a space where alternative realities and different perceptions of the world can be conceived" ("Magic" 55). In this dual spatiality any notion of a single unified worldview or reality becomes problematic. By fusing the real and the fantastic, "magic realism," as Baker points out, "attempts to shake the sense of the normal or rational, opening the way for the reader to question what has previously been accepted as 'real,' and therefore 'true'" ("Magic" 55). This dual space holds immense opportunities for postcolonial nations as well as oppressed minority groups to voice their own realities. As one of the examples of the liberating power of magical realism, Baker points to Aboriginal literature:

> Discourses of colonialism position the Aborigines as objects to be studied, observed and spoken about. The imposed social and political systems of Western culture effectively denied a space in which Aboriginal voices could speak for themselves. The possibility of a "dual spatiality" provided through the deployment of magic realism provides one space where Aboriginal voices can speak and be heard. ("Binarism" 84)

In this light, it is pertinent to rectify the culturalist misinterpretation of magical realism as an essentially Latin American literary mode. Baker's position offers a response to the question posed at the end of chapter 1: how could magical realism so aggressively and persistently claimed by Latin Americans make its way into the postcolonial world? It could do so because magical realism is not the possession of a particular culture or nation, but rather a literary mode that postcolonial nations aptly employ to speak of their hybrid identities.[31] It follows that the reasons behind the wide dissemination of magical realism should be sought in the textual possibilities it offers rather than solely in the cultural endowments of postcolonial countries. In recognition of this fundamental fact, Stephen M. Hart writes,

> It was as a result of its intrinsic heterogeneity rather than its syncretism that the discourse of magical realism was able to migrate from Latin America to various cultural shores around the world. Particularly for writers in countries which had recently escaped from the clutches of colonialism, magical realism appeared to offer a literary idiom which could reflect the raw political tensions which accompanied the movement towards nationhood, this particularly so during the 1980s and early 1990s which may be seen as the highwater mark of globalised magical realism. (11)

In the remaining chapters, the relationship between magical realism and the representations of history and nation in postcolonial literatures shall be analysed. Written in the 1980s and aftermath, the selected novels re-

---

[31] Theo D'haen's study of magical realism can be seen as another contribution to this line of thought. D'haen notes, "it [magical realism] continues to operate from the margins, if not geographical, then social, economic and political. It is now preferred mode for all postcolonial writing, including writers not only from former European colonies, but also from ethnic minorities in the United States and elsewhere, and women" (289).

flect the characteristics of the high-water mark of globalised magical realism, as designated by Stephen M. Hart.

Chapter 3
Reclaiming Indian Past(s): Postmodern Historiography and Magical Realism in the Indian English Novel

> *Warning!*
> *Improbable you say?*
> *No fellers,*
> *All improbables are probable in India.*
> - G. V. Desani, *All About H. Hatterr*

History, or more precisely historiography, has been one of the central issues of postcolonial studies, offering a fertile ground for debates and analyses for scholars and critics working in the field in the last forty years or so. Since the publication of Edward Said's seminal work, *Orientalism* (1978), it has become almost axiomatic in postcolonial studies to view Western historiography as a powerful instrument used by colonial powers to legitimise their presence in foreign lands. While representing the culture of the colonised people as stagnant and their political and social institutions obsolete, the colonisers promoted themselves as the material and spiritual protectors of the "lesser" peoples and hid their economic interests under the pretext of a lofty civilising mission. Particularly after the withdrawal of colonial powers, the former colonies began to challenge and question this Eurocentric version of history and reclaimed their long denigrated past by transforming it into a positive identity affirmation. Hence, as M. H. Abrams and G. G. Harpham succinctly put it, one of the principal preoccupations of postcolonial writing has been:

> [t]he rejection of the "master-narrative" of Western imperialism – in which the colonial "other" is not only subordinated and marginalized, but in effect deleted as a cultural agency – and its replacement by a counter-narrative in which the colonial cul-

tures fight their way back into a world history written by Europeans. (236-237)

Given the fact that India had been subjected to British colonial rule for about a century (1858-1947), it is perhaps not surprising that the Indian novel in English has been an active site of national self-definition through narrativisation of history as an anti-colonial practice. As in other former colonies, a resurgence of interest in indigenous roots marked the early examples of Indian literature in English. Most of the novels written in this period reflected the tenets of the anti-colonial ideology and sought to promote a unified vision of Indian nationhood and nationalism. "One of the most striking trends in the Indian novel in English," Dennis Walder points out, "has been its tendency to reclaim the nation's histories" (103). In the same vein, U. M. Nanavati and Prafulla C. Kar observe, "Indian writing in English published before the 1970s was willy-nilly caught up and embroiled with questions of national identity and some forms of cultural revivalism" (12-13). In this early phase of the Indian novel in English, writers like Chandra Chatterjee, Mulk Raj Anand, R. K. Narayan and Raja Rao embraced the mimetic realism of the nineteenth-century novelists and "exploited English for no better purpose than to vindicate the spirit of India and its quintessential unity" (Nanavati and Kar 12).

There was, however, an increasingly urgent need to represent the sensibilities of the new hybrid identity generated by the experience of colonialism, and change was inevitable. In the late 1970s and the early 1980s, a new mode of writing began to emerge, bringing about a fresh creative breakthrough. Meenakshi Sharma outlines the transformation the Indian novel in English was undergoing in this period as follows,

> Since its inception, Indian English fiction has been dominated (except for sporadic experimental writing) by the monologic, singular and realist narrative aimed at encapsulating the essence

of Indian reality through 'typical' characters, situations, settings and dialogue. With the publication of Salman Rushdie's *Midnight's Children* in 1981 however, a refreshing, productive and invigorating upheaval occurred in Indian English literature. (125)

The distinction between this new generation of writers and their predecessors seems to stem in large from the radical change in the perception of historiography that gradually took hold in the second half of the twentieth century. The novel, that is to say its production and reception as a cultural object, has always responded to the developments in the field of history. However, the relationship between the two had remained controversial until the late twentieth century, mainly because "history defined itself in opposition to literature as an empirical search for external truths corresponding to what was considered to be the absolute reality of past events" (Onega 12). The advent of post-structuralist and postmodern theories in the 1970s had an emancipatory effect on historiography, undercutting the dichotomy between literature and history that had been present ever since Aristotle.[32] Contemporary philosophers of history, such as Hayden White, Paul Veyne and Jacques Ehrmann have repeatedly underscored the fact that historiography, just like literature, is a narrative construct.[33] As a result, from the 1980s onwards, history began to be

---

[32] The relationship between historiography and literary writing has been the subject of debates from Aristotle's *Poetics* to the present day. In *the Poetics* Aristotle makes a straightforward distinction between history as the study of events that actually occurred and poetry as the imagining of possible events. He privileges poetry over history on the grounds that it deals with universal truths and is therefore more philosophical whereas history deals with particular truth. Granting poetry a higher status over history, Aristotle establishes a tension about the value and status of these two practices (Aristotle 17-18).

[33] In this respect Hayden White's contribution is remarkable. He expounded on the similarities between the aims and forms of historical and fictional discourses. In his essays "Tropics of Discourse: Essays in Cultural Criticism," White states, "Although historians and writers of fiction may be interested in different kinds of events, both the forms of their respective discourses and their aims in writing are often the same. In addition, in my view, techniques or strategies that they use in the composition of their discourse can be shown to be substantially the same, however different they may appear on a purely sur-

defined not against, but in relation to literature. It was no longer an inviolable source of absolute truths about the past, but one of the many possible versions of past events.

This postmodernist view of history overlapped to a great extent with postcolonial writing, whose primary intention, according to Leela Gandhi, has been to "fragment or interpellate this [Eurocentric] account with the voices of all those unaccounted for 'others' who have been silenced and domesticated under the sign of Europe" (171). It was within the convergence of postcolonialism and postmodernism in the 1980s that the Indian novel in English experienced its successful proliferation. The novelists started to adopt a sceptical stance towards the privileged status of history as "objective knowledge." Instead of contesting the grand narratives of European history by writing novels with overt national themes, the new generation of Indian novelists intended to disclose the political strategies behind Western historiographic writing. In other words, history became a subversive literary tool in the hands of postcolonial novelists.

Some of the novels written in this period constitute examples of what Linda Hutcheon termed as "historiographic metafiction." Hutcheon employs this term to describe novels that "are intensely self-reflective but that also both reintroduce historical context into metafiction and problematize the entire question of historical knowledge" ("Pastime" 54-55). Contrary to traditional historical novels that pretend to provide an unproblematic access to the past in its fullness and particularity, novels that fall in the category of historiographic metafiction undermine this claim for historical truth by exposing the fictive status of history writing. Hutcheon notes,

---

face, or dictional level of their texts" (121). The historian and the writer do not only share narrative space of textuality, but also use the same narrative devices. Their achievements may look different but, "the process of fusing events, whether imaginary or real, into a comprehensible totality capable of serving as the object of a representation is a poetic process" (White 125).

[h]istoriographic metafiction refutes the natural or commonsense methods of distinguishing between historical fact and fiction. It refuses the view that only history has a truth claim, both by questioning the ground of that claim in historiography and by asserting that both history and fiction are discourses, human constructs, signifying systems, and both derive their major claim to truth from that identity. (*Poetics* 93)

In this respect, Indian novelists can be argued to be artistically more protean than their Western counterparts since the sceptical stance towards history had existed in India's cultural heritage long before the advent of postmodernism in the West. Despite its ancient history, history writing in the European sense does not have a very long tradition in India. Identifying the conceptual difference between Indian and Western notions of history, Nila Shah notes "[s]ignificantly, the idea of history as a linear progression of events, a master narrative with a value of unity, homogeneity, totality, closure and identity has never appealed to the Indian mind nurtured on the concept of karma and dharma" (26). As a result, Indians opted for the interpretations of myths as history instead of official accounts of history in annals or chronicles. Ashis Nandy argues that this common propensity towards evaluating the past through a mythic lens stems from Indian people's deep rooted belief that "they [myths] faithfully contain history, because they are contemporary and, unlike history, are amenable to intervention, myths are the essence of a culture, history being at best superfluous and at worst misleading" (59).

Magical realism has afforded Indian novelists a literary vehicle to combine the traditional sceptical stance towards Western historiography with postmodern experimental writing techniques, for it simultaneously allows writers to employ realism whenever it suits them, but also undermine and question its authority with the incorporation of supernatural and mythical elements in the same textual plane. Linda Hutcheon notes that magical realism with its flexibility as a narrative mode has become a powerful literary catalyst between postmodernism and postcolonialism: "'magic realism' [...] has been singled out by many critics as one of the points of conjunction of post-modernism and post-colonialism. Its challenges to genre distinctions and to the conventions of realism are certainly part of the project of both enterprises" ("Pastime" 55).

The novels selected to be analysed in this chapter, Salman Rushdie's *Midnight's Children* and Shashi Tharoor's *The Great Indian Novel*, present pertinent examples of the incorporation of postmodern writing techniques and magical realism in an attempt to subvert the Western notion of history and more particularly the imperialist record of Indian history. *Midnight's Children,* perhaps the most significant achievement of Rushdie's literary career, was published in 1981 and won that year's prestigious Booker Prize, earning the writer international fame. In 1993, Midnight's Children was chosen as the Booker of Bookers, the best Booker-winning novel from the first twenty-five years of the competition (Reder 146). It has such a powerful hold over the Indian English novel that it has become commonplace among critics to view the novelists publishing novels after *Midnight's Children* as the post-Rushdie generation (Das 55, Nanavati and Kar 14-15). The second novel to be analysed is by one of Rushdie's followers, Shashi Tharoor. Apart from their use of magical realism as the narrative mode in their novels, there are some other similarities between the two novelists that make it meaningful to study their works jointly. Born in the early years of Indian Independence, both novelists have witnessed the utopian expectation set by the independent government as well as their withering away in the era of post-independence. However, instead of upholding a nationalist view of Indian history and culture, they have retained a critical distance towards their indigenous culture. Their magical realist version of Indian history in the selected novels is roughly bracketed by the last days of British colonial rule and the declaration of Emergency Rule by Indira Gandhi. Since both novelists are interested in historiography, particularly the questions of how history is structured and narrated and how the written accounts of history affect our perception of nations, their novels read like running commentaries on the political events that took place in the history of the subcontinent during and after colonialism.

3.1. (Re)imagining India in Salman Rushdie's *Midnight's Children*

In his essay titled "Imaginary Homelands," Rushdie describes *Midnight's Children* as "a novel of memory and about memory" (10). Indeed, the incident that sparked the inspiration for the novel is to be found in a distant memory of Rushdie's childhood, namely a black and white family photograph hanging on a wall in his office in London. The faint memories it evoked propelled Rushdie, after spending almost half of his life abroad, to revisit his hometown, Bombay, and the house where he was born. It was during this expedition that his novel *Midnight's Children* was born. The fruit of his expedition, however, did not come out as a family history as one might expect, but as a national allegory since Rushdie located his mission of restoring the past at a turning point in the history of India as well as his own life: the declaration of India's independence. The novel takes its name from Jawaharlal Nehru's speech delivered at the stroke of midnight on August 14, 1947 as India gained her independence from England. As the country's first prime minister, Nehru stood up in the parliament chamber and announced that after centuries of colonial oppression, India finally gained her independence:

> Long years ago we made a tryst with destiny, and now the time comes when we shall redeem our pledge, not wholly or in full measure, but very substantially. At the stroke of the midnight hour, when the world sleeps, India will awake to life and freedom. A moment comes, which comes but rarely in history, when we step out from the old to the new, when an age ends, and when the soul of a nation, long suppressed, finds utterance. ("Nehru")

Although he draws his material from history, Rushdie does not follow in the footsteps of the masters of historical novel who scrupulously work to record nothing but authentic facts. Instead, he mingles history with fantasy and keeps on switching from one to the other throughout the narrative.

At this critical juncture in Indian history, 1001 babies come into the world "within the frontiers of the infant sovereign state of India" between midnight and 1 a.m. on August 15th, 1947, of whom 581 survive (*MC* 192). As the most significant magical realist element in the novel, the children are "endowed with features, talents and faculties which can only be described as miraculous" (*MC* 193). They have powers of transmutation, flight, prophecy and wizardry. The children's magical powers decrease as the moment of their birth gets further from midnight. Born on the exact moment of India's independence, Saleem Sinai, the narrator of the novel, is given the greatest ability of all midnight's children. He is able to communicate telepathically with other gifted children born within the same hour of India's Independence. He can also turn his mind into a telepathic forum where midnight's children can talk to one another. Together the children represent the future of the new independent nation. However, by the end of the novel midnight's children lose their magical powers as India loses her optimism, dividing into factions under Indira Gandhi's Emergency Rule.

As the novel opens, Saleem, having lost his magical powers, seeks refuge in a pickle factory in Bombay, where he lives with Padma, his loyal and caring companion. With his thirty-first birthday approaching, he decides to write his autobiography in order to save his memory from "the corruption of the clocks" (*MC* 38). Saleem is a typical example of an autodiegetic narrator, where the narrator is also the protagonist of the story he narrates. He can shape his narrative according to his whims. Time seems to be the only obstacle before him. Saleem fears that he may not live long enough to complete his story because his body is literally beginning to crack and fall apart: "I ask you only to accept (as I have accepted) that I shall eventually crumble into (approximately) six hundred and thirty million particles of anonymous, and necessarily oblivious dust. This is why I have resolved to confide in paper, before I forget. (We are a nation of forgetters.)" (*MC* 38). With this unmistakable metaphor, Saleem claims to be the physical embodiment of India. Such allegorical explanations, quite common in magical realist writing, cannot be conveyed in conventional realist novels dominated by the laws of the empirical world.

Anne Hegerfeldt argues that literalisation of metaphor and other related strategies play a crucial role in magical realism's transgression of linguistic and conceptual boundaries in order to destabilise traditional binaries, such as abstract/concrete, word/thing, real/fantastic and past/present. "Magic realist fiction," Hegerfeldt notes, "addresses the traditional Western distinction between the literal and the figurative by rendering the figures of speech oddly real on the level of the text: in magic realist fiction, metaphors become literally true" (56). Seen in this light, Hegerfeldt argues, "Saleem's rather implausible claim to be falling apart [...] can be understood as a projection of India's political and social disintegration onto the physiological level" (240-241). This allegorical interpretation of the text is, however, renounced by Saleem's doctor, a representative of Western science. After carefully examining his patient, the doctor concludes rather briskly: "I see no crack" (*MC* 65). Saleem's reaction to the doctor's diagnosis demonstrates the discrepancy between the Western and the Eastern perception of reality. Saleem blames the doctor for failing to see the cracks in his body: "Damn fool, [...] can't see what's under his nose!" (*MC* 66). Saleem's implausible claim is, thus, left unresolved in the text. This unresolved ambiguity can be interpreted as yet another characteristic of the mode; that is, its ability to represent the hybrid postcolonial identity as a fusion of the Western and indigenous cultural traditions, where neither is dominant. According to Geoffrey Galt Harpham, the blending of two realms, the metaphoric and the literal, in magical realist writing destabilises the Western view of reality that restricts it to what is empirically observable, offering "instead an infinitely inclusive field of significance that embraces contradiction—one in which 'no realm of being, visible or invisible, past or present, is absolutely discontinuous with any other, but all equally accessible and mutually interdependent" (qtd. in Ball 218).

Saleem introduces another literalised metaphor in his account of post-independence India. His father, Ahmed Sinai, suddenly starts to grow pale. While the other family members believe that it is the shock of his friend Dr Narlikar's unexpected death that is responsible for the ailment in his complexion, Saleem offers an alternative explanation. He believes that his father is the victim of a widespread pigmentation disorder that has befallen many Indian businessmen after independence. Saleem writes,

> (although I don't know how much you're prepared to swallow). I shall risk giving an alternative explanation, a theory developed in the abstract privacy of my clocktower… because during my frequent psychic travels, I discovered something rather odd: during the first nine years after Independence, a similar pigmentation disorder (whose first recorded victim may well have been the Rani of Cooch Naheen) afflicted large numbers of the nation's business community. All over India, I stumbled across good Indian businessmen, their fortunes thriving thanks to the first Five Year Plan, which had concentrated on building up commerce… businessmen who had become or were becoming very, very pale indeed! It seems that the gargantuan (even heroic) efforts involved in taking over from the British and becoming masters of their own destinies had drained the colour from their cheeks… in which case, perhaps my father was a late victim of a widespread, though generally unremarked phenomenon. The businessmen of India were turning white. (*MC* 176)

The literalised metaphor here serves to underscore the pervasive effect of the Westernisation on Indian society in the post-independence period. Through his allegorical portrayal of characters like the Rani of Cooch Naheen and Ahmed Sinai, Rushdie seems to imply that although the power of the British came to an end on 15 August 1947, its legacy was inherited by the newly-created nation.

The time constraint in the narrative, that is Saleem's race against the clock, has led some critics to link Saleem with Scheherazade, the legendary Persian queen and the storyteller of *One Thousand and One Nights*. The two narrators (Saleem and Scheherazade), as Saleem reminds us, have different time constraints, though. While Scheherazade needs to stretch her stories to escape her impending death, Saleem has to narrate as many stories as possible because his body is literally falling apart. At the beginning of his narrative, Saleem expounds on this crucial difference:

> Now, however, time (having no further use for me) is running out. I will soon be thirty-one years old. Perhaps. If my crumbling, over-used body permits. But I have no hope of saving my life, nor can I count on having even a thousand nights and a night. I must work fast, faster than Scheherazade, if I am to end up meaning – yes, meaning – something. I admit it: above all things, I fear absurdity. (*MC* 11)

Thus, the similarity between the two narrators, Saleem and Scheherazade, should be sought in the formal structure of their narratives rather than in the question of time constraint. Nancy E. Batty contents that Scheherazade "provides Rushdie with both the precept and organizing principle of his narrative [...] the creation of suspense" (70). That is, Saleem's story is not actually written, as he claims, but told in the ancient pattern of oral tradition. "Padma," Rushdie reveals in an interview, "enabled the book to become an oral narrative, some kind of stylization of such a narrative, if you like" (Durix, "Salman Rushdie" 14). According to Anne Hegerfeldt, the tendency towards oral tradition is another definitive characteristic of magical realist novels: "even where the story is presented as written, or in the state of being written, magic realist fiction tends towards the oral. Frequently, the narrator will address the reader directly, creating the atmosphere of a conversation" (192). In this respect Padma functions as an important textual device, helping Saleem to revise his material in the course of narrative flow. The interaction between the two, along the latter's direct and informal addresses to the reader, gives rise to metafictional moments in the narrative where the process of narrativisation itself is foregrounded. For instance, at the point in the narrative when Padma learns that Saleem is in fact an illegitimate son of William Methwold rather than a member of the Sinai family as he has previously claimed, she feels deceived and storms out of the room. Left in solitude, Saleem cannot continue writing and the narrative action is suspended:

> It has been two whole days since Padma stormed out of my life [...] How to dispense with Padma? How give up her ignorance and superstition, necessary counterweights to my miracle-laden omniscience? How to do without her paradoxical earthiness of spirit, which keeps – kept? – my feet on the ground? I have become, it seems to me, the apex of an isosceles triangle, supported equally by twin deities, the wild god of memory and the lotus-goddess of the present... but must I now become reconciled to the narrow one-dimensionality of a straight line? (*MC* 146)

Saleem's comment on Padma's absence clearly extends to cover the theoretical aspects of the novel. He concedes that it is Padma that lends depth and texture to his otherwise linear narrative written in a conventional style. Thus, his story without Padma's voice risks veering into nineteenth-century realism.

In fact, Saleem lays bare the formal and thematic structure of his narrative, that is, a combination of postmodern writing techniques and magical realism, at the very beginning of the novel when describing the details of his birth that inextricably ties him to the history of India:

> I was born in the city of Bombay... once upon a time. No, that won't do, there's no getting away from the date: I was born in Doctor Narlikar's Nursing Home on August 15th, 1947. And the time? The time matters, too. Well then: at night. No, it's important to be more... On the stroke of midnight, as a matter of fact. [...] thanks to the occult tyrannies of those blandly saluting clocks I had been mysteriously handcuffed to history, my destinies indissolubly chained to those of my country. For the next three decades, there was to be no escape. Soothsayers had prophesied me, newspapers celebrated my arrival, politicos ratified my authenticity. I was left entirely without a say in the matter. I, Saleem Sinai, later variously called Snotnose, Stainface, Baldy, Sniffer, Buddha and even Piece-of-the-Moon, had become heavily embroiled in Fate – at the best of times a dangerous sort of involvement. (*MC* 11)

In this first paragraph of the novel, Rushdie introduces the narrative voice in the novel. Saleem narrates his story in the first person. He directly and informally addresses his audience with what seem to be spontaneous remarks. As his syntactically broken sentences with frequent use of ellipsis indicate, Saleem grapples with the fragmentary and broken pieces of his memory in order to reclaim his past in its entirety. Yet, his view remains fragmented throughout the narrative action. The opening paragraph quoted above also helps introduce magical realism as the dominant narrative mode in the novel. Saleem's intention to begin his autobiography with the stock phrase of "once upon a time" and its immediate rejection in favour of the actual date of his birth can be seen as an indication of the coexistence of the fantastic and the real within the same textual plane. While metafictional comments enable Rushdie to expose the narrative process at work in historical recording, magical realism helps him to convey the multicultural India ignored in monolithic, single-voiced historical accounts. The result is metafictional narrative espoused with a culturally and politically conscious magical realist touch.

The questions that may follow from this are: how does his use of postmodern writing techniques and magical realism relate to Rushdie's position as a postcolonial writer? In what ways does Rushdie's rendition of India differ from his predecessors who claimed to have written an authentic account of Indian culture in an attempt to help decolonise the country's history? To begin with, for Rushdie, the question of authenticity, which has vexed the early generations of Indian postcolonial writers is "the respectable child of old-fashioned exoticism" that "demands that sources, forms, style, language and symbol all derive from a supposedly homogenous and unbroken tradition" ("Commonwealth" 67). It is true that being away from home for such a long time may result in alienation to one's own culture to a certain degree, making it difficult to write about his or her homeland. However, Rushdie believes that migration does not necessarily mean a process of uprooting people from their enduring cultural and social relations and relocating them in an alienating atmosphere. For Rushdie, migration grants one an invaluable multiple perspective to see his or her own country. His writing, therefore, should be regarded as a conscious effort to validate his position as a postcolonial writer nurtured by his bilingual and bicultural background rather than as part of the tradition aimed at creating so-called 'authentic' Indian literature. Rushdie expresses his view of the question of authenticity more clearly when describing the situation of diasporic writers and the way they come to terms with their cultural identity:

> Our identity is at once plural and partial. Sometimes we feel that we straddle two cultures; at other times, that we fall between two stools. But however ambiguous and shifting this ground may be, it is not an infertile territory for a writer to occupy. If literature is in part the business of finding new angles at which to enter reality, then once again our distance, our long geographical perspective, may provide us with such angles. ("Imaginary" 15)

This liminal space that, Rushdie contends, the postcolonial writer occupies seems to correspond to Bhabha's concept of 'hybridity,' where the coexistence of different cultures produces opportunities for cultural interaction and change. As has been made clear in the foregoing chapter, it is in this cultural atmosphere that magical realism has become the dominant literary mode with its ability to present conflicting perceptions of reality within the same textual space.

Rushdie mentions the idea of plurality not only in describing his identity as a diasporic writer, but also India itself. His view of India differs significantly from the mainstream nationalist factions that nostalgically yearn for a unified vision of the country. He defies the concept of a homogenous Indian culture that inspired many writers in the early post-independence days by declaring that "'[m]y' India has always been based on ideas of multiplicity, pluralism, hybridity [...]. To my mind, the defining image of India is the crowd, and a crowd is by its very nature superabundant, heterogeneous, many things at once" ("Riddle" 32). Rushdie denounces the absurdity of continuing to believe that India, home to several different vernaculars and dialects as well as different religions, can be represented monolithically. He writes,

> One of the most absurd aspects of this quest for national authenticity is that – as far as India is concerned, anyway – it is completely fallacious to suppose that there is such a thing as a pure,

unalloyed tradition from which to draw. The only people who seriously believe this are religious extremists. The rest of us understand that the very essence of Indian culture is that we possess a mixed tradition, a *mélange* of elements as disparate as ancient Mughal and contemporary Coca-Cola American. ("Commonwealth" 67)

For Rushdie, realism as practised in the nineteenth century is incompatible with the literary consciousness of the "Third World" countries, where the concept of reality itself has become too complex and intricate to be addressed by essentialist representations. Hence, he proposes magical realism as the most suitable mode of narration to represent India as well as other postcolonial countries;

[…] black and white descriptions of society are no longer compatible. Fantasy, or the mingling of fantasy and naturalism, is one way of dealing with these problems. It offers a way of echoing in the form of our work the issues faced by all of us: how to build a new, 'modern' world out of an old, legend-haunted civilization, an old culture which we have brought into the heart of a newer one. […] Indian writers […] are capable of writing from a kind of double perspective: because they, we, are at one and the same time insiders and outsiders in this society. This stereoscopic vision is perhaps what we can offer in place of 'whole sight' ("Imaginary" 19)

Thus, instead of writing a fantastic story drawing solely upon Indian myths and legends, or a conventional historical novel based on the official history of the subcontinent, Rushdie founds *Midnight's Children* on the liminal space provided by magical realism. In doing so, Rushdie manages to blend traditional binaries (real/fantasy, east/west, secular/religious and myth/history) and foregrounds the hybrid identity of the postcolonial subject and multiculturalism over a uniform view of national identity. This liminal textual space also enables him to question the established history of India. Here, the subversive quality of magical realism that "encourages resistance to monological political and cultural structures" comes to the fore (Bowers 64). *Midnight's Children* depicts a curiously hybrid picture of India, where history, politics, cultural heritage, myths, religion and traditions blend and merge to such a degree that it becomes impossible to distinguish which one of these elements has assumed the dominant role in the follow of narrative. This hybrid portrayal of the subcontinent, in turn, helps to "bring into question the truth of the British version of Indian colonial and postcolonial history" (Bowers 64).

Midnight's Children abounds with fantastic or improbable happenings. It will suffice to remember the 1001 children born with fantastic abilities, Saleem's aunt and Mary Pereira, Saleem's ayah and surrogate mother, who see ghosts of the past around the house and Parvati-the-witch's spiriting Saleem from Pakistan to India in her basket. In fact, it is at the outset of his narrative that Saleem Sinai informs the reader that his story is going to be a mixture of history and fantasy in a statement that reads almost like a definition of magical realism as a literary term: "And there are so many stories to tell, too many, such an excess of intertwined lives events miracles places rumours, so dense a *commingling of the improbable and the mundane!*" (*MC* 11 emphasis added). Furthermore, Saleem justifies the improbable events in the course of his narrative by referring to the multicultural heritage of India, where things that may seem strange in other parts of the world are accepted to be part of daily life. For instance, when commenting on his grandmother Naseem Aziz's eavesdropping on her daughters' dreams to know what they are up to, Saleem remarks, "Yes, there's no other explanation, stranger things have been known to happen in this country of ours, just pick up any newspaper and see the daily titbits recounting miracles in this village or that – Reverend Mother began to dream her daughters" (*MC* 55).

His reference to newspapers to vindicate improbable events taking place in India recalls the prominent Latin American novelists Gabriel García Márquez and Isabel Allende's justification of their magical realist novels as true stories.[34] Magical realism enables Rushdie to reveal the richness of India's cultural and mythic life that, as Rushdie has made it clear, a realistic historical narrative with authorial omniscience is bound to fail to capture.

Although his own pronouncements are not necessarily definitive, Rushdie seems to have left almost no need for critical commentary on his use of metafictional elements in the novel. For Rushdie, the postmodern fragmentation in the novel, like his use of the magical realist narrative mode, is not a matter of artistic preference, but an outcome of his postcolonial identity. Rushdie compares the situation of an Indian writer living abroad yet writing stories set in India to that of a person "obliged to deal in broken mirrors, some of whose fragments have been irretrievably lost" ("Imaginary" 11). Obviously, the broken mirror stands for memory and its fragments for fainted memories that are hard and sometimes impossible to retrieve. Rushdie's metaphor of broken mirror brings two types of distance to the fore: temporal and spatial distance between the writer and his homeland. However, for Rushdie, both of these impediments hold immense possibilities since he believes that "[t]he broken mirror may actually be as valuable as the one which is supposedly unflawed. [...] let me go further. The broken glass is not merely a mirror of nostalgia. It is also, I believe, a useful tool with which to work in the present" ("Imaginary" 11-12).

Viewed from this perspective, Rushdie's metaphor may help identify some of the central formal and thematic concerns of *Midnight's Children*. As the narrative is built on Saleem's fallible memory, it is replete with gaps, discontinuities, fragmentations and random associations, which disrupt the conventional understanding of history as a linear and progressive enterprise. In other words, the image of the writer/narrator

---

[34] See chapter 1, pp. 36-37.

trying to bring the pieces of the broken mirror together to have a meaningful picture of the past recalls the strenuous endeavours of the historian in search of the truth, analysing and interpreting a myriad of documents. With this equation, Rushdie puts forward the postmodernist view of history as fiction, open to interpretation and questions of authorship. There are several textual fissures in Saleem's story that expose the process of narrativisation clearly. For instance, prior to plunging into one of the several digressions in the novel, Saleem talks about Padma's complaints about his narrative style: "I must interrupt myself. I wasn't going to today, because Padma has started getting irritated whenever my narration becomes self-conscious, whenever, like an incompetent puppeteer, I reveal the hands holding the strings" (*MC* 65). Furthermore, Saleem also acknowledges that his account of Indian history is the outcome of highly subjective process of selection and omission. Saleem notes,

> 'I told you the truth,' I say yet again, 'Memory's truth because memory has its own special kind. It selects, eliminates, alters, exaggerates, minimizes, glorifies, and vilifies also; but in the end it creates its own reality, its heterogeneous but usually coherent version of events; and no sane human being ever trusts someone else's version more than his own. (*MC* 253)

Here, Rushdie calls attention to the process how discursive practices, be it a novel or a history textbook, reproduce the so-called 'truth' through selection, alteration, exaggeration and elimination. Saleem also exposes the constant process of revision in his narrative. He stops the narrative flow in order to explain why he has chosen to name a certain chapter of his autobiography "Alpha and Omega." Saleem writes,

> I have titled this episode somewhat oddly. 'Alpha and Omega' stares back at me from the page, demanding to be explained – a curious heading for what will be my story's half-way point, […]

but, unrepentantly, I have no intention of changing it, although there are many alternative titles [...]. But 'Alpha and Omega' it is; and 'Alpha and Omega' it remains. (*MC* 218)

At another point in his narration, while trying to find out the most suitable ending for his book in the final pages of his long narrative, he admits, "[t]he process of revision should be constant and endless; don't think I'm satisfied with what I've done!" (*MC* 433). Given that Saleem's story is the mirror of Indian history, these metafictional moments in the text should not be seen as part of a mere postmodern playfulness. Rather, they seem to serve as a literary device that helps challenge the validity of the colonial account of Indian history as absolute truth by drawing attention to the constructedness of any given text.

Rushdie himself has made clear that his novels aim at questioning the official version of history. "Writers and politicians," he states, "are necessary rivals. Both groups try to make the world in their own images; they fight for the same territory. And the novel is one way of denying the official, politicians' version of the truth" ("Imaginary" 14). Accordingly, Rushdie employs some radical narrative strategies in order to demonstrate the subjective nature of historical recording. Saleem distorts historical facts by assigning wrong dates to the actual historical events. Moreover, he exposes these mistakes by simply admitting, instead of correcting, them. Saleem notes,

> Because I am rushing ahead at breakneck speed; errors are possible, and overstatements, and jarring alterations in tone; I'm racing the cracks, but I remain conscious that errors have already been made, and that, as my decay accelerates (my writing speed is having trouble keeping up), the risk of unreliability grows... [...] in autobiography, as in all literature, what actually happened is less important than what the author can manage to persuade his audience to believe. (*MC* 270-271)

According to Linda Hutcheon, deliberate distortion of historical facts is one of the defining characteristics of historiographic metafiction: "[c]ertain known historical details are deliberately falsified in order to foreground the possible mnemonic failures of recorded history and the constant potential for both deliberate and inadvertent error" (*Poetics* 294). In this respect, it can be argued that *Midnight's Children* presents one of the most remarkable examples of the incorporation of postmodern writing techniques and magical realism since the mnemonic errors in the novel stem from the protagonist's bodily disintegration, which is rendered literally real on the textual plane through magical realism. Rushdie himself acknowledges the function of such deliberate mistakes in the novel as "a way of telling the reader to maintain a healthy distrust" ("Errata" 25). To further pronounce his sceptical stance towards any given monolithic representation of the past, Rushdie has Saleem make one of the most evident mistakes in the novel when dating Gandhi's assassination. "Re-reading my work," Saleem admits unrepentantly, "I have discovered an error in chronology. The assassination of Mahatma Gandhi occurs, in these pages, on the wrong date. But I cannot say, now, what the actual sequence of events might have been; in my India, Gandhi will continue to die at the wrong time" (*MC* 164).

In addition to metafictional commentaries and the deliberate distortion of historical facts, Rushdie also challenges Western historiography by recounting Indian history from Saleem's individual perspective. "Saleem," Michael Reder observes, "creates personal meaning from history, assigning historical events significance in relation to himself as an individual" (226). Throughout the novel, Saleem draws compelling parallels between his family history and that of his country so as to call attention to the subjective nature of historical recording as opposed to the claims to objective history in the Western historiography. For instance, when recounting the outbreak of the Indo-Pakistani War, Saleem asserts,

> Let me state this quite unequivocally: it is my firm conviction that the hidden purpose of the Indo-Pakistani war of 1965 was nothing more nor less than the elimination of my benighted family from the face of the earth. In order to understand the recent history of our times, it is only necessary to examine the bombing pattern of that war with an analytical, unprejudiced eye. (*MC* 324)

Saleem's implausible claims to be at the centre of Indian history can better be understood when considered in relation to the hegemonic nature of colonial historiography. "[I]n the colonial situation," M. Keith Booker argues, "the only true historical event is the process of colonization and its aftermath, leaving no room for the colonized world to have a history of its own independent of the history of the European bourgeoisie" (287). In this perspective, Saleem's autobiography can be regarded as a decolonising attempt to give voice to the suppressed indigenous people.

His miraculous birth is not the only event that ties Saleem to the fate of his country. In the novel, the allegorical role of Saleem as the embodiment of India is underscored time and again. Saleem receives a letter of congratulation form Prime Minister Nehru as a token of the happy accident of his moment of birth. In his letter, Nehru writes, "[y]ou are the newest bearer of that ancient face of India which is also eternally young. We shall be watching over your life with the closest attention; it will be, in a sense, the mirror of our own" (*MC* 122). There are several references to Nehru's letter throughout the narrative, constantly identifying Saleem with the Independent India. Saleem promotes himself as the embodiment of India with all its diversity. "To understand just one life," Saleem cautions, "you have to swallow the world" (*MC* 108). Towards the end of his narrative, he addresses the reader once again and states: "I am the sum total of everything that went before me [...] each 'I', every one of the now-six-hundred-million-plus of us, contains a similar multitude. I repeat for the last time: to understand me, you'll have to swallow a world" (*MC* 370). Thus, by establishing a parallelism between the fate of Saleem Sinai and that of the independent India, Rushdie lends the novel an explicit allegorical quality which otherwise would simply turn into a *bildungsroman*.

The history Saleem records is not only that of his life, it is also that of his family and country. Saleem's magical realist narrative can therefore be regarded as an attempt to encapsulate Indian history with all its multiplicity and diversity. As Saleem's narrative unfolds, it moves out of his household and reaches out to embrace the entire Indian nation with its diverse cultural and religious heritage. In other words, Saleem writes the history of India in the form of his autobiography. His life intersects with many of the historical and political events that took place in the post-independence period. Partition, Amritsar Massacre, India-China War of 1961 the Indo-Pakistani War of 1971, the independence of Bangladesh and the Emergency Rule during Indira Gandhi's reign are just to name a few of them. The remainder of this section shall focus on how Rushdie threads magical realism with postmodern writing techniques in order to present his critical rendition of India, which does not only denounce the colonial version of Indian history, but also the oppressive ideology of the Emergency Rule.

In book 1, Saleem focuses on the formative years of the independence movement and relates the important historical events that took place between 1915 and 1947. The central action of the novel, the birth of midnight's children does not take place until the end of book 1. However, it would be misleading to consider this prolonged introduction to Saleem's birth as a long playful digression as in Laurence Sterne's *Tristram Shandy*, where the narrator sets out to write his autobiography, but does not get around to describing his birth until the third volume. In an interview, Rushdie explains the reason why he did not begin the novel by simply describing Saleem's birth and the subsequent events as follows,

> [...] the reason why in the book there is so much that happens before Saleem is born, is to say 'We do not come naked into the world.' We bring with us an enormous amount of baggage, so therefore, limitation. And that baggage is history, family history, and a broader history too, and we're born into a context, and we're born as the child of our parents, and as the descendant of our family, and as people who live in a certain house, and there's a lot of stuff which is just given – which is not just ours to make. And in order to understand 'us', you have to understand that other stuff. (qtd. in Reynolds and Noakes 17)

Here, Rushdie draws attention to the cultural, national and religious affiliations acquired at birth and the formative role they play in the development of people's identity. The emphasis on the historical context that we are born into also looms large in the novel. Saleem seems to underscore the effect of historical dynamics that shape our identity even before we come into the world when he says, "most of what matters in our lives takes place in our absence" (*MC* 20). Saleem goes on to explain that owing to his magical powers, he is capable of restoring the past down to its minute details, including the events that have taken place before his birth: "I seem to have found from somewhere the trick of filling in the gaps in my knowledge, so that everything is in my head, down to the last detail" (*MC* 20). In this first book of his autobiography, Saleem provides a panorama of the final years of colonial India with all its religious and social conflicts through the story of his grandparents, Aadam Aziz and Naseem Ghani. Saleem's narrative cannot be reduced to the fate of a single family, for his fantastic family history intersects with the national and international political history.

Saleem's story begins in Kashmir in 1915. His grandfather, Aadam Aziz, returns to his hometown in Kashmir after completing his five-year medical education in Germany. In his absence, Aziz's father has had a stroke and his mother has started to run the family business. However, this unfortunate event is not the only reason that has dragged Aziz back home. He has grown impatient with the colonial arrogance prevalent in Europe. When his close friends Oskar, Ilse Rubin and Ingrid upset Aziz with their colonist remarks, he resolves to leave Europe for good. Saleem writes,

> Heidelberg, in which, along with medicine and politics, he learned that India – like radium – had been 'discovered' by the Europeans; even Oskar was filled with admiration for Vasco da Gama, and this was what finally separated Aadam Aziz from his friends, this belief of theirs that he was somehow the invention of their ancestors. (*MC* 13)

But Aadam Aziz does not receive a warm reception in Kashmir as he expects. He is now perceived as a "foreigner" by the inhabitants of Kashmir because of his Western education. Ostensibly, Aziz, in Homi Bhabha's famous formulation, is a postcolonial hybrid subject, living between two cultures with no complete attachment to either of them. Saleem sets the old boatman Tai, who represents the collective voice of Kashmir, as a foil to Aziz. "I have," Saleem remarks, "Tai-for-changelessness opposed to Aadam-for-progress" (*MC* 107). Tai is a mythical figure. He claims to have seen baby Jesus and the Emperor Jehangir and keeps the entire community aware of its past with his tales. Tai sees Aziz's medical bag as a representation of Western knowledge and ridicules him with his sarcastic remarks: "We haven't got enough bags at home that you must bring back that thing made of a pig's skin that makes one unclean just by looking at it? Sistersleeping pigskin bag from Abroad full of foreigners' tricks. Big-shot bag. Now if a man breaks an arm that bag will not let the bone-setter bind it in leaves" (*MC* 21). Tai later decides to give up washing "as a gesture of unchangingness in defiance of the invasion of the doctori-attache from Heidelberg," and he keeps his vow until his tragic death in a dispute between Pakistan and India over Kashmir in 1947 (*MC* 28). His death is a harbinger of the inevitable changes awaiting India in the era of independence.

The perception of Aziz as a threat to the enduring Kashmiri community is further reinforced when he is called upon to treat Naseem, the daughter of a wealthy landowner called Ghani. At the landowner's house, Aadam Aziz finds the patient hidden behind a white sheet in the centre of which there is a seven-inch hole. Seeing that Aziz is overwhelmed with the scene, Ghani chides, "You Europe-returned chappies forget certain things. Doctor Sahib, my daughter is a decent girl, it goes without saying. She does not flaunt her body under the noses of strange men" (*MC* 24). Aziz starts paying regular visits to Ghani's house to examine Naseem, who develops a series of ailments in different parts of her body in the following years. Aziz is only allowed to see the affected area through the seven-inch hole. Naseem's father's resolution to hide his daughter behind a sheet does not prevent the blossoming of an unusual romance between the two. The phantasm of the partitioned woman starts to haunt Aziz. However, he cannot get sight of Naseem's face since she never complains of a headache. It is on the day when the First World War ends that Naseem eventually complains of a headache, and Aadam Aziz receives the long-awaited permission to set his eyes upon Naseem's face, whom he marries soon after. This is the first of the several moments in Saleem's narrative where personal history intersects with world history, balancing the magical atmosphere with historical background.

The perforated sheet is also a functional narrative device, regarded by many critics as the most obvious metaphor of postmodern fragmentation in the novel (Gopal 98-99). Like the narrative structure, the characters and their stories fragment and then unite. When she falls out of love with her husband, Naseem's daughter Amina trains herself to love her husband in parts. "That perforated sheet," Saleem writes, "which doomed my mother to learn to love a man in segments, and which condemned me to see my own life – its meanings, its structures – in fragments also; so that by the time I understood it, it was far too late" (*MC* 106). In an interview Rushdie himself acknowledges the metaphoric quality of the perforated sheet: "[w]ell, having found the image of the sheet with the hole, it began immediately to feel like a metaphor for the way in which the whole book was written [...]" (qtd. in Reynolds and Noakes 12). Both Rushdie and his protagonist imply that India can only be understood in fragments. Just as Aadam Aziz could see his future wife in bits and parts, so Saleem also could see Indian history in fragments. While he hastens to complete his family history before his death, he fragments Indian history into meaningful chapters.

Disenchanted by the treatment he has received from the Kashmir community, the newly married Aziz leaves the city with his wife for Amritsar, the burning centre of anti-colonial protests. As the religious connotation of his name indicates, Aadam is the progenitor of the Aziz family. Thus, his expulsion from Kashmir, described as idyllic setting well-preserved from colonial expansion, leads to the inauguration of a series of events. When Aadam and Naseem arrive in Amritsar on April 6, 1919, they find themselves in the middle of Hartal, a call for a day of mourning, issued by Mahatma Gandhi to protest the British presence in India. Saleem describes the scene through a playful interjection of directorial comments into the narrative:

> Close-up of my grandfather's right hand [...] my grandfather was holding a pamphlet [...] Now, looking out of his window, he sees it echoed on a wall opposite; and there, on the minaret of a mosque; and in the large black type of newsprint under a hawker's arm. Leaflet newspaper mosque and wall are crying: Hartal! Which is to say, literally speaking, a day of mourning, of stillness, of silence. But this is India in the heyday of the Mahatma, when even language obeys the instructions of Gandhiji, and the word has acquired, under his influence, new resonances. Hartal – April 7, agree mosque newspaper wall and

pamphlet, because Gandhi has decreed that the whole of India shall, on that day, come to a halt. To mourn, in peace, the continuing presence of the British. (*MC* 33)

Here, Saleem manages to convey a glimpse of Mahatma Gandhi's influence in the anti-colonial movement. However, anti-colonial protests are not always peaceful. The Sinais also witness the political turbulence accompanied by violence in the long process of liberation movement. Saleem describes the Amritsar Massacre (also known as Jallianwala Bagh Massacre) with some minute historical details:

It is April 7th 1919, and in Amritsar the Mahatma's Grand design is being distorted. […] Doctor Aziz, leather bag in hand, is out in the streets, giving help wherever possible. Trampled bodies have been left where they fell. They have fired a total of one thousand six hundred and fifty rounds into the unarmed crowds, […] killing or wounding some person. (*MC* 35-36)

It is in the midst of the anti-colonial resistance that the couple starts questioning their own place in the changing face of India. While Aziz tries to come to terms with his national identity by participating in the anti-colonial protest and treating the injured, his wife struggles between her traditional upbringing as a Muslim woman with certain limitations and the demands of her western-educated husband, who imposes upon her a secular lifestyle with his exhortation: "Forget about being a good Kashmiri girl. Start thinking about being a modern Indian woman" (*MC* 35). The tension between the two rises with the birth of their children: three daughters, Emerald, Alia, Mumtaz and two sons, Hanif, and Mustapha. Aziz dismisses the religious tutor, thinking that he teaches them to hate other religions: "'[h]e was teaching them to hate, wife. He tells them to hate Hindus and Buddhists and Jains and Sikhs and who knows what other vegetarians. Will you have hateful children, woman?'" (*MC*

42-43). Saleem also presents a view of a "muhalla" where neighbours with different religions and languages are depicted with daggers drawn at each other's throat so as to demonstrate the racial and religious intolerance prevalent in the pre-independence period.

At this point in the narrative Saleem makes a leap of twenty-three years from 1919 to 1942 so that he can conclude his account of the colonial past by relating the transfer of assets between a leaving British gentleman and his parents, Amina and Ahmed Sinai. When Ahmed Sinai loses his business in Delhi in a fire started by religious extremists, the Sinai family moves to Bombay on June 4, where he wants to enter the property business. On the same day, Earl Mountbatten of Burma holds a press conference and announces the Partition of India seventy days later. Soon after their arrival in Bombay, Ahmed Sinai goes into a bargain with William Methwold, a departing British estate owner. Saleem explains that Methwold is named after William Methwold, the first East India Company officer to envision Bombay as a British colony. As a representative of the British colonial mind, Methwold sees British forces in the Indian subcontinent as a civilising power. He reminds Ahmed, "[y]ou'll admit, we weren't all bad: built your roads. Schools, railway trains, parliamentary system, all worthwhile things. Taj Mahal was falling down until an Englishman bothered to see to it" (*MC* 95-96). Methwold's schedule for transfer further explicates the details of his colonial mind. The four identical villas in Methwold's estate, named after famous European palaces (Versailles, Buckingham, Escorial and Sans Souci), are "sold on two conditions: that the houses be bought complete with every last thing in them, that the entire contents be retained by the new owners; and that the actual transfer should not take place until midnight on August 15th" (*MC* 95). Hence, the transfer of assets between Methwold and the Sinais is a symbolic rendition of the transfer of political power. As David W. Price notes, "Methwold seeks to preserve the traditions of the British Raj through the very materiality of his estate. His hope is that the object will affect the new occupants in such a way that the traditions of the past will be preserved" (95). Indeed, Methwold's plan seems to work for a short period of time as Saleem observes,

> [...] things are settling down, the sharp edges of things are getting blurred, so they have failed to notice what is happening: the Estate, Methwold's Estate, is changing them. [When he] comes to call they slip effortlessly into their imitation Oxford drawls; and they are learning, about ceiling fans and gas cookers and the correct diet for budgerigars, and Methwold, supervising their transformation, is mumbling under his breath [...] All is well. (*MC* 99)

But once he leaves for England, Methwold's colonist gambit starts to lose its effect on the new occupants of the estate.

As the time of Indian independence draws closer, Vanita and Amina Sinai are revealed to get in labour simultaneously, lying in adjacent wards at Dr Narlikar's Nursing Home. Two children are born at the stroke of midnight: Saleem and Shiva. The former is the illegitimate child of Vanita, the minstrel Wee Willie Winkie's wife and William Methwold and the latter is the child of Ahmed and Amina Sinai. However the nurse Mary Pereira changes the babies' nametags. She gives Saleem, the son of Vanita and William Methwold to Amina, and Ahmed Sinai as a gesture to her revolutionary lover, Joseph D' Costa, who believes that the struggle in India is not between religious or ethnic groups, but the classes, the rich and the poor. Saleem makes a distinction between himself and Shiva, whom he calls his alter ego, along the mythological lines:

> [...] two of us were born on the stroke of midnight. Saleem and Shiva, Shiva and Saleem, nose and knees and knees and nose [...] to Shiva, the hour had given the gifts of war (of Rama, who could draw the undrawable. bow; of Arjuna and Bhima; the an-

cient prowess of Kurus and Pandavas united, unstoppably, in him!) [...] and to me, the greatest talent of all – the ability to look into the hearts and minds of men. (*MC* 196)

Shiva is not the only mythological character in the novel. Ganesh and Parvati are other deities of the Hindu pantheon mentioned in the novel. With his unmistakable reference to Saleem's enormous nose, Rushdie manages to establish a parallelism between Saleem and Ganesh, elephant-headed Hindu god, the scribe of the epic *Mahabharata*. Saleem even compares himself to Ganesh: "[n]ote that, despite my Muslim background, I'm enough of a Bombayite to be well up in Hindu stories, and actually I'm very fond of the image of trunk-nosed, flap-eared Ganesh solemnly taking dictation!" (*MC* 146). Through these mythological names, Rushdie succeeds in connecting the past with the present so as to help revive in the readers a sense of India's ancient past, often excluded in the official versions of the country's history. They also help foreshadow the course of events in the novel. Like Ganesh, associated with wisdom and overcoming difficulties, Saleem represents optimism and democratic ideals of independence while Shiva, the god of procreation and destruction, stands for the authoritarian rule that shall eventually lead to the destruction of midnight's children.

When Mary Pereira's secret is revealed nine years later, Saleem's parents continue to accept him as their own. "We all found that it made no difference!" Saleem writes, "I was still their son: they remained my parents. In a kind of collective failure of imagination, we learned that we could not think our way out of our pasts" (*MC* 118). Rushdie, thus, manages to convey the essence of the modern nation-state through the stories of the Aziz and the Sinai families that are not linked to each other by blood. Like the Sinai family, the nation is an imagined community; its legitimacy lies not in its absolute homogeneity, but on the contrary, in its diversity and the collective willingness of its citizens to believe to be the part of the same community. In other words, the modern nation-state is "premised on an imagined homogeneity in the face of actual heterogeneity" (Gopal 97). Accordingly, Saleem's description of the Indian nation-state seems to concur with Benedict Anderson's concept of the nation as an imagined community;

> a nation which had never previously existed was about to win its freedom, catapulting us into a world which, although it had five thousand years of history, although it had invented the game of chess and traded with Middle Kingdom Egypt, was nevertheless quite imaginary; into a mythical land, a country which would never exist except by the efforts of a phenomenal collective will – except in a dream we all agreed to dream; it was a mass fantasy shared in varying degrees by Bengali and Punjabi, Madrasi and Jat, and would periodically need the sanctification and renewal which can only be provided by rituals of blood. India, the new myth – a collective fiction in which anything was possible, a fable rivalled only by the two other mighty fantasies: money and God. (*MC* 111)

Rushdie's magical realist plot starts to unfold with the declaration of Indian independence and, more significantly, with the birth of midnight's children. "Think of this," Saleem asserts, "history, in my version, entered a new phase on August 15th, 1947" (*MC* 194). At the centre of Saleem's alternative history lies the literalised metaphor that lends its name to the title, *Midnight's Children*. Like other literalised metaphors in the novel, Saleem explains the meaning of midnight's children in a detailed metafictional commentary:

> Reality can have metaphorical content; that does not make it less real. A thousand and one children were born; there were a thousand and one possibilities which had never been present in one place at one time before; and there were a thousand and one

dead ends. Midnight's children can be made to represent many things, according to your point of view: they can be seen as the last throw of everything antiquated and retrogressive in our myth-ridden nation, whose defeat was entirely desirable in the context of a modernizing, twentieth-century economy; or as the true hope of freedom, which is now forever extinguished; but what they must not become is the bizarre creation of a rambling, diseased mind. No: illness is neither here nor there. (*MC* 197)

The fate of midnight's children mirrors the fate of democratic India. Through the story of midnight's children Rushdie manages to demonstrate how the ideals of democratic and egalitarian India, as represented by the Midnight's Children's Conference are shattered by subsequent political developments, namely Indira Gandhi's Emergency Rule. The optimism of the early days of independence turns into a time of pain and mourning.

At the age of nine, Saleem receives the first telepathic messages from other midnight's children while hiding in his mother's washing chest, but he mistakes them for the voices of the angels. When he tells his family that he can speak to angels, his parents grow angry with him. His mother calls him "a madman" and his father hits him on the side of his head, permanently impairing the hearing in his left ear. Fearing that his parents' reaction might lead to a withdrawal of their love, Saleem tries to suppress his ability of telepathy. However, he cannot escape from what is awaiting him. Saleem notes, "at a crucial point in the history of our child-nation, at a time when Five Year Plans were being drawn up and elections were approaching and language marchers were fighting over Bombay, a nine-year-old boy named Saleem Sinai acquired a miraculous gift" (*MC* 170). This short passage presents a pertinent example of the magical realist commingling of reality and fantasy. Magical realist fiction establishes a subtle equilibrium between the quotidian and the fantastic, thereby normalising the latter as part of everyday life.

Saleem's realisation of his magical powers, thus, takes place in a washing chest, which is revealed as a child's resolution to hide from the fear of failure. Similarly, it is in a bicycle accident that he discovers the voices filling his head do not belong to the angels, but midnight's children. In doing so, Rushdie seems to debunk fantasy for its own sake since by itself the fantastic can never be the answer. It is only through a commingling of the two opposing ontological domains, the fantastic and the real that the subversive nature of the former can be revealed.

The moment when Saleem realises his magical power is significant in terms of history as well. During the summer of 1956, protestors march in the streets of Bombay, demanding that the city should be partitioned along linguistic lines. It is at this historical juncture that Saleem starts to hear multitudinous voices from different parts of the Indian subcontinent, and beneath the trans-subcontinental rambles he hears the voice of the other midnight's children, sending "here-I-am signals" (*MC* 184). The multiplicity of languages in Saleem's head, ranging from Urdu to Tamil, creates a stark contrast with the language marches that end in the partition of Bombay. Akin to the religious faction that has led to the partition of India and Pakistan, the protestors in language marches advocate a singular, shared identity, undermining the cultural and linguistic diversity in the country. In this respect, magical realism can be regarded as complementary to the postmodern writing techniques in the novel that aim at bringing multiperspectivity to the established historical truth since it clearly favours multiplicity over a shallow homogenisation. In explaining the role of magical realism in *Midnight's Children*, Wendy Faris makes a subtle generalisation about the mode and its subversive function in literature:

> These texts [magical realist texts], which are receptive in particular ways to more than one point of view, to realistic and magical ways of seeing, and which open the door to other worlds, respond to a desire for narrative freedom from realism,

and from a univocal narrative stance; they implicitly correspond textually in a new way to a critique of totalitarian discourses of all kinds. ("Scheherazade" 179-180)

Rushdie voices similar ideas about magical realism through his narrator Saleem in the novel. Saleem underscores the functional role of fantasy in unveiling the alternative realities when he writes, "sometimes legends make reality, and become more useful than the facts" (*MC* 47). Furthermore, when commenting on the significant number of midnight's children, Saleem writes, "1001, the number of night, of magic, of alternative realities – a number beloved of poets and detested by politicians, for whom all alternative versions of the world are threats [...]" (*MC* 212). It is in the "third space" provided by magical realism that Saleem relates his alternative history of India.

On his tenth birthday, Saleem resolves to create his own gang, namely the Midnight's Children Conference. The conference can be regarded as the climax of Rushdie's pursuit of heteroglossia in the novel. A multiplicity of contesting ideas and discourses come into play in the Conference, disrupting the seeming homogeneity of ideology and language in the novel. In recognition of the collective aspect of the Conference, Priyamvada Gopal states, "[t]heir Conference gives a necessary collective dimension to the national allegory that might otherwise only be Saleem's life story. [...] [It] represents the richness of the historical moment of India's transition to nationhood that brought many political and social ideas into the fray" (96). In the telepathic meetings convened by Saleem, the geographical, linguistic and ethnic boundaries prevalent in India are eliminated. Children freely discuss their ideas. Saleem records the minutes of one of their conferences in which the children discuss the meaning of their gathering and their purpose in life. Rushdie reflects the exuberance present in the conference in a celebratory tone with a paragraph that runs on without any use of periods:

I record, faithfully, the views of a typical selection of the Conference members [...]: among the philosophies and aims suggested were collectivism – 'We should all get together and live somewhere, no? What would we need from anyone else?' – and individualism –' You say 'we; but we together are unimportant; what matters is that each of us has a gift to use for his or her own good' – filial duty – 'However we can help our father-mother, that is what it is for us to do' and infant revolution – 'Now at last we must show all kids that it is possible to get rid of parents!' – capitalism – 'Just mink what businesses we could do! How rich, Allah, we could be!' – and altruism – 'Our country needs gifted people; we must ask the government how it wishes to use our skills' – science – 'We must allow ourselves to be studied and' – religion – 'Let us declare ourselves to the world, so that all may glory in God' – courage – 'We should invade Pakistan!' – and cowardice – 'O heavens, we must stay secret, just mink what they will do to us, stone us for witches or what-all!'; there were declarations of women's rights and pleas for the improvement of the lot of untouchables; landless children dreamed of land and tribals from the hills, of Jeeps; and there were, also, fantasies of power. 'They can't stop us, man! We can bewitch, and fly, and read minds, and turn them into frogs, and make gold and fishes, and they will fall in love with us, and we can vanish through mirrors and change our sex... how will they be able to fight?' (*MC* 222-223)

Metaphorically, The Midnight Children's Conference expresses Rushdie's belief that "the defining image of India is the crowd, and the crowd is by its very nature superabundant, heterogeneous, many things at once" ("Riddle" 32). As mentioned earlier, Saleem and his alter ego, Shiva, represent two opposing political ideologies. While Saleem represents liberal democratic ideals, Shiva is the spokesperson of brute dictatorship. Shiva explains that the political conflict between the two results from class distinction: "'Rich kid,' Shiva yelled, 'you don't know one damned thing! What purpose, man? What thing in the whole sister-sleeping world got reason, yara? For what reason you are rich and I'm poor?... Man, I'll tell you – you got to get what you can, do what you can with it, and then you got to die. That's reason, rich boy.' (*MC* 220-221). The fact that Saleem is not really a rich boy reveals Rushdie's attitude towards identities as fictive and unstable entities.

The Midnight's Children Conference gradually disintegrates. Saleem explains that the Conference fails partly because the children begin to replicate the poison of their parents' prejudices and thus can no longer collaborate: "Children, however magical, are not immune to their parents; and as the prejudices and world-views of adults began to take over their minds, I found children from Maharashtra loathing Gujaratis, and fair-skinned northerners reviling Dravidian 'blackies'; there were religious rivalries; and class entered our councils" (*MC* 248). The other reason that leads to the betrayal of the Conference is Indira Gandhi's oppressive rule between 1974 and 1977 known as the Emergency. It was during the Emergency, Rushdie contends, " [that] the Congress, and the government of Mrs Gandhi, abandoned its policy of representing the coalition of minorities, and began to transform itself into an overtly Hindu party. [...] From Hindu nationalism sprang separatism of all sorts; if Hindustan was really to be turned into the home of Hindus, no wonder some Sikhs began to talk of a homeland" ("God" 386). With the final book of Saleem's autobiography where he relates the days of Emergency, the narrative gains an elegiac tone. In this time of political oppression, a liberal formation as the Midnight's Children Conference cannot be tolerated. Saleem and the other midnight's children undergo operations of sterilisation. Shiva helps helping sterilise his fellow midnight children by "strewing bastards across the map of India" (*MC* 395). When they are finally released in late March of 1977, it is not only midnight's children, who have lost their procreative power, but also India as well. Saleem describes the sterilisation process by coining a new term "sperectomy" which means "the draining-out of hope" (*MC* 455). The subsequent annihilation of midnight's children by Indira Gandhi marks the climax of gradual betrayal of ideals of independence. Thus, Saleem confesses that his "historic mission to rescue the nation from her fate" has failed (*MC* 381). In the final part of his autobiography, Saleem makes a future projection and describes his death. His body breaks and falls apart, reducing him to 600 million specks of dust as he has prefigured at the beginning of his narrative.

Saleem's lengthy narrative, thus, ends in the darkness of the Emergency. Some critics have blamed Rushdie for portraying a pessimist picture of India. Rushdie's reply to the critics helps delineate magical realism's function in portraying India as a country of diversity and multiplicity in the novel. He contends,

> What I tried to do was to set up a tension in the text, a paradoxical opposition between the form and the content of the narrative. The story of Saleem does indeed lead him into despair. But the story is told in a manner designed to echo, as closely as my abilities allowed, the Indian talent for non-stop self-generation. This is why the narrative constantly throws up new stories, why it 'teems.' The form – multitudinous, hinting at the infinite possibilities of the country – is the optimistic counterweight to Saleem's personal tragedy. I do not think that a book written in such a manner can really be termed a despairing work. ("Imaginary" 15)

His magical realist rendering of India endowed with myths and legends of the past makes it possible to imagine the multiplicity of Indian society that is largely ignored in the official accounts of history. The textual space provided by magical realism enables Rushdie to blend India's vast cultural identity with contemporary history. Thus, mythic characters, such as Ganesh and Shiva appear on the same textual plane as the founding figures of independent India, Gandhi and Nehru.

3.2. Mythologising Indian History: Shashi Tharoor's *The Great Indian Novel*

Published eight years after Rushdie's *Midnight's Children*, *The Great Indian Novel* marked the debut of a new literary talent, Shashi Tharoor, who followed in the footsteps of Rushdie into the realm of magical realism and postmodern historiography. In his hasty note of disclaimer in the preface to the novel, Tharoor explains that the primary source of inspiration for the novel is a two-thousand-year-old Indian epic, the *Mahabharata*, whose Sanskrit name means 'Great India.' The epic serves as an interpretative strategy in the novel. Tharoor rigorously reinvents the *Mahabharata* as a satirical retelling of twentieth-century India, from the British colonial days to the post-independence years. Not only does he establish parallelism between the themes and events in each book of the novel and those in the epic, but he also transforms the political figures from Indian history into mythical characters. In other words, Tharoor presents contemporary Indian history through a mythic lens. In addition to the thematic issues, the structure of the novel also mirrors the ancient epic of the *Mahabharata*, consisting of eighteen books divided into one hundred and twenty three sections. The *Mahabharata* is not the only text subjected to Tharoor's postmodern subversion. Tharoor incorporates a plethora of narratives on and of India within the textual space of the novel, which, in turn, gives rise to what Roland Barthes calls a "writerly text."[35] The titles of the books in the novel bear allusions to

---

[35] Translated from Barthes' neologisms *lisible* and *scriptible*, the terms "readerly" and "writerly" mark the distinction between traditional literary works with established conventions and those that violate the conventions of realism, and thus force the reader to produce a meaning or meanings. Barthes writes, "The writerly text is a perpetual present, upon which no consequent language (which would inevitably make it past) can be superimposed; the writerly text is ourselves writing, before the infinite play of the world (the world as function) is traversed, intersected, stopped, plasticized by some singular system

several fictional accounts of India. With titles like "Passages Through India," "The Bungle Book," "The Duel With the Crown," "Midnight's Parents" and "The Far Power-Villain" Tharoor refers to some famous works of literature written by E. M. Forster, Rudyard Kipling, Paul Scott, Salman Rushdie and M. M. Kaye. Some of the fictional characters from these works of literature and their writers also appear in the novel.

As a reworking of the ancient epic, it is almost impossible to read the novel without some understanding of the story narrated in the *Mahabharata* and its characters.[36] It is, therefore, necessary to provide an outline of the ur-text from the outset. Traditionally, the age old tale of the *Mahabharata* is ascribed to Maharishi Ved Vyasa, who is believed to have narrated the epic to Lord Ganesh of Hindu mythology. The main theme of the epic is the dynastic struggle between the Pandavas, the five sons of Pandu, and the Kauravas, the hundred sons of Pandu's half-brother Dhritarashtra, which culminates in the great battle of Kurukshetra. In moral terms, it is also traditionally read as a struggle between the forces of good and evil, *dharma* and *adharma*. Cheated of their royal rights by the Kauravas and forced into exile, the Pandavas return to reclaim their birthright. The climactic battle of Kurukshetra is a vindication of the Pandavas, although the cost of battle is so high that there seem to be no real victors in the struggle.[37] In his allegorical interpretation of the epic, Tharoor recasts events, episodes and characters from the *Mahabharata* in the context of the Indian independence movement and the first three decades of the post-independence period. Almost all of the characters in the novel bear the names of characters from the *Mahabharata*. Gan-

---

(Ideology, Genus, Criticism) which reduces the plurality of entrances, the opening of networks, the infinity of languages" (5).

[36] Pamela Lothspeich goes as far as to claim that *The Great Indian Novel* cannot appeal to general readership, but only to a select few: "Both in terms of its content (Indian history through an epic lens) and its style (magical realism), *The Great Indian Novel* speaks to an elite, Western or Westernized, English-speaking audience" (82).

[37] In this study, two English translations of the *Mahabharata* have been used as reference sources: *The Mahabharata* Translated by Chakravarthi V. Narasimhan and *The Great Epic: The Stories of the Ramayana and the Mahabharata* by John Campbell Oman.

gaji/Ganga is Mahatma Gandhi, Dhristarashtra is Jawaharlal Nehru, and Priya Duryodhani is Indira Gandhi. Tharoor's opus roughly covers the same period as Rushdie's *Midnight's Children*. The novel begins with the rise of Gangaji (Gandhi) as a political leader and the emergence of popular nationalism and moves to the days of Jawaharlal Nehru as the first Prime Minister of India, and then to Lal Bahadur Shastri and Indira Gandhi. The novel ends with the days of National Emergency and the formation of the Janata Party, its grand alliance, success in the elections and eventual defeat.

In his collection of essays on writing and writers, titled *Bookless in Baghdad*, Tharoor explains his aim in writing *The Great Indian Novel* as follows:

> My motivation was a conscious one. Most developing countries are also formerly colonized countries, and one of the realities of colonialism is that it appropriated the cultural definition of its subject peoples. Writing about India in English, I cannot but be aware of those who have done the same before me, others with a greater claim to the language but a lesser claim to the land. Think of India in the English-speaking world even today, and you think in images conditioned by Rudyard Kipling and E.M. Forster, by the Bengal Lancers and "The Jewel in the Crown." But their stories are not my stories, their heroes are not mine; and my fiction seeks to reclaim my country's heritage for itself, to tell, in an Indian voice, a story of India. Let me stress, a story of India; for there are many other stories, and many other Indians to tell them. (257)

Here, Tharoor clearly pinpoints the fact that *The Great Indian Novel*, like most of the Indian English novels written in the 1980s, is located at the crossroads of postmodern and postcolonial influences. While his intention to present Indian history from an indigenous perspective is markedly postcolonial, his immediate caution that the novel is one of the myriads of possible renditions of the country's ancient history indicates the postmodern understanding of history as a human construct.[38] Needless to say, magical realism functions as an enabling literary device in the novel. It is through the third space provided by magical realism that Tharoor successfully threads history and myth together and thereby dismantles the scientific pretensions of a colonial history. Exempt from the limitative borders of empirical realism, Ved Vyas incorporates a variety of texts in the narrative, ranging from history to literature, from politics to mythology. For instance, while describing the situations and characters in the novel, he uses literary terms drawn from classical literature, such as "nemesis" (*GIN* 138), "hubris" (363) and "bathos" (402), and when he intends to criticise the imperial policies of the British administration, he borrows from the colonist terminology and refers, for instance, to the colonial motto of the Roman empire "divide et impera," divide and rule (134).

That Tharoor looks to the ancient epic for inspiration is hardly surprising since he is well aware of the vital place of myths in any given culture, including his own. He writes, "my novel is about the kind of stories a society tells about itself. In many cultures, myths and epics both contribute to and reflect the national consciousness [...] what, I asked to myself, would a 20th century Veda Vyas tell about the great events of his time?" (qtd. in Rao 62). Therefore, a more pertinent question related to Tharoor's use of the ancient epic would be "why has he chosen the *Mahabharata* from innumerable Indian epics to model his novel on?" In his vigorous study of the epic and its relevance in the contemporary Indian culture, titled *Transmission of the Mahabharata Tradition*, C. R. Deshpande provides an unequivocal answer to this question.

---

[38] In an interview, Tharoor states: "History is not created by some sort of inscrutable force; it is created by human beings. It is not, as the old saying goes, a web woven by innocent hands. Rather history emerges as a result of people either wilfully using memory to drive others into oblivion or allowing the experience of recent oblivion to create new antagonistic memories" ("Of Novels" 81).

He aptly demonstrates that the ancient Indian epic has been one of the major sources of inspiration for Indian literature in the last four centuries or so. Deshpande identifies twenty re-writings of the *Mahabharata* in verse and prose forms alike. According to Deshpande, one of the reasons for the popularity of the ancient epic in the contemporary literary scene stems from the fact that it is inscribed in the collective memory of the Indian nation. Like William Shakespeare's Falstaff or Charles Dickens' Ebenezer Scrooge in English culture, the characters in the *Mahabharata* have become part of India's popular culture, signifying some of the stereotypical characteristics of the Indian nation. "Call a man Bhīṣma, Karṇa or Abhimanyu" C. R. Deshpande points out, "and any Indian will immediately understand your estimate of the character of the person concerned" (3).

This is, of course, true for the English-speaking Indian public who are familiar with the ur-text itself. For the non-Indian readers, *The Great Indian Novel* presents a completely different reading experience mainly because it invites the reader to look at an emerging nation through its ethos inscribed in an ancient indigenous epic. In recognition of this crucial fact, the influential postcolonial critic Bill Ashcroft, argues that "Tharoor's novel is consciously counter-discursive in its reproduction of history through a Hindu lens, reversing the historical gaze by putting the reader in the place of the Indian consumer of a dominant but culturally alien discourse" (*Post-colonial* 106). Tharoor invites the reader to make a comparative reading, trying to identify the links between the ur-text and his novel. Yet, *The Great Indian Novel* embodies other challenges for the Western reader as well,

> The process of using the *Mahabharata* as the 'transparency' of history has a formidable counter-discursive function. For the non-Indian reader the access to Hindu cosmology occurs in exactly the same way that the Indian readers of the Great Tradition of English literature were expected to absorb the values of

Western civilization from their reading. This reversal is a profound reversal of the strategy of reading. *The Great Indian Novel* demonstrates not only the process of the postcolonial interpolation of history but the kind of 'resistance' which can be achieved by an interpolation of the category 'literature' itself. What we find is not a simple reversal of history; at one level the narrative of history is left untouched. But the layering of the transparency of Indian cosmology, values, assumptions, world view upon that history via the *Mahabharata* enacts the civilizing mission *in reverse*. (*Postcolonial* 108-109 emphasis original)

In other words, in *The Great Indian Novel*, Shashi Tharoor challenges the Western reader who has grown adept at deciphering the mythological codes in the canonical works of literature, such as T. S. Eliot's *The Waste Land* and James Joyce's *Ulysses* with an equally legitimate claim for the canon as reflected in the title of the novel.

The content of the novel constitutes only one part of Tharoor's postcolonial project. The other part of the project rests on the postmodern view of history as a narrative construct, "nonlinear, cyclic, indeterminate, discontinuous [and] contingent;" one that can no longer make claims to universality (Lather 161). Well-versed in history, Tharoor once said of his writing: "I am a student of history and I am concerned with the recording of history – my work is conscious about the various ways that history can be told and recorded" (qtd. in Kanaganayakam 121). In *The Great Indian Novel*, he subtly experiments with the ancient epic text and opens up a textual space in which he could challenge and subvert the tenets of Western historiography. The omnipresent narrator, Ved Vyas (also referred to as VV or VVji), functions as the most important narrative device in Tharoor's experiment with history and myth. Ved Vyas declares early in his story that "what I am about to dictate is the definitive memoir of my life and times [...] in my epic I shall tell of past, present and future, of existence and passing, of efflorescence and decay, of death and rebirth, of what is, of what was, of what should have been" (18). Ved Vyas' initial intention reminds us the traditional duty of the historian, recounting the past events with a vision for the future. However, it is only few lines later that Ved Vyas renounces his claim for historical truth: "This my story, the story of Ved Vyas but it could become nothing less than *The Great Indian Novel*" (18). Indeed, as history is transformed into myth and the epic characters become figures of contemporary history, the dividing line between fact and fiction gets blurred.

From a broader perspective, Tharoor's narrator can be seen as an extension of an Indian understanding of history that does not classify myth and history in separate compartments. In the Indian tradition, the Vedas, a large body of texts originating in ancient India, are considered to be both stories and chronicles. In his magical realist rendering of Indian history, Tharoor successfully establishes a parallelism between the modern Ved Vyas and the narrator of the ancient text of the *Mahabharata*, Ved Vyasa. For instance, Ved Vyas' penchant for narrating the past, present and the future within his narrative echoes the original claim. Maharishi Ved Vyasa, the narrator of the *Mahabharata*, is believed to have been a seer with magical powers. As Kevin McGrath notes, "Vyâsa's comprehension is total, there is no further reference, he is *pratyakṣadarśī* [...] *bhūtabhavyabhaviṣyavit*, 'one who has before his eyes the past, present and the future'" (70). The verbal similarity between the two narrators' claims for historical truth is a clear indication of Tharoor's subtlety in his interweaving ancient myth and contemporary history.

In the course of the narrative, Tharoor puts the established tenets of Western historiography on trail. Ved Vyas questions the received histories of India in his narrative. His method of criticism varies widely. Sometimes, he makes a direct comment on the histories laid down by the British. For instance, in one of his addresses to Ganapathi, his young scribe, Ved Vyas questions the established view of India as a poverty-stricken country and the English as a civilising humanitarian power:

> It is difficult for you, living now with the evidence of that poverty around you, taking it for granted as a fact of life, to conceive of an India that was not poor, not unjust, not wretched. But that was how India was before the British came, or why would they have come? Do you think the merchants and adventurers and traders of the East India Company would have sailed to a land of poverty and misery? No, Ganapathi, they came to an India that was fabulously rich, and prosperous, they came in search for wealth and profit, and they took what they could take, leaving Indians to wallow in their leavings. (*GIN* 95)

Leaving no space for ambiguity, Ved Vyas asserts, "[w]rite this down: the British killed the Indian artisans, they created the Indian 'landless labourer,' they exported our full-employment and they invented our poverty" (*GIN* 95). Tharoor's critique of Western historiography is not always straightforward. His self-reflexive narrative challenges the traditional conception of history as an unbiased reporting of past events, encouraging the reader to ponder upon the intricacies of the Western historiography. In this respect, the process of narrativisation becomes more important than the narrative itself. Through Ved Vyas' comments on the concepts of truth, reality and history, Tharoor draws attention to the "constructedness" of narrative and thereby disrupts the traditional distinction established between history and literature. Tharoor demonstrates that history, hitherto considered as a scientific discipline, in fact, bears affinities with literature, for the act of narrativisation, interpretation and perspective play an important role in shaping the documentation of the past. At one point in his narrative, Ved Vyas suspends the narrative and expounds on the fact that an account of any given past event inevitably requires a selective view. In a lengthy address to Ganapathi, he explains that his story is not exempt from the pitfalls of historiography either:

> Independence was not won by a series of isolated incidents but by the constant, unremitting actions of thousands, indeed hundreds of thousands of men and women across the land. We tend, Ganapathi, to look back on history as if it were a stage play, with scene building upon scene, our hero moving from one action to the next in his remorseless stride to the climax. Yet life is never like that. […] the recounting of history is only the order we artificially impose upon life to permit its lessons to be more clearly understood.
>
> So it is, Ganapathi, that in this memoir we light up one corner of our collective past at a time, focus on one man's actions, one village's passion, one colonel's duty, but all the while life is going on elsewhere. […] It is no different for the protagonists of our story, the little band of individuals and families selected from the swirling mists of an old man's memory to represent a past in which others too have played a significant but unrecalled part. (*GIN* 109-110)

Through such commentaries on his own narrativisation of Indian history, Ved Vyas hints at similar processes in Western historiography. By "emphasizing and asserting the porousness of genres and blurring the boundaries between history and fiction," the novelist enables readers to "make their own evaluation of what they are told and […] compels them to rethink the distinction that is traditionally made between history and fiction" (Salat 130). Ved Vyas goes on to confide in his amanuensis:

> For every tale I have told you, every perception I have conveyed, there are a hundred equally valid alternatives I have

omitted and of which you are unaware. I make no apologies for this. This is my story of the India I know, with its biases, selections, omissions, distortions, all mine. But you cannot derive your cosmogony from a single birth, Ganapathi. Every Indian must for ever carry with him, in his head and heart, his own history of India. (*GIN* 373)

Here, Tharoor clearly advocates that there is more than one truth, more than one way of looking at history and myths that have shaped Indian culture. Yet, the illusion that there is one unified history is to be sustained since, as increasingly voiced by contemporary critics such as Benedict Anderson and Homi Bhabha, at the very foundation of the nation state lies this collective illusion, the belief that there is a unified, traceable national past.

Ved Vyas' selective view of history is nowhere more evident than in his attitude towards the separatist groups in Indian history. In *The Great Indian Novel*, Shashi Tharoor, like Salman Rushdie in *Midnight's Children*, speaks passionately in favour of Indian pluralism. It is, therefore, not surprising that V.V. excludes civil strife from his story. Towards the end of the novel, Ved Vyas notes,

I have portrayed a nation in struggle but omitted its struggles against itself, ignoring the regionalists and autonomists and separatists and secessionists who even today are trying to tear the country apart. To me, Ganapathi, they are of no consequence in the story of India; they seek to diminish something that is far greater than they will ever comprehend. (*GIN* 412)

Ved Vyas' explanation becomes more meaningful when considered in relation with his earlier assertion that "[w]hat is left out matters almost as much as what is said" (*GIN* 411). Thus, by leaving out the separatist groups, V. V. emphasises the necessity of cultural pluralism and tolerance at a national level. Viewed in a broader perspective, the exclusion of separatist movements from the novel is not Tharoor's/Ved Vyas' personal preference, but a prerequisite imposed by the ancient epic text itself. The *Mahabharata* is believed to draw its unifying power from the plurality of the ethnic groups that constitute India. In explaining the distinctive place of the *Mahabharata* in Indian culture, the anthropologist K. S. Singh states

> A remarkable feature of the *Mahābhārata* from an anthropological angle is that it presents in its present form a grand assembly of all ethnic groups and of the peoples of all territories constituting almost the whole of Bharat. The present day *Mahābhārata* consists of 125,000 verses, as stories and legends churned out by various communities and territorial groups were incorporated into this corpus. This is probably the finest example of the making of the consciousness of a people, of a civilisation and of a moral order, from the interaction of various communities and their cultures in the geographical area lying south of the Himalayas and bounded by the oceans. (6-7)

By the same token, another critic, O. P. Juneja, argues that the *Mahabharata* and its rewritings point towards a "polyphonic heteroglossic dialogism," which he regards as an inherent characteristic of Indian culture (qtd. in Wiemann 89). At the risk of perpetrating a gross anachronism, Jueneja goes as far as to categorise the ancient myth as a postmodern text: "[t]he postmodern condition which was already, always there in the Indian soil produced post-modern texts like the *Mahabharata* and its contemporary rewritten texts like *The Great Indian Novel* by Shashi Tharoor" (qtd. in Wiemann 89). In this light, it can be argued that in *The Great Indian Novel* Shashi Tharoor attempts to remind Indian people not only of their shared national struggle for independence and constitution of democracy, but also of their common duty to protect the democratic and pluralistic face of the country. The ensuing pages aim at demonstrating how Tharoor employs magical realism in his revitalisation of the ancient text of the *Mahabharata* in the contemporary context.

The twentieth century Ved Vyas is a former politician of the Kaurava Party (the Indian National Congress). He has been involved in the political life of the country and witnessed the momentous events during India's struggle for independence. As an insider and a participant of Indian political history, he sees himself as "destiny's observer" (*GIN* 216). Having retired at the age of eighty-eight, Ved Vyas, like Saleem Sinai, settles down to write the definitive memoir of his life. Ved Vyas exacts his friend Brahm to find him an amanuensis to dictate what he believes to be the Song of Modern India. The next day, a young South Indian scribe called Ganapathi shows up in his office. Ved Vyas describes the young scribe as having "a big nose and shrewd, intelligent eyes" (*GIN* 18). The strange thing is that he has an "elephantine treat, broad forehead," a "substantial belly" and "an enormous trunk behind him" (*GIN* 18). The description points to the elephant-headed Hindu god Ganesh, who is believed to have written Vyasa's account of the *Mahabharata*. Thus, as a tale dictated to an elephantine scribe by a veteran politician, *The Great Indian Novel* earns its magical realist credentials from the outset. Unlike Padma in Rushdie's *Midnight's Children*, Ganapathi remains silent throughout the novel. The expressive gestures on his face are read out by Ved Vyas. It is Ved Vyas' digressive narrative style that vexes the young scribe most. He shows his reaction by turning his trunk into a question mark, yet Ved Vyas ignores Ganapathi most of the time since he sees digressions as an integral part of life: "I know this is a digression – but my life, indeed this world, is nothing more than a series of digressions" (*GIN* 28).

The narrator, Ved Vyas, stands as the embodiment of the Indian nation. Like Saleem, V.V. claims that he has a profound correspondence with India at large, embodying the cultural practices of both the pre- and post-colonial eras: "[l]ike India herself, I am at home in hovels and palaces [...], I trundle in bullock carts and propel myself into space, I read the *vedas* and quote the laws of cricket" (*GIN* 65). Therefore, *The Great Indian Novel,* as V.V. points out, is "my story, the story of Ved Vyas [...] and yet it is also the story of India, your country and mine" (*GIN* 46). The novel begins with Ved Vyas' repudiation of the westernised intellectuals' claim that India is an underdeveloped country:

> They tell me India is an underdeveloped country. They attend seminars, appear on television, even come to see me, creasing their eight-hundred-rupee suits and clutching their moulded plastic briefcases, to announce in tones of infinite understanding that India has yet to develop. Stuff and nonsense, of course. I tell them that if they would only read the *Mahabharata* and the *Ramayana,* study the Golden Ages of the Mauryas and the Guptas and even of those Muslim chaps the Mughals, they would realize that India is not an underdeveloped country but a highly developed one in an advanced state of decay. (*GIN* 17)

Here, Tharoor does not only oppose the popular perception of India as an underdeveloped country, but also traces its roots in the ignorance of the Indian nation about their cultural and historical heritage. It is important to note that contrary to Western understanding, progress, for Ved Vyas, does not mean economic or technological development, but a firm, shared cultural heritage. In this respect, Tharoor's novel itself can be seen as an instrument of decolonisation, intended to alert the Western readers and perhaps more importantly the Indian reading public to the fact that Indian history does not begin with the colonisation of the subcontinent.

The first book of the novel has a self-explanatory title, "The Twice-born Tale," which indicates the palimpsest nature of Tharoor's novel as a retelling of *the Mahabharata.* In a parallel fashion to the ancient epic structure, the narrator, V.V., recounts the genealogy of his family wherein he touches upon the caste system prevailing in ancient India. In the past, Brahmins, the travelling sages, journeyed through the country, honouring different households with their visits. They were offered a lodging, food and bed with the host's daughter. On one such occasion, Ved Vyas is born out of seduction of Satyavati, a poor fisherman's daughter by Parashar, a travelling Brahmin. Ved Vyas explains, "I was born with the century, a bastard, but a bastard in a fine tradition, the offspring of a fisherwoman seduced by a travelling sage" (*GIN* 19). With her father's consent, Parashar takes Satyavati away for religious training, promising that he shall return her as a virgin within one year. Satyavati returns home after giving birth to Ved Vyas in an old midwife's home in the forest. Her virginity has remained intact by the dint of Parashar's magical powers.

Later, Shantanu, the king of Hastinapur, seeks Satyavati's hand in marriage. The king has been married to an exquisite Maharani who has suffered from seven successive miscarriages and disappeared after giving birth to a son, Ganga Datta. The fisherman agrees to marry his daughter, Satyavati, to the king provided that no one else, but her son shall be his heir. Tharoor successfully builds a correlation between ancient Hastinapur and colonial India and recounts the increasing power of the British rule over the Indian sub-continent. Shantanu explains to his son Ganga Datta that his marriage is not a mere pursuit of fleshly pleasure, but a procreative plan that shall ensure the continuation of the kingdom in the face of the growing threat of annexation: "[t]he damned Resident [the British] has already run over three people in that infernal new wheeled contraption of his. I'm not saying that that could happen to you, but one never knows, does one? [...] Something happens and sut! the British swoop in and take over your kingdom claiming the lack of a legitimate heir" (*GIN* 22). Thus, Hastinapur demands more than one heir. When the king reveals the details of his marriage pact with Satyavati's father, Ganga Datta takes a vow of chastity and renounces his claim to the throne in order to enable his father's second marriage. From then onwards he is named "Bhishma, the One Who has Taken a Terrible Vow" (*GIN* 24).

The allegorical framework starts to emerge with the appearance of Ganga Datta, who stands for none other than the founding father of the nation Mahatma Gandhi himself. Tharoor reveals the historical figures behind the mythic characters by providing their distinctive physical features and detailed biographical information. For instance, he presents some information about Ganga's past through an overheard dialogue: "courtiers at the door swore they heard the words "South Africa", "defiance of British laws," "arrest," "jail" and "expulsion" rising in startled sibilance at various times" (*GIN* 25). It is only one page later that Ganga is described as having a "balding pate and oval glasses," so as to assure that readers do not fail to recognise the correlation between the two (*GIN* 26).

Ganga occupies a central role in politics. Like his father, he is most concerned with the procreation of progeny that shall secure the dynastic succession. Hence, when Satyavati gives birth to two sons, Chitrangada and Vichitravirya, Ganga becomes increasingly involved in the dynastic issues, serving his half-brothers as the Regent of Hastinapur. Chitrangada's premature death hastens Ganga to arrange Vichitravirya a marriage with two sisters, Ambika and Ambalika in order to assure the continuation of the dynastic family, but Vichitravirya dies childless as well, which causes consternation in the royal palace. At this point, Ved Vyas suspends his narrative to make a passing comment about the British colonial policy and the Indians' armed rebellion against it, known as the Mutiny of 1857:

> Whereas in the past the royal house could simply have adopted a male child to continue the family's hold on the throne, this was not quite as easy under the British, who had a tendency to declare the throne vacant and annex the territory for themselves.

(We even fought a little war over the principle in 1857 – but the British won, and annexed a few more kingdoms). (*GIN* 30)

In his collection of political writing titled *India: From Midnight to the Millennium and Beyond,* Tharoor expounds on the importance of the Mutiny in the history of the Indian independence movement. According to Tharoor, India had never been communally united until the so-called Mutiny of 1857. Hence, it should be seen as a unique expression of solidarity between the largest ethnic and religious groups in India, namely Muslims, Hindus and Sikhs. Tharoor states, "[t]he sight (and the dismaying prospect) of Indians of varying faiths and regions united in a shared struggle against alien rule struck more terror into the hearts of the British than their actual revolt, which was put down by the force of superior arms" (*India* 14-15). Tharoor's interpretation of the so-called Mutiny in the novel reflects his misgivings about the official accounts of Indian history downplayed by Western historians. V.V. begins his description of the revolt by asserting that it was "disparaged by imperial historians" as "the 'Sepoy Mutiny'" (*GIN* 135). He, then, invites Ganapathi, his amanuensis, and thus the reader, to reassess the national revolt of 1857 from an indigenous perspective by emphatically asserting: "[i]magine the horror of the British in 1857 when their paid Indian soldiers revolted. Hindus and Muslims rallying jointly to the standard of the faded Mughal Emperor, deposed princes and disgruntled peasants making common cause against the alien oppressor" (*GIN* 134).

Despite the success of the revolt, the British administration continues to be a major threat for the kingdom of Hastinapur, which is left with no known eligible heir to the throne after the death of the two young princes. When Ganga Datta pronounces that he shall remain faithful to his vow of celibacy, Satyavati calls upon her son Ved Vyas as a last resort and instructs him to inseminate Ambika and Ambalika so that they can have a rightful heir to the throne. Thus, Ved Vyas, re-enters the story. Following his mother's injunction, he unites with both sisters, Ambika and Ambalika and with the latter's maidservant as well. From Ambika emerges Dhritarashtra, blind heir to Hastinapur throne, from Ambalika emerges Pandu the pale, his half brother and from the servant girl Vidur the wise, counsellor to the kings. The three brothers correspond to the politicians involved in India's struggle for independence: Jawaharlal Nehru (Dhritarashtra), Subhas Chandra Bose (Pandu) and Sardar Vallabhbhai (Vidur).

Tharoor borrows the epithets of his characters from the epic. According to the ancient text of the *Mahabharata*, appalled by their ravisher's advances, Ambika closes her eyes tightly while Ambalika turns pale. As a result, they give birth to a blind and a pale son, respectively. With a magical realist twist, Tharoor transforms this supernatural incident into one of the most important metaphors in the novel through which he reveals the political inclinations that the princes of Hastinapur shall develop in the future. V.V. explains that the meaning of their epithets is more than a mere physical description. Dhritarashtra is a Fabian Socialist and he has "the blind man's gift of seeing the world not as it [is], but as he want[s] it to be" (*GIN* 85). Pandu bears the epithet "the pale" because his ideology is mimicry of the white colonists'. V.V. says that "he saw the world very differently from his blind half-brother. Pandu believed in taking stock of reality, preferably with a clenched fist and eyes in the back of one's head. He balanced an hour of meditation with an hour of martial arts" (*GIN* 85). In other words, Pandu is a reminder of the indigenous elite that Frantz Fanon subjects to critique in his *Black Skins White Masks*, particularly for their tendency to model their government on the policies inherited from the colonial administration.

Ved Vyas declares to Ganapathi that the three bothers shall be the main characters of his narrative: "Can't neglect the little blighters because this is really their story, you know" (*GIN* 39). However, Ganga Datta continues to be the most important figure in colonial Hastinapur. Tharoor confirms the centrality of Gandhi in the narrative of the nation through Ved Vyas' explanation: "it was, indeed, Gangaji, who brought up my sons – as if, I must admit, they were his own children" (*GIN* 41). Ved Vyas marks the beginning of Ganga's (Gandhi's) rise to national leadership with a passage that echoes the invocation of the muse in the epic tradition:

> How shall I tell it, Ganapathi? It is such a long story, an epic in itself, and we have so much else to describe. Shall I tell of the strange weapon of disobedience, which Ganga, with all his experience of insisting upon obedience and obtaining it toward himself, developed into an arm of moral war against the foreigner? Shall I sing the praises of the mysterious ammunition of truth-force; the strength of unarmed slogan-chanting demonstrators falling defenceless under the hail of police lathis; the power of wave after wave of *khadi*-clad men and women, arms and voices raised, marching handcuffed to their imprisonment? Shall I speak, Ganapathi, and shall you write, of the victory of non-violence over the organized violence of the state; the triumph of bare feet over hobnailed boots; the defeat of legislation by the awesome strength of silence? (*GIN* 46)

Tharoor successfully sketches Gandhian philosophy in his renderings of Ganga's movements against the British colonial policies in two books aptly titled as The Duel with the Crown and The Powers of Silence. Ganga's urge to follow the dictates of conscience rather than the British law and his willingness to accept the punishment for his violations so as to prove the strength of one's convictions are further illustrated in Forbidden Fruit, devoted to a satirical rendition of Gandhi's Salt March as the Great Mango March.

In The Duel with the Crown, a satirical allusion to Paul Scott's novel *The Jewel of the Crown*, Tharoor introduces two representatives of British administration, Sir Richard and his equerry, Heaslop. Heaslop expresses his dismay for Ganga's personal eccentricities, such as his talk about equality and justice as well as his practices that undermine the caste distinctions. For instance, he cleans his own toilet and prepares his own enema, suggesting that "[u]ntouchables are just as good as he is" (*GIN* 37). Heaslop considers Ganga's activities a major threat to colonial rule since the caste system, dividing the society along the lines of various social ranks and religions, has served the British policies in India eminently. He is surprised at this sudden change in Ganga's attitudes since he has been part of the British community, attending receptions and contributing to their charity organisations, such as the Ambulance Association. "But of late," Heaslop states, "he has been known to say things about *swaraj*, you know, sir, self-rule. And about pan-Indian nationalism. No one seems to know what started him off on that track. They say he reads widely" (*GIN* 38). However, after arranging marriages for Ved Vyas' three sons, Ganga resigns from the regency and retreats to his ashram and pursues a spiritual life until one day he is summoned by a peasant from Motihari, an impoverished district of Hastinapur. The peasant insists that Ganga should come and see the terrible conditions of his fellow peasants and convince the British to change their indigo policy. In Motihari, three tenths of every peasant's land have to be consecrated to indigo because the British need cash-crops more than wheat. But the local people do not earn any profits from this trade since they have to sell their crop at a fixed price determined by the British administration.

The reluctant Ganga finally agrees to visit Motihari. He goes straight to the Planters' Club to talk to "English sahibs," but is denied entry. He stands outside the clubhouse and gazes at the people around him. Tharoor presents the ruthless intensity of the divide between the coloniser and the colonised through Ganga's discerning eyes:

> He [Ganga] saw men whose fatigue burrowed into their eyes and made hollows of their cheeks. He saw women dressed day after day in the same dirty sari because they did not possess a second one to change into while they washed the first. He saw

children without food, books or toys, snot-nosed little creatures whose distended bellies mocked the emptiness within. And he went to the Planters' Club and saw the English and Scots in their dinner-jackets and ballroom gowns, their laughter tinkling through the notes of the of the club piano as waiters bearing overladen trays circled their flower-bedecked tables. (*GIN* 50)

Next morning Ganga announces his protest campaign. To openly defy the indigo laws, Ganga plucks an indigo plant and sows a symbolic fistful of grain in its place. Ved Vyas dictates to Ganapathi that it is a pivotal moment in the history of India, changing the destiny of Indian people. "Even we who were with him then," Ved Vyas expounds, "were conscious of the dawn of a new epoch. […] A new nation was rising, with a small, balding, semi-clad saint at its head" (*GIN* 51). Seeing an incredulous gesture on Ganapathi's face, Ved Vyas chides him, saying "[yo]u can't know, you with your ration-cards and your black markets and the cynical materialism of your generation, what it was like in those days, what it felt like to discover a cause, to belong to a crusade, to *believe*" (*GIN* 52; emphasis original). Ved Vyas' reflection indicates the waning of Gandhian ideals in contemporary Indian society. He complains that the young generation seems to have already forgotten their great leader, thinking that he is a saint, or Nehru's biological father, or even a mythical character in *the Mahabharata*: "It was only two decades after Gangaji's death, but they were already unable to relate him to their lives. He might as well have been a character from the *Mahabharata*, Ganapathi, so completely had they consigned him to the mists of myth and historical legend" (*GIN* 47). However, his own portrayal of Ganga is far from flattering. He confesses "Let us be honest: Gangaji was the kind of person it is more convenient to forget. The principles he stood for and the way in which he asserted them were always easier to admire than to follow. While he was alive, he was impossible to ignore; once he had gone, he was impossible to imitate" (*GIN* 47). It becomes increasingly evident with the novel's progress that Tharoor endeavours to demystify the legendary figure of Gandhi by drawing a down to earth picture of him. He does not miss any chance to intersperse his own comments on the legend of Gandhi through Ved Vyas. For instance, while describing the momentous success he achieved in his mango march, V.V. cautions Ganapathi, "don't ever forget, young man that we were not led by a saint with his head in the clouds, but by a master tactician, with his feet on the ground" (*GIN* 122). Tharoor readily concedes that behind the myths attributed to Gandhi in the national grand narrative lies a shrewd politician who knows how to defeat his rivals through political gambits.

The British follow Ganga's political manoeuvres in Motihari with watchful eyes. His sedition in Motihari has served as the last straw for the British administration. Sir Richard, filled with anger and spite, annexes Hastinapur, pleading that Gangaji has failed to notify the imperial administration about his resignation from the regency of Hastinapur even though such a procedure is required by law. He has therefore visited a territory under the British administration as an official representative of Hastinapur and committed a violation. Ganga resolves to address a mass rally at the Bibigarh Gardens to protest the annexation. Daunted by Ganga's previous marches, Sir Richard instructs Colonel Rudyard to disperse the protesters. Rudyard's order to shoot the protesters without any reminder of the illegality of their congregation turns the peaceful protest into one of the bloodiest massacres in the history of Hastinapur. Tharoor includes the official numbers provided by the British administration: 1600 bullets were shot against the unarmed protestors, killing 397 and leaving 1,137 injured. As the historical facts suggest, this bloody military operation corresponds to the Amritsar massacre during the Indian independence movement. The power of Tharoor's critique of colonisation becomes nowhere more evident than in his portrayal of oppressions and cruelties of the imperial administration:

> He [Rudyard] just acted in the way dictated by the simple logic of colonialism, under which the rules of humanity applied only to the rulers, for the rulers were people and the people were objects. Objects to be controlled, disciplined, kept in their place and taught lessons like so many animals; yes, the civilising mission upon which Rudyard and his tribe were embarked made savages of all of us, and all of them. (*GIN* 80)

Through his cantankerous narrator, Tharoor also extends his criticism to Western historiography that seeks to reduce the effect of the atrocity committed by the colonial administration by using the almost euphemistic appellation of massacre for it:

> Historians have dubbed this event the Hastinapur Massacre. How labels lie. A massacre connotes the heat and fire of slaughter, the butchery by bloodthirsty fighters of an outgunned opposition. There was nothing of this at the Bibigarh Gardens that day. Rudyard's soldiers were lined up calmly, almost routinely; they were neither disoriented nor threatened by the crowd; it was just another day's work, but one unlike any other. [...] I think of the Bibigarh Gardens Massacre as a frozen tableau from a silent film, black and white, an Indian Guernica. (*GIN* 81)

Here, Tharoor seeks to redeem the biased view of Indian history by offering an alternative view of the Amritsar massacre from an indigenous perspective. His description of the scene through a reference to Picasso's *Guernica* demonstrates the Westerners' indifference to the atrocities committed in the former colonies. It is only through a familiar artefact that the Westerners can understand the enormity of the atrocities committed in the name of colonialism's civilising mission in India. Tharoor, then, extends his critique of colonisation through the fictional character of Colonel Rudyard. The colonel, rewarded with a half-million-pound pension for his "service", goes back to London, where two Indian nationalists await his return. They want to exact the revenge for their fellow Indians by killing the colonel. However, they kill a racist professor called Kipling, mistaking him for Colonel Rudyard. With his witty play upon the name of the famous English colonial poet Rudyard Kipling, Tharoor does not let anyone who took part in the colonisation of India escape his satirical gaze.

The Bibigarh Gardens Massacre had a great resonance in the Indian independence movement, stirring the nationalist feelings in the public. It is with this rising tide of Indian nationalism that Ved Vyas' sons embark on their political careers. They start to work together under the roof of the Kaurava Party, which corresponds to the National Congress. While Dhritarashtra (Nehru) becomes the head of the party, attending meetings and press conferences in urban India, Pandu (Bose), the party's chief organiser, carries the party's banners to the most distant villages through the mud and grime of the countryside. As a result of this division of labour, Dhritarashtra becomes the most famous political leader after Ganga, overshadowing Pandu's political campaigns in villages. Soon a rift develops between the two brothers. Although Pandu manages to become the president of the Kaurava Party, he is soon outmanoeuvred by Gangaji, who designates Dhritarashtra as his successor. At this point in his narrative, Ved Vyas flings himself into verse and recites his longest poem for his son's fall from grace. The poem reads like a lampoon, detailing Pandu's final days before his death in a plane crash. At the heart of Tharoor's criticism lies Bose's political inclination towards fascism. As an allegorical counterpart of Subhas Chandra Bose, Pandu is in favour of armed resistance against the colonial rule. Ved Vyas' thus begins his poem by highlighting Pandu's critique of Ganga's philosophy of non-violence to attain independence:

> 'Away with Tolstoy, Ruskin, Buddha:
> Their ideas just make little men littler.
> No more "truth force", only *yuddha* –
> It's time to learn from that chap Hitler.'
>
> So saying, our angry hero
> Became the country's first Fascist;
> Admiring Roma's latest Nero
> He practised how to clench his fist. (*GIN* 176)

Ved Vyas' long poem does not only diverge from the events as recorded in the verses of the *Mahabharata*, but also from the historical facts since Bose never went to Germany. In spite of this clear divergence from historical facts, Ved Vyas claims that his story is true:

> The song I sing is neither verse nor prose.
> Can the gardener ask why he is pricked by the rose?
> What I tell you is a slender filament,
> A rubbing from a colossal monument;
> But it is true. (*GIN* 164)

The concept of "truth" is one of the issues that Tharoor grapples with throughout the novel. Perhaps foreseeing the criticism his novel would receive for its clear divergence from history, Tharoor has Ved Vyas declare, "It is my truth, Ganapathi, just as the crusade to drive out the British reflected Gangaji's truth, and the fight to be rid of both the British and the Hindu was Karna's truth. Which philosopher would dare to establish a hierarchy among such verities?" (*GIN* 164).

Although V.V. admits that his story is the fruit of "the faltering memory of an old man" (*GIN* 163), he insists on its truth-value. V.V's contradiction reflects the essence of the postmodernist view of history that validates different versions of the past by underscoring the multiple nature of historical truth. In the same breath, Ved Vyas poses some questions about the validity of historical truth: "Question, Ganapathi. Is it permissible to modify truth with a possessive pronoun? Questions Two and Three. How much may one select, interpret and arrange the facts of the living past before truth is jeopardized by inaccuracy?" (*GIN* 164). Ved Vyas provides an answer to these questions later in the novel when he expounds on the nature of history. For Ved Vyas, history, like any other discursive practice, is in constant evolution, and for this reason the historian cannot have the final say on the past as it is impossible to provide a definitive, unified version of the evolving historical reality. What s/he attempts to provide can only be different versions and interpretations of it: "History, [...] indeed the world, the universe, all human life, and so, too, every institution under which we live – is in a constant state of evolution" (*GIN* 245).

As the narrative unfolds, Ved Vyas starts to complain about the increasing number of characters that populate his story. Addressing Ganapathi, he says, "I don't imagine this is particularly easy for you, is it, with so many dramatis personae to keep abreast of, so many destinies to persue. But what we're talking about is the story of an entire nation, a nation of 800 million people" (*GIN* 91). No matter how many new characters emerge in his story, V. V. cannot steer clear of Ganga, and thus he resolves to devote two successive books of his epic narrative to the heirs born to two brothers, Dhritarashtra and Pandu. In book eight, titled "Midnight's Parents," Ved Vyas recounts the childhood and education of the five Pandavas and the Kauravas. The title bears a clear allusion to Rushdie's *Midnight's Children*, suggesting that the Pandavas and their niece Priya are the generation that would parent the children of independence. Pandu has five sons, known as the Pandavas of the epic: Yudishthir, Bhim, Arjun and the twins, Nakul and Sahadev. Unlike other characters in the novel, Pandu's sons, except for Yudhishtir, who represents the honest but ineffective fourth prime minister of India, Morarji Desai, do not correspond to historical figures, but civil and governmental organisations of independent India. His second son Bhim represents the Indian Army, which is regarded as the sole incorruptible governmental organisation in Indian society. The third Pandava, Arjun, represents the Indian news media and the twin brothers Nakul and Sahadev, the Civil Service and the Foreign Service, respectively. Unknown to him, Pandu also has a step-son by his first wife Kunti, Muhammed Ali Karna. As the unmistakable verbal similarity suggests, he corresponds to Muhammed Ali Jinnah.

Blind king Dhritarashtra of the *Mahabharata* has one hundred sons, known as the Kauravas, by his wife Gandhari. Diverging from the original text to comply his characters in the modern context, Tharoor, compresses the entire progeny of Dhritarashtra's into a single female character: Priya Duryodhani, who metaphorically stands in for Indira Gandhi. Like Priya Duryodhani of the epic, her counterpart in Tharoor's novel is greeted with sinister omens of violence and bloodshed, foretelling Indira Gandhi's Emergency Rule. Ved Vyas, attending the birth at hospital, prophesises, "[y]our daughter Gandhari [...] will be equal to a thousand sons. This I promise you. [...] Gandhari would not live long to know it, but her sombre-eye daughter [...] would grow up one day to rule all India" (*GIN* 74). Thus, the two feuding houses of Hastinapur, the Pandavas and the Kauravas, find their allegorical doubles in the novel as the political leaders of Indian Independence.

With the extension of the dynastic family, the Indian nationalist movement starts to divide into factions. Muhammed Ali Karna becomes the leader of the Muslim Group, corresponding to the Muslim League in Indian history. For V. V, who sees British policies in the subcontinent as an extension of the Roman policy of "divide and rule," the Muslim Group is yet another divisive political manoeuvre introduced by the colonial administration; a Trojan horse aimed at the integrity of the Indian society. Like many other ills of colonisation, it is the British administration that is behind the disintegration of the society. V. V. explains with a religious allusion that social and religious differences have never been carried into the political arena until "the British civil serpent [...] made our people collectively bite the apple of discord" (*GIN* 134). He advocates that the Kaurava Party, which includes every one of the minority groups that make up India, could claim to be able to speak on their behalf. The British, however, V. V. notes, have always intended to introduce as many divisive elements as possible into the Indian political scene in order to reassure the world public opinion that "Indians can never agree amongst themselves, we [the British] really have no choice but to continue ruling them indefinitely *for their own good*" (*GIN* 115; emphasis original).

Indeed, the British succeed in partitioning India, creating a new nation state for the Muslims, Karnistan, which allegorically stands for Pakistan. The British administration assigns the job of partitioning India to a certain Mr Nichols, a satirical rendering of Sir Cyril Radcliffe, who was appointed to the same position particularly because he "virtually knew nothing about India" and thus could act impartially exercising his professional judgement (Collins and Lapierre 179). In Tharoor's version of Indian history, the act of partition gives rise to one of the most humorous, yet bitterly satirical scenes in the novel. Bending over the map of the subcontinent, Mr Nichols speaks confidently:

> One takes a given cartographical area – there – one checks the census figures for religious distribution and then one applies the basic principles of geography, choosing natural features as far as possible for the eventual boundary, studying elevation and relief - see these colours here? – not forgetting, of course, heh heh, the position of these thin lines, which are roads or rivers, and then... then one draws one's boundary line v-e-r-y carefully, like this. [...] That, ladies and gentlemen [...] will be the new frontier between India and Karnistan in this area. (*GIN* 224)

Mr Nichols' explanation is immediately ridiculed by an Indian veteran administrator named Basham. He derides Mr Nichols' plan to partition India, and thus the depravity of British colonisation as follows,

> You have just succeeded in putting your international border through the middle of the market, giving the rice-fields to Karnistan and the warehouses to India, the largest pig-farm in the zilla to the Islamic state and the Madrassah of the Holy Prophet to the country the Muslims are leaving. Oh, and if I understand that squiggle there correctly, […] the schoolmaster will require a passport to go to the loo between classes. Well done, Mr Nichols. I hope the rest of your work proves as – easy. (*GIN* 225)

Basham's humorous remark lays bare the absurdity and callousness of imperial policies that simply ignore the rights and even the lives of the people living in colonies. From the colonist perspective, they are but part and parcel of the colonised territories that can be sold, transferred or passed over to others. Through Basham's comment, Tharoor also manages to convey a glimpse of the geographic, social and cultural proximity between the two states, which immediately renders Mr Nichols' effort absurd.

Tharoor deliberately introduces anachronism within the allegorical framework of the novel whenever it suits him. Ganga's assassination by Amba is a case in point. Historically, Nathuram Godse killed Gandhi on January 30, 1948, approximately five months after the declaration of independence. Tharoor's Amba kills Gangaji on the day of Indian independence. With his deliberate anachronism, Tharoor's seems to remind the devastating effect of India's partition from Pakistan on Gandhi. Indeed, as Ved Vyas informs, the prospect of partition has already marked the end of Ganga's legacy: "that night the Kaurava Party resolved anonymously to accept in principle the partition of the country. It was the first time we had ever gone against the expressed wishes of Gangaji. His era was over" (*GIN* 223). Therefore, it is not surprising that Tharoor has chosen the day of independence for Ganga's assassination.

In this anachronistic rendition of Gandhi's death, Tharoor also manages to combine the epic storyline with the novel, giving rise to one of the most evidently magical realist scenes in the novel. In the *Mahabharata*, Amba is turned down by her lover, King Salva. She begs Bhishma to marry her to save her from disgrace, but Bhishma refuses her since he has taken a vow of celibacy. Enraged by the fact that she is going to die a virgin, Amba swears to kill Bhishma. She turns to princes and tries to persuade them to kill Bhishma for disgracing her. However, no one takes up her deadly mission. She then retreats to the forest vulva where she undergoes strict austerities and changes into a male, adopting the name Shikhandi. Her desire is fulfilled in the great battle at Kurukshetra. Shikhandi, accompanied by Arjuna, gives fatal wounds Bhishma.

In the novel, Ganga abducts Amba to marry her with his half-bother Vichitravirya, thereby blighting her nuptial bliss with King Salva. Amba vows to take her revenge and begins looking for an assassin. However, nobody agrees to kill Ganga, whose fame has spread beyond the borders of Hastinapur. Amba resolves to do the task herself. She grows obsessed with the thought of her overwhelming clamour of retribution and embarks on the magical rites of Tantrism with the hope of being granted the power to defeat her enemy. Eventually, she is informed by "an ethereal voice" that Ganga Datta can be killed only by "a man made unlike all other men" (*GIN* 208). Amba hastens to a sharp-toothed surgeon in a small clinic in the backstreets of Mumbai and asks him to transform her into a man just as the mythic character of Amba in the *Mahabharata*. Now as a man named Shikhandin, Amba arrives at Ganga's office straight from the small clinic where she has had her gender transformation. S/he finds Ganga grieving over the news of Karnistan's independence, blaming himself for the partition of India. S/he attacks old Gangaji verbally at first and then shoots him three times:

> What a wreck you are, Bhishma! [...] What a life you've led. Spouting on and on about our great traditions and basic values, but I don't see the old wife you ought to be honouring in your old dotage. Advising everyone about their sex life, marrying people off, letting them call you the Father of the Nation, but where is the son you need to light your funeral pyre, the son of your own loins? [...] You make me sick, Bhishma. Your life has been a waste, unproductive and barren. You are nothing but an impotent old walrus sucking other reptiles" eggs, an infertile old fool seeking solace like a calf from the udders of foreign cows, a man who is less than a woman. The tragedy of this country springs from you [...] you have lived long enough. (*GIN* 232)

Upon the news of Ganga"s death, Mohammed Ali Karna hastens to the funeral house to seek his forgiveness and blessings. Karna explains to the dead Ganga that his political role in the formation of Karnistan is part of his karma; thus, he cannot be blamed for doing something in fulfilment of his destiny.[39] Tharoor uses this critical juncture to introduce yet another magical realist scene in the novel. Dead Ganga pats Karna"s shoulder as a sign of forgiveness:

> Then – *and this is where I really part company with the popular version* – as the unacknowledged son of Kunti [Karna] rose to leave, the story goes, a hand slipped out from under the shroud and grazed his shoulder. Gangaji disagreed with no man more profoundly, yet he would not deny Mohammed Ali Karna his blessing when he asked for it. That, at least, is the story as it is told; make of it what you will. (*GIN* 234-235; emphasis added)

---

[39] In his glossary to the novel, Shashi Tharoor explains karma as the "Hindu cycle of predestined birth and rebirth, destiny" (422).

This seemingly trivial magical realist scene provokes the reader to reassess one of the most tumultuous political conflicts in Indian history, namely the Partition, regardless of the established historical facts. Ved Vyas' emphatic exhortation at the end, "make of it what you will," indicates yet another defining quality of magical realism. Unlike conventional realism, where only one possible version of history can be narrated as absolute truth, magical realism privileges textual ambiguity, blending both sides of the binaries myth/history, reality/fantasy and coloniser/colonised. The passage above, thus, aptly demonstrates an example of magical realist interrogation of received histories in the novel where the reader is provoked to ponder upon such speculative questions about Indian history as "would it be possible for Mahatma Gandhi to forgive Muhammed Ali Jinnah for the Partition?" or "would it be possible for Gandhi to come to terms with the idea of Pakistan as a separate nation state?'

With the declaration of independence, the nationalist resistance against Bitish rule leaves its place for the political struggle among the Kaurava Party members for the presidency of democratic India. Utilising the liberating power of magical realist writing, Tharoor shifts the narrative mode from parody to allegory in this second part of the novel and introduces Indian democracy as one of the characters in the novel: Draupadi Mokrasi, the illegitimate daughter of Dhritarashtra (Nehru, the first president of independent India) and Georgiana Drewpad (Edwina Mountbatten), the wife of the last British Viceroy. As has been discussed at length in the first part of this chapter, literalisation of metaphor and related strategies have an important function in magical realist fiction. Tharoor highlights the stages Indian democracy has undergone through the allegorical character of Draupadi. Her birth, parentage, education and marriage all bear historical and political implications beyond the literal meaning of the text.

Ved Vyas begins narrating the history of independent India by announcing the birth of Draupadi Mokrasi and notes that she shall dominate the rest of the story:

> At last, on 26 January 1950, as the Constitution of the new Republic of India was solemnly promulgated by its founding fathers, Georgina Drewpad, her face awash with tears, delivered herself of a squalling, premature baby. [...] She was to be adopted; neither of her parents could openly acknowledge the intimacy that produced her. The baby was called Draupadi, a subtle Indianization of her mother's family name, and she took the uncouth patronymic of her adoptive father, Mokrasi. Draupadi Mokrasi. Remember the name well, Ganapathi. You will see a lot more of this young lady as she grows up in independent India. [...] [her] life gives meaning to the rest of our story. (*GIN* 244-245)

Tharoor's Draupadi Mokrasi bears striking similarities with Rushdie's Saleem Sinai. As her mixed parentage suggests, Draupadi is the fruit of postcolonial India, begotten by the first president of India and the last vicereine of the British colonial administration. Tharoor reveals the indigenous characteristics of Indian democracy through Draupadi's complexion: "Ours was inevitably a darker democracy, and all the more to be cherished for the Indianness of her colouring" (*GIN* 309). Her birth, like that of Saleem Sinai, coincides with a defining moment of Indian history. She is born on India's Republic Day, January, 1950. In his account of Draupadi Mokrasi's childhood and education, V.V's underlines two qualities associated with democratic rule, namely liberty and equality. "Draupadi's beauty," he notes, "was public. [...] The more people beheld her, the more beautiful she seemed" (*GIN* 309). He also quotes from one of her teachers, professor Jennings: "she added an open manner, an ability to learn from and adapt to the conditions in which she found herself, and a willingness to play with all the children in the neighbourhood, irrespective of caste, creed or culture" (*GIN* 262). Despite her premature birth, which implies the fact that Indian democracy was born rather frail and prone to political ailments, Draupadi survives and grows into a beautiful young lady. It is not surprising that Tharoor has chosen to depict democracy as an attractive young woman given the two parties vying for presidency: the Pandavas (Yudhishtir, Arjun, Bhim, Nakul and Shadev) and the Kauravas (Indira Gandhi). With the introduction of Draupadi, the ground for political confrontation is prepared. While the young and attractive Draupadi has led to contention among the Five Pandavas, she has only provoked jealousy in Priya Duryodhani, who shall attempt to replace democracy with her authoritarian rule.

In addition to the literalisation of allegory, Tharoor also makes intensive use of yet another major magical realist convention in this part of the novel devoted to the history of independent India: dreams. The narrator Ved Vyas plunges into five dreams that are set in the epic era, yet not populated by gods and goddesses, but by the contemporary political figures of Hastinapur. In dreams, Vyas summarises the three major political developments in the post-independence period: the first democratic election, the Indo-Pakistani War of 1971, Indira Gandhi's misconduct in the elections and the declaration of the Emergency Rule. His mythic dreams interwoven with the political developments help reveal Tharoor's magical realist narrative structure in the novel:

> They were extraordinarily vivid dreams, in full costume and colour, with highly authentic dialogue delivered (for they were clearly set in the epic era of our national mythology) in Sanskrit. Yes, Ganapathi, I dreamt in Sanskrit, and I dreamt of our traditions. Yet my dreams were populated not by the Ramas and Sitas of your grandmother's twilight tales, but by contemporary

characters transported incongruously through time to their oneiric mythological settings. (*GIN* 355)

Ved Vyas goes on to explain that he has chosen to relate his dreams because he believes that dreams have explanatory power. "Sometimes, Ganapathi," he asserts, "dreams enable you to see reality more clearly" (*GIN* 383). Ved Vyas' assertion reads like a homage paid to magical realism itself. Dreams, visions and even hallucinations have a central role in magical realist writing and are treated. In explaining the narrative possibilities provided by such magical realist devices, Anne Hegerfeldt notes,

> Using an ensemble of literary techniques, magic realist fiction insists that the concept of reality cannot be confined to the empirically perceivable. Rather, people's multiple ways of perceiving and constructing their world must be acknowledged as real. [...] In rendering metaphors, stories, dreams or magical beliefs real on the level of the text, magic realist fiction re-evaluates modes of knowledge production generally rejected within the dominant. (3)

In this light, the historical moment when V.V. starts to have his mythic dreams becomes meaningful. He informs Ganapathi that he starts to dream just immediately after the Bangladesh War, when Priya Duryodhani is not only declared a national heroine, but also deified with the appellation of Ma Duryodhani or Duryodhani Amma, a reminder of the Indian Mother Goddess, Shakti. It is at this historical moment that Duryodhani's rule starts to grow increasingly oppressive and subsequently culminates into her authoritarian Emergency Rule. Tharoor's extensive use of magical realist devices in this part of the story can thus be seen as a clear indication of the mode's power to provide alternative perspectives on the received ideas.

In the first of the several magical realist scenes that dominate this last part of the novel, Ved Vyas relates the story of Draupadi's suitors in a dream vision. The Pandavas lay their eyes on Draupadi for the first time in a political training camp convened by Ved Vyas to discuss the future of the party in the absence of a leader of national stature to succeed Dhritarashtra. Priya Duryodhani immediately orders Ved Vyas to get Draupadi married since her beauty distracts the Pandavas from their political training. Then, a competition is organised for Draupadi's hand. Everyone in the meeting hall goes to the ballot box and drops the ballot papers into it in a silent ethereal procession. Then, Ved Vyas places Draupadi in the box, announcing that the first one to let her out of it shall be her husband. Among the attendant people, Ved Vyas counts several politicians that range from the dead Karna to American, Chinese and British diplomats. Ved Vyas cautions Ganapathi that the rest of the story is not a dream but reality. It is Arjun (the media), who manages to open the ballot box and thus becomes Miss Mokrasi's husband. At this juncture, Tharoor introduces yet another humorous reversal in order to thread the epic and the novelistic plots together. The Draupadi of the *Mahabharata* is married simultaneously to the five Pandavas. A misunderstanding leads to polyandry in the novel. Arjun calls his mother Kunti to tell her that they are coming home with a surprise. But her mother wants them to share whatever Arjun has for her. Committed by their solemn oath to obey their mother's every injunction, the five Pandavas resolve to share Draupadi Mokrasi.

Given that the five brothers allegorically stand for the national institutions, their strange marriage is laden with social and political resonance. Dirk Wiemann outlines the details of the political allegory of the Pandavas' marriage with Draupadi as follows,

> By virtue of their common marriage to democracy, the Pandavas seem to function as a collective allegory of the postcolonial *nation* while they actually stand in for the postcolonial national

elite whose very eptiomes (and nothing much else besides) they embody. [...] Clearly the impotence of these five husbands in protecting their shared wife from public humiliation and enslavement at the hands of the plotting Kauravas subjects precisely the 'national institutions' they represent to a severe critique and thus emphasises their collective failure as custodians of democracy in the face of Indira Gandhi's emergency [...]. (97)

Ved Vyas devotes the last two books of his epic narrative to one of the most painful periods of Indian political history, namely Indira Gandhi's Emergency Rule and the ensuing uprisings to restore Indian democracy. Shashi Tharoor's portrayal of Priya Duryodhani (Indira Gandhi) is no less vitriolic than that of Salman Rushdie's, who degrades her with the appellation of "the widow" in his *Midnight's Children.* Tharoor's cantankerous narrator, Ved Vyas, calls Priya "a new Queen-Empress" indicating the fact that life in India under her rule was not very different from that of the colonial administration. Tharoor reflects the rise of political tension between the Pandavas and the Kauravas (Priya) through Draupadi Mokrasi, one of the key literalised metaphors in the novel. Her health starts to deteriorate with Priya's increasingly oppressive regime. At end of each book, V.V. describes her changing health. When Yudhishtir resigns from the cabinet, Ved Vyas reports, "Draupadi Mokrasi, running a fever, [take] to bed, complaining of alternating hot flushes and chills" (*GIN* 343). And when Duryodhani starts to rule the country with the support of a vast majority, "Draupadi Mokrasi," Ved Vyas informs, "is diagnosed as asthmatic, her breath coming sometimes in short gasps" (*GIN* 352).

Jayaprakash Drona, the instructor of the Pandavas and their mentor, organises a People's Uprising against the dishonesty and cynicism of Priya Duryodhani's government. It is a non-violent mass movement aimed at "[restoring] India's ancient values to its governance" (*GIN*

361). As the political tide start to turn decisively away from her, Duryodhani declares a Siege, a satirical rendition of Indira Gandhi's Emergency Rule, suspending certain fundamental civil rights, such as free speech, assembly along with a strict censorship of the press. Ved Vyas tells that most Indians have accepted the Siege without reaction. It is not surprising for a nation that has been detached from the processes of their own governance for two hundred years. He confides in Ganapathi that he "couldn't, at that stage, think of the issue simply as one of freedom versus tyranny" because he feared that "Drona's idealistic but confused Uprising […] could have led the country nowhere but to anarchy" (*GIN* 369). V.V. reveals that it is his dreams of the legends past that have helped him to see the ploy behind Duryodhani's policies and begins relating his third and longest dream. Ved Vyas dreams of the incidents narrated in the book of the *Mahabharata*. His dream recounts Indira Gandhi's Emergency Rule in terms of the Kauravas' attempt at disrobing Draupadi Mokrasi. Shakuni, Duryodhani's uncle, challenges Yudhishtir in a dice game with a pair of crooked dice. Yudhishtir loses all his wealth, including his kingdom. He then wagers his brothers, himself, and finally their common wife Draupadi in servitude and loses. The victorious Kauravas start to humiliate all the Pandavas and physically abuse Draupadi, disrobing her in front of the entire court. When she is about to be stripped naked, Draupadi invokes Krishna, who comes to her rescue and creates an endless supply of cloth around her. Krishna's face appears on the ceiling as he addresses the Kauravas: "However hard you try, Priya Duryodhani, […] you and your men will never succeed in stripping Draupadi Mokrasi completely. In our country, she will be always enough to maintain her self respect. But what about yours?" (*GIN* 382). As Arjun prepares to challenge Priya with his own pair of dice, Ved Vyas wakes from dream with a prophetic vision that prefigures the fate of Priya Duryodhani's/Indira Gandhi's political career: "And as she prepared to throw them, Ganapathi, I realized even in my sleep that I didn't need to dream anymore […] she was going to lose" (*GIN 383*).

Ved Vyas declares a decisive political campaign against Duryodhani's Siege and instructs the five Pandavas with different responsibilities. Soon Priya Duryodhani is obliged to suspend the Siege and calls free general elections, paving the way for the most participative election campaign in Indian history. For Ved Vyas, the election signifies a nation's decision between democracy and dictatorship, but also "between dharma and adharma" (*GIN* 391). The moral conflict in the epic is, thus, projected on the political contest between liberal democracy and electoral authoritarianism. At this juncture, Ved Vyas informs: "I saw Draupadi's face glowing in the open, the flame of her radiance burning more brightly than ever" (*GIN* 392). As in the ancient text of the *Mahabharata*, Krishna, depicted as a local South Indian politician in the novel, is invoked to support the Pandavas, securing their victory in the elections. Yet Ved Vyas hastens to note that the result of the election is "not a climactic triumph but a moment of bathos" (*GIN* 402) since soon the unity of the Front starts to crumble and Priya Duryodhani returns to power with an overwhelming majority in the following elections.

In V.V.'s final dream, Tharoor integrates myth, politics and the Indian concept of dharma together. Yudhishtir gets into a political dispute with Dharma, god of justice and righteousness, who is irreverently depicted as a dog in Ved Vyas' dream. Yudhishtir charges Dharma for failing to accept pluralism and its concomitant ambiguity:

> Derive your standards from the world around you and not from a heritage whose relevance must be constantly tested. Reject equally the sterility of ideologies and the passionate prescriptions of those who think themselves infallible. Uphold decency, worship humanity, affirm the basic values of our people – those which do not change – and leave the rest alone. Admit that there is more than one Truth, more than one Right, more than one dharma... (*GIN* 418)

In this spontaneous fusing of history, myth and dream, Tharoor underlines the importance of the multiplicity of truth once again. "Envisaging many *dharmas* instead of one," Dirk Wiemann notes, "Yudhishtir has not come to cut the ropes with tradition completely but to reform old legacies in order to make them match the present" (100). With his irreverent depiction of a deity and charges directed at him, Tharoor repudiates the essentialist view of his predecessors. The promotion of indigenous culture through a mapping of myths and legends do not concur with the intricacies of the postcolonial identity, which is now perceived as open to international effects. Thus, it is only through magical realist subversion that the cultural heritage may offer some insights into the present. "By applying the *Mahabharata* to the events of India's contemporary political history," as Bill Ashcroft points out, "Tharoor manages to open up a site for both a vigorous and controversial debate over the historical truth as well as problematisation of history writing at large" (107). Ved Vyas interprets his dream of Yudhishtir as an indication of the fact that he has told "the story from a completely mistaken perspective" and that he has to retell his story right from the start (*GIN* 418). Thus, the theme of multiplicity of truth and reality is vindicated at the formal level of the story.

Chapter 4
The Yarns of the Black Continent: Magical Realism in the African English Novels

> It is precisely in a broken age that we need mystery and a re-awakened sense of wonder: need them in order to be whole again
> - Ben Okri

4.1. An *Abiku* Nation: Ben Okri's *The Famished Road*

Ben Okri's *The Famished Road*, acclaimed and often cited by scholars today as "a classic hallmark of magical realism,"[40] was published in 1991 and awarded the Booker Prize of the same year on the grounds that it was a "beautifully written and moving novel [that] convey[ed] Nigerian peasant life in a changing world" (qtd. in Cooper 14). Surprisingly enough, Okri does not offer any specific detail about the setting in the novel. As David C. L. Lim notes, "Nigeria is scarcely ever mentioned by name" in Okri's works of fiction and non-fiction, which distinguishes him from pioneering Nigerian writers like Chinua Achebe and Wole Soyinka, who wrote about the country extensively (60). In explaining why he avoids any direct reference to Nigeria in his writings, Okri asserted, "[t]he first thing I'd say is that I think it's important to understand that a piece of writing is, first of all, a piece of writing. By that I mean that one may be writing about Nigeria, but that terrain may be the place in which one can best see very strong universal concerns" (qtd. in Lim 60-61). Okri's impressions on writing and his homeland might suggest that he evades his postcolonial identity in order to cater to an international reading public. However, his works bear witness to the ills of colonialism. He is particularly concerned with the African conscious-

---

[40] In their introduction to *A Companion to Magical Realism*, Stephen M. Hart and Wen-chin Ouyang regard Ben Okri's *The Famished Road* as a classic hallmark of magical realism. They also list a number of contemporary critics who discuss the novel in terms of magical realism (10).

ness, and the way it may help redeem the damage caused by colonialism. Okri believes that the colonial powers might have succeeded in exploiting the wealth of African countries, but they failed to dominate African people's consciousness and culture. In an interview with Jane Wilkinson, Okri states,

> There's been too much attribution of power to the effect of colonialism on our consciousness. Too much has been given to it. We've looked too much in that direction and have forgotten about our own aesthetic frames. Even though that was there and took place and invaded our social structure, it's quite possible that it didn't invade our spiritual and aesthetic and mythic internal structure, the way in which we perceive the world. If one were going to be investigative, one would probably say that a true invasion takes place not when a society has been taken over by another society in terms of its infrastructure, but in terms of its mind and its dreams and its myths, and its perception of reality. If the perception of reality has not been fundamentally, internally altered, then the experience itself is just transitional. There are certain areas of the African consciousness which will remain inviolate. Because the world-view it is that makes a people survive. (86)

The reclamation of indigenous traditions as a means of cultural healing is an issue extensively addressed by postcolonial critics as well. For instance, in seeking to explicate the place of magical realism in postcolonial literature, Michael Dash clearly reiterates Okri's ideas quoted above when he states,

> [...] the Third World writer [engages in] an investigation of his past which goes beyond the documented privations of slavery and colonization to a more speculative vision of history in

> which the consciousness of the dominated cultures would predominate. In order to tap this consciousness, [he returns] to the myths, legends and superstitions of the folk in order to isolate traces of a complex culture of survival which was the response of the dominated to their oppressors. That is to say that colonization and slavery did not make things of men, but in their own way the enslaved peoples might have in their own imagination so reordered their reality as to reach beyond the tangible and concrete to acquire a new re-creative sensibility which could aid in the harsh battle for survival. The only thing they could possess (and which could not be tampered with) was their imagination and this became the source of their struggle against the cruelty of their condition. (150-151)

The striking verbal similarity between the arguments put forward by Okri and Dash reveals the former's capacity to understand and reflect on the problems inflicting postcolonial societies. In this light *The Famished Road* can be seen as an attempt to rediscover and revitalise what Okri believes to be the "inviolate" part of Africa's cultural heritage latent in the continent's pre-colonial past.

Okri draws extensively from traditional African beliefs and cultural practices in his quest for a primeval cultural source. However, he is also well aware of the fact that such a quest has its attentive risk of generating a "static, homogenous African authenticity" that vexed the works of many of the earlier African novelists (Cooper 37). This is where Okri differs from his predecessors since he does not designate the pre-colonial traditions as a pristine form of the African self, but as a site that allows cultural interaction, transformation and hybridisation. In other words, African culture, whose definition of reality is less strict than that of the Western world, provides Okri with the double vision he needs as a postcolonial subject. "Africans," as Nelson Hayashida points out, "integrate with their total environment. Both physical and spiritual become possible as people relate to the ancestors, the divinities and to God" (41). Within this cultural context, dreams, myths, folk tales and legends are treated as an integral part of everyday life, serving as a means to perceive social reality and history. They are at the heart of African aesthetics and consciousness, helping people to overcome the psychic trauma inflicted upon them by colonialism.

Although dreams and visions are powerful narrative elements in *The Famished Road*, the key to Okri's magical realist vision is the myth of *abiku*, "the willful spirit child, who masquerades as human baby, only to recurrently 'die' and be re-born, causing grief and mischief among the living" (Cooper 50). In the novel, Okri recounts the story of Azaro, an *abiku* child caught between the world of the spirits and the living. It is also the story of his poverty-stricken family and their neighbours living in the same ghetto, also referred to as the compound. They struggle to survive in a country that has recently gained her independence and is still suffering from the maladies of post-independence politics. Azaro's liminal existence as well as his magical powers, his ability to envision the past and the future in particular, affords Okri to open a window in the history of Nigeria for the reader to witness the different phases of the country's long history. For instance, in one of the several magical realist scenes, Okri presents a glimpse of Nigeria as she goes through pre-colonial, colonial and postcolonial stages through Azaro's magical vision. Looking in the eyes of a duiker, Azaro starts to envision Nigeria's past. First, he sees "the forms of serene ancestors, men and women for whom the stars were both words and gods, for whom the world and the sky and the earth were a vast language of dreams and omens" (*FR* 456). Soon this pre-colonial tableau of peace and tranquillity is disturbed by the colonial invasion of the country. In the lengthy quotation below, Azaro describes the environmental and cultural damage caused by the colonial powers:

The ghost ships of centuries arrived endlessly on the shores. I saw the flotillas, the gunwales, the spectral great ships and the dozens of rowing boats, bearing the helmeted ones, with mirrors and guns and strange texts untouched by the salt of the Atlantic. I saw the ships and the boats beach. The white ones, ghost forms on deep nights, stepped on our shores, and I heard the earth cry. The cry scared me. Deep in the duiker's eyes, I ran through the yellow forests, through deluded generations, through time. I witnessed the destruction of great shrines, the death of mighty trees that housed centuries of insurgent as well as soothing memories, sacred texts, alchemical secrets of wizards, and potent herbs. I saw the forests die. I saw the people grow smaller in being. I saw the death of their many roads and ways and philosophies. Their precious stones and rocks of atomic energies were drawn from the depths of their ancestral memories. I saw the trees retreat screaming into the blue earth. I heard the great spirits of the land and forest talking of a temporary exile. They travelled deeper into secret spaces, weaving spells of madness round their arcane abodes to prevent humans from ever despoiling their transformative retreat from the howling feet of invaders. I saw the rising of new houses. I saw new bridges span the air. The old bridges, invisible, travelled on by humans and spirits alike, remained intact and less frequented. As the freedom of space and friendship with the pied kingfisher and other birds became more limited with the new age, something died in me. (*FR* 457)

Despite this terrifying portrayal of the colonial invasion quoted above, Okri, as shall be seen in the pages to follow, still has a positive, if not celebratory, attitude towards the change and transformation introduced by the contact with the Other. His choice of an *abiku* as his narrator and protagonist is regarded by critics as an indication of his acceptance of the idea of cultural transformation and hybridity. John Hawley, for example, argues that Okri's "choice of a liminal figure like the *abiku* to serve as his spokesman, straddling both worlds and drawing power from both, summarizes his determination to imagine something new" (36). Sharing the same view, Brenda Cooper maintains, "Ben Okri's hope and goal in *The Famished Road* is to see with a new 'third eye'" (67). Magical realism functions as a literary catalyst in the text. Within the third space provided by magical realism, Okri combines the ancient indigenous traditions with the elements of Western modernisation, stressing the necessity to form a new hybrid identity in postcolonial cultures.

The novel opens with Azaro's detailed introduction to the myth of *abiku* and related beliefs. Azaro informs the reader that as they approach the moment of their incarnation, some spirits make pact that they shall return to the spirit world at the first opportunity. The ones who have made such vows are known as *abiku*, or spirit-children. He describes himself and his spirit companions as "the strange ones, with half of our beings always in the spirit world" (*FR* 4). Spirit-children have the ability to will their deaths. Those who break their pacts are assailed by their spirit companions with hallucinations and nightmares. They can only find consolation when they return to the land of the unborn. *Abiku* children have their own particular spirit tokens that bind them to the other world. They hide their tokens, for if others find and destroy them, they cannot return to the land of spirits. Azaro is a rebelling spirit that chooses life on earth over his spirit existence. Hence, his spirit companions constantly try to lure him back to "the world of pure dreams, where all things are made of enchantment, and where there is no suffering" (*FR* 4). Azaro is fully aware of what is in store for him in the world of the living: "the rigours of existence, the unfulfilled longings, the enshrined injustices of the world, the labyrinths of love, the ignorance of parents, the fact of dying, and the amazing indifference of the Living in the midst of the simple beauties of the universe" (*FR* 3). He is punished for his refusal to return to the land of spirits by constant hallucinations. It is in one of these spiritual assaults that his parents come to the realisation that their child is an *abiku*, but since they cannot find the tokens that connect him to the world of spirits, Azaro oscillates between the two worlds. It is the interspace where the phenomenal world intermingles with dreamscape. Azaro has vivid dreams, foretelling the future, and he can see spirits interacting with the living in broad daylight. The result is a unique blend of physical and spiritual landscapes within a radically unpredictable textual context.

Okri writes in eloquent yet simple language since the whole novel is narrated from a child's perspective. Compared to the large epic canvas of the other magical realist novels studied here, *The Famished Road* has fewer characters and a relatively simpler plot. Azaro's adventures are articulated within a limited constellation of characters and settings, including his home and his parents (simply named Mum and Dad); the shrewd, magisterial bartender called Madame Koto and her bar peopled with politicians and prostitutes; the forest surrounding the ghetto where spirits and other supernatural beings dwell. Life in the ghetto is monotonous. Nothing much happens except for the brief moments of rebellion and ensuing cacophony caused by the two political parties' struggle for dominance over the compound, namely the Party of the Poor and the Party of the Rich. Thus, it is mostly through the articulation of myths, folk tales and dreams that Okri manages to convey his magical realist view of Nigerian history.

African mythology, particularly the *abiku* myth, does not only provide the necessary ground for magical realism to flourish in the course of narrative flow, it also earns the novel its postcolonial content. Margaret Cezair-Thompson terms *The Famished Road* a "decolonized fiction" because "the origin of the 'famished road' lies in myth, not history. And so the fate of colonialism in *The Famished Road* is that not only is it disqualified in its claim to be a devouring force, colonialism itself becomes devoured, as mythopoeia overwrites history" (qtd. in Faris, *Ordinary*, 158). In other words, Okri challenges the tenets of colonialism through his magical realist revision of national history that combines the mythic with the contemporary. In *The Famished Road*, myths and folk tales are not treated as authentic cultural artefacts, but as dynamic discursive agents providing commentary on the social and political problems prevailing Nigeria. There are two key myths that Okri recounts to unravel the themes of poverty and political oppression. These myths also help reveal the socio-economic conditions in which Azaro's family and other families live in the compound. It is thus fitting to explore at the outset the two complementary myths told by Azaro's parents.

The first is the myth of the stomach which explains how hunger descended into the world. As the family's financial condition worsens, they can only afford one meal a day. Mum and Azaro wait for Dad's return at night so that they can share what they have got for the day. When Azaro complains of hunger, Mum relates the myth of the stomach to divert his attention from his grumbling stomach. In the story, a man without a stomach annually travels to a distant land to worship at a great shrine. On his way to the shrine, he meets a stomach without a body which immediately jumps on him and becomes part of his body. Soon the man starts to feel hungry, the stomach orders the man to feed him, but he refuses to eat, saying, "when I didn't have you I travelled far, was never hungry, was always happy and contented, and was strong. You can either leave me or be quiet" (*FR* 80). Azaro falls asleep before his mother finishes the story only to wake up to the bitter realities surrounding his family. Azaro's Dad, who has just returned from work, complains in a ghostly and exhausted voice that "[t]hey have begun to spoil everything with politics [...]. Now they want to know who you will vote for before they let you carry their load. [...] If you want to vote for the party that supports the poor, they give you the heaviest load. I am not much better than a donkey" (*FR* 81). The myth of the stomach told to a starving child and Dad's complaints about work describe Nigeria's economic and political dilemmas as an emerging independent country. Like the stomach in the story, political leaders in the emerging nation-state fasten themselves on the national wealth of the country. Consequently, it becomes almost impossible for the poor to survive, and the ghetto dwellers are condemned to live below the poverty line. Azaro describes the ghetto as "a world drowning in poverty," "eating the food of suffering" (*FR* 281, 326).

The second myth in the novel, the King of the Road, arises from a similar circumstance. As the political polarisation in the society gets worse, it becomes more difficult for Azaro's parents to earn their living mainly because they refuse to support the Party of the Rich. To punish the family, the landlord, a member of that Party of the Rich, raises their rent more than any other tenant in the compound. When Mum suggests that they should sleep on empty stomachs in order to afford the exorbitant rent, Azaro wants Dad to tell him a story because his mother's talk about food reminds him of his terrible hunger. This is when Dad tells Azaro the myth of the King of the Road, a giant with a huge stomach and an insatiable appetite who competes with other forest monsters for strange things to eat. But, "when the Forest started to get smaller because of 'Man', when the giant couldn't find enough animals to eat, he changed from the forest to the roads that men travel" (*FR* 258). People start to leave him sacrifices or he does not allow them to pass, and sometimes he eats them alive. When a famine breaks out because of the insatiable hunger of the giant, people decide to send a delegate to reason with him, but the King of the Road eats the delegation. Beset by his insatiable hunger, the giant starts to eat himself till only his stomach remains, which melts in the rain and becomes part of all the roads in this world. Dad ends his story with a warning for Azaro:

> He is still hungry, and he will always be hungry. This is why there are so many accidents in the world. And to this day some people still put a small amount of food on the road before they travel, so that the King of the Road will eat their sacrifice and let them travel safely. But some of our wise people say that

there are other reasons. Some say people make sacrifices to the road to remember that the monster is still there and that he can rise at any time and start to eat up human beings again. Others say that it is a form of prayer that his type should never come back again to terrify our lives. That is why a small boy like you must be very careful how you wander about in this world. (*FR* 261)

The famished giant is an obvious symbol of greed and abuse of power. The context in which Dad tells the myth to his starving child makes it possible to consider the King of the Road in relation to the modern manifestations of greed, namely colonialism and abuse of power by the politicians of independent Nigeria. For instance, in her reading of the myth Felicia Oka Moh contends: "[t]he King stands for the archetypal predator who has such an insatiable appetite that he preys on everything and everyone for self-preservation. The road is famished because the rulers are monsters and oppressors. The road becomes a symbol of the Nigerian nation which has unjust predatory rulers" (77).

At another level of interpretation, Dad's tale can be regarded as a reflection of the colonised people's desire to retrieve and reassert their indigenous cultural traditions and histories. Michael Dash points out that magical realist novelists resort to the myths, legends and superstitions of the folk in order to "shatter the myths of 'historylessness' or 'nonachievement'" imposed on the colonised peoples by the West (151). When asked to comment on the reference to history in *The Famished Road*, Okri notes that he "is very interested in history and the book is about history. [...] History is actually in the book right from the beginning" (Wilkinson 86). What Okri describes as history is the myth of beginnings related by Azaro in the opening paragraph of the novel: "In the beginning there was a river. The river became a road and the road branched out to the whole world. And because the road was once a river it was always hungry" (*FR* 3). It is only half way through the novel that the reader fully understands the significance of Azaro's ambiguous introduction through Dad's tale. The road is always hungry because it was once a greedy giant. Thus, Okri conflates "the mythic" and "the historical" time through Azaro's opening statement in the novel. This historical and cultural retrieval of the past also help challenge Western epistemology that makes a distinction between history and mythology in line with its scientific worldview. As can be seen in Dad's tale, African culture does not separate the two domains of knowledge. In African tradition, history is not construed as documentation of past events, but also of mythic, religious and cultural beliefs.

Although laden with myths, legends and folk tales, Okri's narrative never undermines the political reality of the society that it sets out to describe. As a defining characteristic of magical realism, Azaro's fantastic narrative is anchored in the socio-political realities of independent Nigeria. "What is curious […] about Okri's text," Stephen M. Hart and Wenchin Ouyang observe, "is the fact that – even while it fuses the magical with the real, and the animal with the human, the spiritual with the material, and the natural with the supernatural – it never loses its political relevance" (10). Sharing a similar view, Abubakar Liman describes *The Famished Road* as "a way of depicting the life of the poor in Nigeria who are caught between the urge to life, a better life and the difficulties of a system built on injustice and exploitation of man by man" (70). Indeed, it is a riot that triggers the unfolding events in the novel. One night a fire starts and burns the compound where Azaro's family live to the ground. The landlord forces the tenants to pay for the damage the fire caused. When the colonial police arrive at the compound, a riot breaks out. "That night," Azaro informs the reader, "our life changed" (*FR* 9). During the riot, Azaro is kidnapped by a group of witches. He manages to escape from them but only to end up in the house of a corrupt policeman where he witnesses the bribes collected and shared by the policeman and his gang. Assailed by his spirit companions, Azaro has the strangest nightmares in the policeman's house. Eventually, his mother rescues him and takes him to their new compound.

Okri reveals the exploitation of the poor by the rich through his vivid depiction of the life in the compound. The family is now crammed into a single room with almost no furniture. The detailed description of their room presents an index of the poverty of the inhabitants of the compound. A rope stretched between the walls functions as a wardrobe, and Azaro sleeps on a mat spread on the floor. The sanitary condition of their habitation is very poor. Fleas, mosquitoes and rats are part of every household. The wide gulf between the rich and the poor is reflected from Azaro's naïve perspective:

> I was home. And being at home was very different from being in the comfortable house of the police officer. No spirits plagued me. There were no ghosts in the dark spaces. The poor also belong to one country. Our surroundings were poor. We didn't have a bathroom worth speaking of and the toilet was crude. But in that room, in our new home, I was happy because I could smell the warm presences and the tender energies of my parents everywhere. (*FR* 32-33)

While Azaro's parents try to make ends meet, the election campaigns start to heat up. Politics is everywhere; Madame Koto's bar, the marketplace where Azaro's mother sells her provisions, the garage where his father works as a carrier reverberate with conversations about the burgeoning Nigerian independence politics. The communal interest in politics gradually gives way to a radical polarisation in the society along the lines of two parties and eventually leads to violence. Dad and his neighbours are subject to constant exploitation by the landlord. Despite the terrible condition of the houses in the ghetto, the landlord increases the rent and threatens the tenants with his thugs. Madame Koto, the mysterious bartender, starts to grow indifferent to the inhabitants of the ghetto as she negotiates with the members of the Party of the Rich. While most of the tenants seem to be less concerned, Azaro's Dad becomes an active political figure, trying to draw attention to the injustices in the society. He has once announced loudly that "some people have too much, and their dogs eat better food, while others suffer and keep quiet until the day they die" (*FR* 380). When pressurised by the landlord to vote for the Party of the Rich, he bursts out in rage, "[w]hat right has the landlord to bully us, to tell us who to vote for, eh? Is he God? Even God can't tell us who to vote for. Don't be afraid. We may be poor, but we are not slaves'" (*FR* 206). However, his effort is not enough to start a serious and purposeful political movement among the deprived masses.

Jeremiah, a photographer living in the same ghetto as Azaro's family, is also reflective of the tragedies experienced in the post-independence period. He earns his living by taking photographs of the inhabitants of the ghetto on special occasions. He also exhibits these photographs in the little cabin in front of his house. His life changes with a visit by the members of the Party of the Rich. They distribute powdered milk, which turns out to be rotten and makes everyone in the compound sick except for Azaro's family as his father has turned down the party's handout in the first place. When the party members return later to see the effect of their campaign, the compound people attack them. The party van is burned and becomes a "landmark" of the short-lived riot in the compound. The photographer manages to take pictures of the incident and have them published in an international newspaper. Azaro describes the astonishment of the compound people when they see themselves in the paper as follows,

> For the first time in our lives we as a people had appeared in the newspapers. We were heroes in our own drama, heroes of our own protest. There were pictures of us, men and women and children, standing helplessly round heaps of the politicians' milk. There were pictures of us raging, attacking the van, riot-

ing against the cheap methods of politicians, humiliating the thugs of politics, burning their lies. The photographer's pictures had been given great prominence on the pages of the newspaper and it was even possible to recognise our squashed and poverty-ridden faces on the grainy newsprint. There were news stories about the bad milk and an editorial about our rage. We were astonished that something we did with such absence of planning, something that we had done in such a small corner of the great globe, could gain such prominence. (*FR* 156)

The attention his photographs receive makes Jeremiah a political target. He is arrested and tortured, which leads him to embark on a nocturnal existence. He stays away from the compound during the day and returns to Azaro's room at night to show him the photographs of the social and political corruption he has taken: "I took photographs of women at the market being attacked by thugs. The women fought them back. I took pictures of riots against our white rulers. I took pictures of a policeman taking bribes. The policeman saw me and pursued me. I escaped" (*FR* 232). The ordeals of the photographer encapsulate the life of journalists, writers and freedom fighters in African countries who have been either murdered or kept in prison by the government or the military forces for questioning or challenging their authority.

It is not only the society that changes in the country, fragmenting into different political factions. The country itself also undergoes a dramatic change as new roads and buildings are constantly being built. With the advent of industrialisation, the forest moves away from the city as prefigured in the myth of the King of the Road. Magical realism is instrumental in Okri's treatment of the changes taking place in the country. In one of his several solitary wanderings in the forest, Azaro discovers "a village of spirits" in the middle of a clearing (*FR* 246). With the serenity of the scene, he falls asleep. When he wakes up, he sees a construction machine destroying the village of the spirit. In another magical realist scene, Azaro foresees the things in store for Nigeria with an eye opened at the centre of his forehead:

> I had emerged into another world. All around, in the future present, a mirage of houses was being built, paths and roads crossed and surrounded the forest in tightening circles [...] The world of trees and wild bushes was being thinned. I heard the ghostly wood-cutters axing down the titanic irokos, the giant baobabs, the rubber trees and obeches. There were birds' nests on the earth and the eggs within them were smashed, had fallen out, had mingled with the leaves and the dust, the little birds within the cracked eggs half-formed and dried up, dying as they were emerging into a hard, miraculous world. Ants swarmed all over them. (*FR* 242)

Here, Azaro subverts the Eurocentric view of history as a forward progression through his magical realist viewpoint that blurs the conventional boundaries. The natural world dies out as Western modernity makes its progress through the thick African forest. However, Azaro's vision goes beyond this mere criticism of the colonial idea of economic development. As mentioned earlier, the forest is inextricably linked with African cultural beliefs; it is the dwelling of spirits and other supernatural beings. The compound people are depicted performing religious rituals in the forests on several occasions. It functions as their shrine and spiritual sanctuary. Therefore, the destruction of the forest also suggests the destruction of African cultural heritage by the West.

Azaro's critical view of colonialism is further reinforced by his mother's account of the arrival of the colonising powers in Africa. Having encountered a white man (an engineer at work in the forest) for the first time, Azaro asks his mother in amazement to tell him a story about the white people. In her story, Mum subverts the colonial claim of introducing civilisation to the masses living in the distant lands of the world.

She contends that when the white people first set foot on the African continent, they were, in fact, inferior to the blacks:

> 'When white people first came to our land,' she said, as if she were talking to the wind, 'we had already gone to the moon and all the great stars. In the olden days they used to come and learn from us. My father used to tell me that we taught them how to count. We taught them about the stars. We gave them some of our gods. We shared our knowledge with them. We welcomed them. But they forgot all this. They forgot many things. They forgot that we are all brothers and sisters and that black people are the ancestors of the human race. The second time they came they brought guns. They took our lands, burned our gods, and they carried away many of our people to become slaves across the sea. They are greedy. They want to own the whole world and conquer the sun. Some of them believe they have killed God. Some of them worship machines. They are misusing the powers God gave all of us. They are not all bad. Learn from them, but love the world.' (*FR* 282)

Despite her final reconciling remark, Mum's story reflects an idealised view of Africa and the superiority of the black culture as prefigured in the Négritude movement.[41] It retains the essentialist view of races as well as the established binaries between the coloniser and the colonised.

However, it would be a mistake to assume too readily that Okri advocates an essentialist view of African culture, following in the footsteps of the realist tradition of African literature. It is again through tales and dreams narrated by Azaro's parents that Okri reveals the crucial role of transformation and change in postcolonial societies. Later in the novel, Mum tells Azaro and his friend Ade, who is also an *abiku* child, a very strange, yet as she insists, a true story. One day while selling her provi-

---

[41] See chapter 2, pp. 62-64.

sions in the marketplace, Mum meets a white man who has been in Africa for ten years and wants to find a way to leave. She says she can help him in exchange for his blue sunglasses. However, she baffles the man with an enigmatic saying that she has heard from a tortoise: "all things are linked" (*FR* 483). Next time when Mum sees the man, she cannot recognise him as he has transformed into a black Yoruba man with magical powers. Seeing the incredulous look on her face, the man tells Mum what has happened after their first encounter:

> When I left you, […] I became feverish in the head and later in a fit of fury over a small thing I killed my African servant. They arrested me. I sat in a cell. Then they released me because I was a white man. Then I began to wander about the city naked. Everyone stared at me. They were shocked to see a mad white man in Africa. Then a strange little African child took to following me around. He was my only friend. All my white colleagues had deserted me. Then one day my head cleared. Five hundred years had gone past. The only way to get out of Africa was to become an African. So I changed my thinking. I changed my ways. I got on a plane and arrived in England. I got married, had two children, and retired from government service. I was in the Secret Service. Then before I turned seventy I had a heart attack and died. They buried me in my local parish cemetery with full national honours […] Time passed. I was born. I became a businessman. (*FR* 483-484)

Through this seemingly trivial magical realist story, Okri manages to provide insights into the identity crisis caused by the interaction of different cultures. Particularly the transformation in the white man's resolution from "[t]he only way to get out of Africa is to get Africa out of you," into "[t]he only way to get out of Africa was to become an African" demonstrates that it is only through acceptance and internalisation of certain aspects of the Other's culture that the subject may find comfort (*FR* 483, 484).

Okri seems to sustain his double vision throughout the novel by looking at the same issue from different points of view. Thus, the white man's story in Africa is counterpoised later in the narrative by an account of Dad's nightmare. To underscore the interpretative power that dreams and visions have in African culture, Dad reminds Azaro that "[a] man can wander the whole planet and not move an inch […]. My son, I dreamt that I had set out to discover a new continent" (*FR* 436). However, he dreams the continent away because it is inhabited by white men dressed in strange clothes. When he dreams again, Dad finds himself on a strange island where the inhabitants are all white and treat him badly, but this time he does not stop dreaming. He finds it difficult to live on the island because people are afraid of his different colour. Dad undergoes a physical transformation in order to accommodate himself to the island. He shrinks the continent in him and then turns white (*FR* 437). That both the white man and Dad have to undergo transformation in order to come to terms with their identity signifies postcolonial societies' urge to (re)construct their national identity as a fusion of two cultures. In her reading of the two magical realist scenes explicated above, Brenda Cooper draws a similar conclusion, stating that they can be seen as Okri's "love of change and celebration of the transformations arising out of interactions with other cultures" (74).

Yet, cultural transformation entails a long painful process of negotiation between the local and the colonial communities. Madame Koto's bar, which Brenda Cooper describes as "the barometer for the nature of the modernizing, Westernizing changes," presents one of the most concrete examples of this process (84). The bar is located between the road and the forest, that is to say, the phenomenal world and the world of spirits. Many of the technological developments, such as electricity, gramophone and the motor car are introduced to the compound people in Madame Koto's bar. However, the bar is also homse for malevolent *abiku* children trying to lure Azaro back to the world of spirits. This hybrid space affords Okri to present his satirical view of indigenous cultural practices in the changing world. When Madame Koto buys a car, she wants a herbalist to perform a protective ritual. Okri depicts Nigerians' efforts to come to terms with the changing cultural scene of the country in a humorous scene:

> When the day arrived for Madame Koto to wash her new car, many people came to celebrate the ritual with her. Our landlord was present. People brought their bicycles and scooters. Many came on foot. There were old men whom we had never seen before. And there were a lot of powerful strange women with eyes that registered no emotion. We saw chiefs, thugs, and there were even herbalists, witch-doctors and their acolytes. They gathered in the bar and drank. They talked loudly. Eventually everyone was summoned for the washing. They formed a circle round the vehicle. The great herbalist amongst them was a stern man with a face so battered and eyes so daunting that even mirrors would recoil and crack at his glance. He uttered profound incantations and prayed for the car. (*FR* 380)

The mood of the gathering suddenly changes as the herbalist prophesies that the car shall become a coffin unless the proper sacrifice is performed. Then he demands one of the prostitutes in Madame Koto's bar to drive the coffin away from the car. The great herbalist walks into the forests, shouting his drunken lamentations: "Too many roads! Things are CHANGING TOO FAST! No new WILL. COWARDICE everywhere! SELFISHNESS is EATING UP the WORLD. THEY ARE DESTROYING AFRICA! They are DESTROYING the WORLD and the HOME and the SHRINES and the GODS! THEY are DESTROYING LOVE TOO" (*FR* 382). Indeed, soon after the herbalist's prophecy, Madame Koto's driver runs over Ade, an *abiku* child. Azaro believes that the King of the Road is awakened that night when Ade's blood is spilled on the road. "I think," Azaro says, "most of real troubles began that night" (*FR* 424). Brenda Cooper interprets the ritual washing of Madame Koto's car as an expression of the impotency of the African cultural heritage in the face of drastic changes the West has introduced. "[T]he car ritual in *The Famished Road*," Cooper argues, "is pervaded by Okri's consciousness of the changing times and the futility of the libations in the face of the evil with which the society is about to be overtaken" (85).

In *The Famished Road*, Okri brings together a multitude of views on colonialism, but the idea of transformation, as reflected in the tale and the dream narrated by Azaro's parents, is a leitmotif. Like other magical realist novelists discussed in this study, Okri sees cultural transformation and transgression as part and parcel of postcolonial societies. Thus, he searches for new and more fruitful ways in which the new hybrid culture, originating from colonialism, may contribute to the present predicament of Nigerian society. In an interview, Okri reveals, "I am interested in affecting consciousness. I do not have time for idle exercises on colonisers and so on. It seems to me defeatist. I am much more interested in transforming consciousness, which goes beyond colonialism" (qtd. in Oliva 182). The idea of transformation is presented in relation to the world of spirits or through the devices of dream and vision in the novel. Azaro's description of the spirit king presented at the outset of the novel is instructive in this respect:

> He [The spirit king] had been born uncountable times and was a legend in all worlds, known by a hundred different names. It never mattered into what circumstances he was born. He always lived the most extraordinary of lives. [...] Sometimes a man, sometimes a woman, he wrought incomparable achievements from every life. If there is anything common to all of his lives, the essence of his genius, it might well be the love of transfor-

mation, and the transformation of love into higher realities. (*FR* 3-4)

As the excerpt above suggests, the cycle of death and rebirth brings spiritual wisdom and arcane knowledge. The idea of spiritual transformation dominates the last part of the novel, where Dad decides to become a boxer to make some money from bets. He trains dementedly all hours of the day except when he works and sleeps. He punches at flies, jabs at mosquitoes and flying ants, fights with his own shadow and spars with the air. Dad is like a champion boxer, fighting with "imaginary foes as if the whole world was against him" (*FR* 353). Through his incessant trainings and matches with party members and spirits, he undergoes a spiritual transformation. In three near death experiences he has after the matches, Dad is symbolically reborn. Each has a different significance.

Dad's first match is against the spirit of a deceased legendary boxer called Yellow Jaguar, who miraculously appears out of the blue and challenges him. The match provides Dad with his initiation into the world of spirits. During the match he undergoes a magical transformation: "[…] I saw how Dad was transforming. He was going back to simple things. He was going back to water, to the earth, to the road, to soft things. He shuffled. He became fluid. […] I felt a great strange energy rising from him" (*FR* 357). The primordial energies he has evoked help Dad knock out Green Jaguar, who disappears into the earth with Dad's fatal blow. The bout with Yellow Jaguar leaves Dad "in a state of shock between agony and amnesia" that lasts for six days (*FR* 359). They have to feed him pap "as if he were the biggest newborn baby in the world" (*FR* 359). He sleeps for long hours, day and night, drooling and passing gas indiscriminately. On the seventh day, Dad rises miraculously from his bed. He is symbolically reborn "with fresh energies" (*FR* 363) and develops "interesting powers and a kind of madness" (*FR* 364). This is a spiritual rebirth as well as a physical one, for he has now acquired a new vision since to enter the world of spirits is to negotiate with their primordial wisdom: "'I am,' he confides in Azaro, "beginning to see things for the first time. This world is not what it seems. There are mysterious forces everywhere. We are living in a world of riddles'" (*FR* 388).

As evidenced by his rhetorical question to Azaro, "Maybe you have to overcome things first in the spirit world, before you can do it in this world, eh?" (*FR* 364), the boxing match with Green Jaguar prepares the necessary ground for Dad's long and painful transformation. His second match is against a man of the Party of the Rich named Green Leopard, "a legendary personage, the most feared fighter, and terroriser in many of the ghettos" (*FR* 393). Before the match, Dad promises that he will beat Green Leopard and disgrace the philosophy of the Party of the Rich (*FR* 396). Dad knocks Green Leopard out after a gruelling fight. His victory is succeeded by a three-day period of recuperation. Azaro's mother, Madame Koto and a reincarnated herbalist perform a ritual together to call his spirit from the Land of the Fighting Ghosts. When he wakes up, Dad tells them about his delirious dreams, how he has fought malevolent spirits. He is, thus, reborn a second time, bustling with energy. If Dad's first symbolic death and rebirth brings him a spiritual awakening, his second charges him with a humane and political vision. Dad starts to talk about "becoming a politician and bringing freedom and prosperity to the world and free education to the poor" (*FR* 408). Despite his illiteracy, he spends most of the money he has made from the bets on books. In the evenings, he has Azaro read them for him. When they hear Dad's promise to save the poor from starvation, the beggars in the neighbourhood begin to gather in his garden, saluting him as their leader. He grows the strange habit of keeping the door of his house open as a political gesture in Gandhian style. He does not work as much as he used to. As part of his political campaign, he visits the compound people asking for votes for the party he intends to start soon. In his speeches, he urges them to see what possibilities the future holds. When the crowd does not respond as enthusiastically as he expects, he starts blaming them for "not thinking for themselves, [...] their sheep-like philosophy, their tribal mentality, their swallowing of lies, their tolerance of tyranny, their eternal silence in the face of suffering" (*FR* 420).

Explaining the reason behind his interest in politics, Dad remarks, "[i]deas, dreams, my son, [...]. Since fighting the Green Leopard the world has changed. The inside of my head is growing bigger" (*FR* 433). His equation of dreams and ideas as mental faculties is an expression of African heritage where there is no rigid distinction between scientific thinking and mythic belief systems. They both help people to understand social and political realities. Okri expatiates on the African perception of dreams as a means of access to knowledge about the world and a way of transforming it as follows,

> The greatest inspiration, the most sublime ideas of living that have come down to humanity come from a higher realm, a happier realm, a place of pure dreams, a heaven of blessed notions. Ideas and infinite possibilities dwell there in absolute tranquillity. [...] We should return to pure contemplation, to sweet meditation, to the peace of silent loving, the serenity of deep faith, to the stillness of deep waters. We should sit still in our deep selves and dream good new things for humanity. We should try and make those dreams real. We should keep trying to raise higher the conditions and possibilities of this world. Then maybe one day, after much striving, we might well begin to create a world justice and a new light on this earth that could inspire a ten-second silence of wonder – even in heaven. (*Birds* 12-14)

Many of these sentiments are echoed in the story of Dad's transformation. Dreams and visions precede action in *The Famished Road*. Thus, towards the end of the novel Dad exhorts Azaro to trust dreams as a guiding principle in life: "We can redream this world and make the dream real" (*FR* 498). Moreover, he explains his political projection for the future in a utopian dream,

> He [Dad] conjured an image of a country in which he was invisible ruler and in which everyone would have the highest education, in which everyone must learn music and mathematics and at least five world languages, and in which every citizen must be completely aware of what is going on in the world, be versed in tribal, national, continental, and international events, history, poetry, and science; in which wizards, witches, herbalists and priests of secret religions would be professors at universities; in which bus drivers, cartpullers, and market women would be lecturers, while still retaining their normal jobs; in which children would be teachers and adults pupils; in which delegations from all the poor people would have regular meetings with the Head of State; and in which there would be elections when there were more than five spontaneous riots in any given year. (*FR* 409)

Dad's dream represents magical realism's desire to articulate change and transformation through its utopian impulse. With his third and the last match with an anonymous man, referred to as "a man in a white suit," Dad's transformation is completed. "[T]he third transformation," David C. L. Lim maintains, "marks the ultimate traversal of fantasy and metamorphosis of the very kernel of his being" (86). Devastated physically, Dad drifts into restless dreams once again, in which he searches for answers to the suffering in his community. In his dreams, he comes to the realisation that "all nations are born children; […] a spirit-child nation, one that keeps being reborn and after each birth come blood and betrayals, and the child of our will refuses to stay till we have made propitious sacrifice and displayed our serious intent to bear the weight of a unique destiny" (*FR* 494). As Dad's explanation suggests, if the nation is to survive, she is to transcend the threats against herself. Azaro's liminal existence, thus, turns into a metaphor for the Nigerian nation. His unrelenting choice to stay alive metaphorically stands for Nigeria's struggle to form and sustain her national identity. In keeping with Dad's epiphanic illumination, the reader is invited to reconsider the events in the novel, particularly the family's struggle to keep their son alive in the face of extreme poverty and socio-political corruption under a new light.

It should however be noted that Azaro is not the only *abiku* child in the novel. Madame Koto is pregnant with three *abikus,* and there is also Azaro's friend, Ade. In explaining the metaphoric function of *abikus* in the novel, Brenda Cooper notes, "Nigeria is not only the wicked *abikus* in Madame Koto's belly, it is a combination of Azaro and his *alter ego*, Ade, the sweet ethereal spirit child who is determined to keep dying and returning to his spirit companions" (91). Ade and Azaro have different dispositions to life. While Azaro sees himself as a "spirit-child rebelling against the spirits, wanting to live the earth's life and contradictions", he observes that "Ade wanted to leave, to become a spirit again, free in the captivity of freedom" (*FR* 487). Ade is optimistic that his beleaguered country shall break the cycle of social, economic and political problems. He conceives that "[o]ur country is an *abiku* country. Like the spirit-child, it keeps coming and going. One day it will decide to remain. It will become strong. I won't see it" (*FR* 478). But, the survival of the nation will not be easy. Through his prophetic vision, Ade foretells what the future holds for Nigeria,

> There will be changes. Coups. Soldiers everywhere. Ugliness. Blindness. And then when people least expect it a great transformation is going to take place in the world. Suffering people will know justice and beauty. A wonderful change is coming from far away and people will realise the great meaning of struggle and hope. There will be peace. Then people will forget. Then it will all start again, getting worse, getting better. Don't

fear. You will always have something to struggle for, even if it is beauty or joy. (*FR* 478)

Despite his optimism, Ade does not rebel against the relentless cycle of the *abiku* like Azaro, which turns him metaphorically into a foil for the nation. Comparing the two *abiku* children's disposition to life, Abiodun Adeniji concludes that "[t]he decision of Okri's Azaro to stay is [...] a ray of hope for the nation. At the first level of signification, it implies the survival of the nation in spite of the many problems besetting her" (204). Adeniji goes on to argue that Okri's positive reconstruction of the *abiku* myth is a "paradigm shift" from the literary image of the spirit-child who torments his parents by his or her constant coming and going between the worlds of the living and the dead as depicted in the works of Fagunwa, Tutuola, Soyinka and Clark-Bekederemo (204-205). In the same vein, Brenda Cooper maintains that "[t]he hope of the novel lies in Azaro successfully repudiating the *abiku* within himself and thereby, denying the inevitability of that mythical, Tutuolan road with its hungry waiting monster [...] Here Okri appears to contradict earlier reservations and to assert passionately the possibility of change" (92). This paradigm shift epitomises magical realism's capacity to provide new ways of seeing the indigenous cultures. The magical realist novelist returns to the indigenous past only to recreate anew by incorporating the mythical with the modern in the third space.

The *abiku*, as a metaphor for the nation, is also an explicit indication of the relationship between magical realism and postcolonial writing. In her article titled "Transfiguring: Colonial Body into Postcolonial Narrative," Elleke Boehmer explores the function of art as a means of giving voice to the silent or the silenced in postcolonial societies. For Boehmer, self-representation of "the colonial body" has become "one of the key distinguishing features of the postcolonial" since it serves as a counter-discourse to the colonizing powers which, in their authoritative rule, seized the sole right of representing the colonised masses in their political and literary narratives ("Transfiguring" 272). Boehmer observes that "in postcolonial nationalist discourses of the last number of decades, images of the scrutinized, scored subject body have become the focus of attempts at symbolic reversal and transfiguration. Representing its own silence, the colonized body speaks; uttering its wounds, it negates its muted condition" (272). In *The Famished Road*, Okri manages to combine the abiku myth with the political realities of postcolonial society through his magical realist writing. Azaro speaks for the nation. His will to live in the face of poverty and political oppression represents the nation's determination to preserve its independent existence.

African traditional beliefs that Okri draws from in order to create his magical realist vision include myths, folk tales and dreams, constantly shifting the boundaries between the established binaries. The deliberate ambiguity created in the text instils in the reader the possibility of seeing reality from a different point of view. The evident conflation of the mythic and the realistic in *The Famished Road* does not only provide the necessary textual space for magical realism to flourish but also helps challenge the Western concepts of identity and progress, as they are constantly destabilised. His use of magical realism, particularly his articulation of the *abiku* myth, also coincides with his view of African aesthetics, which he contends, "is bound to a way of looking at the world in more than three dimensions. It's the aesthetic of possibilities, of labyrinths, of riddles [...] of paradoxes" (Wilkinson 87-88). Ben Okri employs magical realism in *The Famished Road* to reinvest in the Nigerian cultural heritage in order to generate a narrative that resists the monological understanding of Western historiography.

4.2. A Black Odyssey Home: Syl Cheney-Coker's *The Last Harmattan of Alusine Dunbar*

The fourth and the last of the novels to be studied within the present framework is Syl Cheney-Coker's debut novel *The Last Harmattan of Alusine Dunbar*, which was published in 1990 and awarded the Commonwealth Writers' Prize of the following year. In the novel, Cheney-Coker addresses one of the darkest chapters of colonial history, the legacy of slavery in Sierra Leone, through the lives of a group of liberated slaves who return to West Africa in 1787. Like other postcolonial writers who have experimented with magical realism, Cheney-Coker has a profound interest in the history of his country of origin. In an interview with Brenda Cooper, Cheney-Coker explains how the unique history of Sierra Leone has shaped his artistic sensitivity and vision as follows:

> If you have read my poetry, and of course my novel, it is clear that I am a Sierra Leonian with roots in the history of the middle passage. Initially, I was trying to define what that history has meant for me and how in some ways it makes me slightly different, or so people feel, from other West African Writers. It is clear that if you are dealing with other West African Writers who write in English, their mindsets, the traditional norms and forms that make themselves known in their poetry now and then, image clusters so to speak which they have inherited, have remained intact. But in my case it's quite different because I'm having to contend with the admixture of an African life and the history of slavery – what those two have meant for us Sierra Leonian Creoles. (qtd. in Cooper 118)

In the same interview, Cheney-Coker also draws attention to the experience of slavery and its indisputable effect on the identity of the Sierra Leonean people. It is his interest in the Creole identity that has served as a source of inspiration for *The Last Harmattan of Alusine Dunbar*:

By telling the history of what slavery produced in Sierra Leone, however fictional it was going to be, but along historical lines, I wanted to show how these remarkable people, in two hundred years (mind you it's longer than two hundred years in my novel) did so much, not just for Sierra Leone but for West Africa. It was for me an act of celebration. I think in some ways I was trying to do what in a much larger context Derek Walcott has done in his poetry. (qtd. in Cooper 120)

It is clear from his comments above that Cheney-Coker, like the other magical realist novelists addressed in this study, recognises the value of cultural heterogeneity generated by the colonial experience, for it provides a direct contact with "the Other." Having said this, it is equally important to emphasise the fact that he does not acknowledge the colonial experience as the beginning of his country's initial contact with the so-called civilisation as claimed in the Western historiography. Rather, he tends to view colonialism as a transitory phase in the country's history, and he explores the predicaments of slavery in a wider historical context. Accordingly, the chronological span of his novel extends as far as to the slave plantations in America, where the Sierra Leonean were transported as part of the transatlantic slave trade.

Despite his initial plan to write a novel about the history of Sierra Leone, Cheney-Coker's epic novel is set in a fictional country, Malagueta. Evidently, the fictional setting affords the novelist greater freedom than the traditional historical novel as he can handle the historical material without being constrained by it. Through the unfolding history of Malagueta, Cheney-Coker addresses many of the issues and themes that can be found in other major postcolonial novels, such as the shallow mimicry of Western cultural patterns and political corruption in the indigenous government. Despite its imaginary existence, the history of Malagueta is interwoven with pivotal events in world history. There are sporadic references to the American War of Independence and the Second World War. Yet, at the core of the novel lies the turbulent political history of Sierra Leone. Most of the major events in the novel allude to the history of the country. Consequently, critics tend to consider *The Last Harmattan of Alusine Dunbar* as a historical novel. For instance, George Elliott Clarke argues that Cheney-Coker's Malagueta is a novelisation of Sierra Leonean history since most of the events in the text are predicated on the historical account of the country (126-128). Similarly, Eustace Palmer considers *The Last Harmattan of Alusine Dunbar* as historical fiction written in a magical realist fashion (202-203).

There are a number of parallels between the history of Sierra Leone and Cheney-Coker's fictional country of Malagueta. The first settlement in Sierra Leone, known as Freetown, was established by the formerly enslaved African Americans who returned to their homeland in two groups in 1787 and 1792, respectively (Clifford 110-111). In the novel, Cheney-Coker recreates the experience of the original settlers and relates the history of Malagueta through the lives of the founding families, such as the Cromantines, the Martins, Thomas Bookerman, Phyllis Dundas and the Farmer brothers. Their collective story sheds light on the history of Sierra Leone from slavery to colonialism and to the subsequent post-independence period. Cheney-Coker also draws heavily from historical material to shape the thematic structure of the novel. As historian Mary Louise Clifford notes, the early phase in history of the country is marked with a cultural crisis caused by the distinction between the returnees and the local African people: "The Creoles of Sierra Leone have always considered themselves a special group. Indeed, the designation Creole has a special meaning as it is used in Sierra Leone, for it embraces all the descendants of the freed Negroes whom the British settled on the peninsula to make a new life for themselves in the continent of their origin" (110). In the novel, Cheney-Coker explores the painful process of nation building with all its accompanying difficulties and problems, including ethic essentialism inflicting the Creole community of Sierra Leone.

The novel consists of four books framed by a prologue and an epilogue, which helps communicate the cyclical nature of history. In the prologue, General Tamba Masimiara is depicted in his prison following his failed attempt of military coup against the corrupt dictatorship Sanka Maru. The general is imprisoned in the same dungeon "where, in centuries past, the blood of his countrymen and women had mixed with their own excreta and vomit, before they were transported across the treacherous sea to die in the swampy bleakness of another world" (*LHAD* vii). This specific location can be regarded as an indication of the fact that although the colonial powers have been defeated, the country cannot be saved from the tyrannical forces. In his cell, the general reflects on the series of events that have led him to ploy a military coup against the corrupt government. He condemns the post-independence politicians' for their pursuit of Eurocentric values which, he thinks, has led to the fall of Malagueta:

> Modes of behaviour long abandoned in the factories and gutters of England were still being copied with diligence by the despicable lot who made up the middle and upper classes. They were men and women whose other passion was to drink tea in the afternoon in the ovens of their drawing rooms and parlours modelled on the antediluvian style of pre-abolition America while worrying about the cost of taking holidays in England. (xiii)

Like many other events in the novel, the failed coup presented in the prologue and the epilogue corresponds to a recorded event in the history of Sierra Leone, namely the execution of General John Bangura by Siaka Stevens, the first president of Sierra Leone (Palmer 130; Clarke 210). However, as part of Cheney-Coker's magical realist scheme, the political agenda of the novel is revealed through the prism of fantastic events that take place in Malagueta. Magic carpets, prophetic visions and haunting ghosts figure amidst the events that parallel Sierra Leone's political history. The blend of the fantastic and the historical epitomises Cheney-Coker's magical realist vision, which is, in fact, reflected in the self-explanatory subtitle of the novel: *A Novel of Magical Vision*. In an interview, Cheney-Coker explains that his writing style is a reaction to the reductive view that categorises African writers along the lines of two founding figures of the African novel, Chinua Achebe and Ngugi wa Thiong'o:

> [...] the novel in Africa has been as it were cloistered within very prescribed forms. It was either you had a sociological view of the novel within the Achebean definition, or you were a political novelist within the Ngugian concept of it. There were all these perceived notions of what the African novel should be like. One hears so much about it – this novel should be written in this or that form because this is the way African literature is perceived. For me this was rather an intellectual humbug. I felt the need for new kinds of directions [...]. (qtd. in Cooper 119)

In this light, Cheney-Coker's choice of magical realism in *The Last Harmattan of Alusine Dunbar* can be considered as part of his rejection of the categorical constraints of African literature. It is in the fertile third space of magical realism that Cheney-Coker interpolates the social and political history of Sierra Leone with its indigenous cultural heritage. His double vision demonstrates the liberating power of magical realism as it allows the historical and the fantastic to be presented together within the body of a single text.

In explaining the functional role of magical realism in the novel, Ato Quayson argues that Cheney-Coker's "focus is more on magical realist characters, as opposed to events as such," for these characters help the novelist integrate "mythical elements into the narration of a foundational saga that is supposed to bear historical significance for present-day Sierra Leone" (170). There are two key magical realist characters in the novel: Sulaiman the Nubian, otherwise known as Alusine Dunbar and Fatmatta the Bird-Woman. Both characters are significant for a critical interpretation of the novel not only because they are fundamental to the plot structure as argued by Quayson, but also because they function as the agents of anti-colonial resistance in the text. The magical vision referred to in the subtitle of the novel is revealed by Sulaiman the Nubian, a magician and a seer with a remarkable power of premonition. He arrives among the people of Kasila, the African town that shall grow into Malagueta, accompanied by a local gold merchant called N'jai. The merchant announces the crowd gathering around his caravan that he has encountered a mysterious man while travelling, and that he is going to read the life of Kasila in the mirror. Sulaiman the Nubian foretells all the unfolding events in the novel:

> Everything was mirrored in the looking-glass: the octoroon woman who would bring the potato plague, the albino who would marry the most beautiful woman in the world, the man who would be afraid of snakes and would use the skull of his father as a guiding light, and the one-eyed man who would lead a great mission in the atmospheric darkness of the forest tracing the first strangers who would be wiped out because of the potato plague. (*LHAD* 25)

In this enigmatic premonition, Sulaiman identifies many of the key events that shall take place in the future Malagueta, such as the arrival of diasporic Africans from across the Atlantic, the founding of a new settlement (a palimpsest of Freetown), and the coming of the English colonisers led by Captain Hammerstone. His vision, therefore, proves an ideal instance of the blending of the fantastic and the historical. Starting from the first line of the novel, there are constant references to Sulaiman the Nubian's prophecy in the novel: "She had been prophesied in the looking-glass of Sulaiman the Nubian of Khartoum, a hundred years ago" (*LHAD* 1), "Just as Sulaiman the Nubian had predicted many years earlier" (*LHAD* 100), "just as Sulaiman the Nubian, otherwise known as Alusine Dunbar had seen them in the magical mirror many years earlier" (258). It can therefore be argued that Cheney-Coker denies the authority of Western historiography from the outset of the novel as the large portion of the history of this fictional country is recounted by a seer instead of a historian.

As mentioned earlier, the magical realist characters function as decolonising agents in the narrative. It is revealed at the outset of the novel that Sulaiman the Nubian is an adamant opponent of any form of racial or cultural abuse. He rescues N'jai from a group of Arabs abusing him simply because he cannot bear "the thought that another person, however different, should be made to suffer in another country at the hands of human pirates" (*LHAD* 19). This seemingly trivial scene is in fact a foreshadowing of the events that take place at the end of the novel. Sulaiman the Nubian returns to the town and rescues its people from the dictatorship of Sanku Maru by unleashing a strong harmattan (a dust-laden wind that sometimes blows in the area), killing the dictator and condemning his supporter Colonel Lookdown Okongo to an eternal public disgrace.

The other key magical realist character in the novel is Fatmatta the Bird-Woman. She is the daughter of Sulaiman the Nubian and Mariamu, N'Jai's wife. Upon receiving the news that her husband has returned to the town with a man of unearthly powers, Mariamu resolves that he can help her to conceive a child that she has desperately longed for. Out of their secret union is born Fatmatta the Bird-Woman. Like her father, she is endowed with supernatural powers. She can read other people's mind, talk to animals, move objects merely by looking at them, and change the colour of water just by touching it. When she is sold into slavery, she uses her magical powers to resist the white slave owner's sexual abuses. However, this should not be seen as a mere act of chastity, but as an act of anti-slavery. As Angela Davis states, slave women "were simply instruments guaranteeing the growth of the slave labour force. They were breeders—animals, whose monetary value could be precisely calculated in terms of their ability to multiply their numbers" (7). In this light, Fatmatta's "female body," Brenda Cooper asserts, "is cast into the mould of the struggle against slavery, against colonialism [...]" (126).

After her death, Fatmatta the Bird-Woman is reincarnated as the spiritual protector of the founding families of Malagueta. The interaction between the worlds of the living and the dead constitutes the most consistent magical realist strategy in the novel. Cheney-Coker's magical realist vision seems to be rooted in indigenous cultural practices of African people. As Mary L. Clifford points out, the belief system of the indigenous Sierra Leoneans is primarily based "on the obedience of the elders and the spirits with whom they mediate" (126). In keeping with this holistic view of the world, the dead in the novel do not only inhabit the land of the living, but also watch over their descendants. Fatmatta's actions have some political resonances as she protects the leaders of the anti-colonial group: Emmanuel Cromantine and Thomas Bookerman. First, she appears to Jeanette Cromantine while she is labouring to give birth to her son Emmanuel. As the labour reaches an unbearable stage, Jeanette sees the celestial face of Fatmatta the Bird-Woman, and the pain that is tearing her apart stops. Cheney-Coker portrays the bond between the Malaguetans/Sierra Leoneans and their ancestors in a beautifully written magical realist scene:

> She had lost the premature wrinkles of old age, which years of labouring in the fields and in the kitchens of supercilious brides had left on her face. She barely gave Jeanette Cromantine time to wonder where she had come from or at the astonishing power of her transformation, before the pregnant woman began to feel the child in her belly moving into position. 'Move over, sister' said Fatmatta the Bird-Woman. She held the hand of Jeanette Cromantine; then, as if she was transmitting her strength to the

woman who was losing hers [...] 'Now, you goin to deliver,' she told the raving woman. (*LHAD* 109)

Similarly, Fatmatta's spectral apparition resists colonialism. When the British colonisers, led by Captain Hammerstone, attempt to establish their rule in Malagueta, they encounter Thomas Bookerman's resistance group. At a decisive moment, when Captain Hammerstone aims his gun at Bookerman, Fatmatta's spectre appears and makes him miss his target.

The first book of the novel covers the span of time between the last days of the American Civil War and the establishment of the first settlement in Malagueta. As the novel opens, a group of freed slaves are depicted as they are about to embark on their return journey to Africa. Cheney-Coker exposes the terrible conditions in the American slave plantations through their story. The first character that appears in Cheney-Coker's large epic canvas is Jeanette Cromantine, an octoroon born of a slave woman called Sophie Mahogany, who has been seduced and impregnated by a white plantation owner, Willie Blackburn. Sophie gives her daughter away for adoption to a free black pastor who vows to protect the little child from her mother's fate. Despite the pastor's efforts to keep Jeanette away from the miseries of slavery, she learns about the suffering black men and women are condemned to on the plantations by eavesdropping upon the conversations between the pastor and his black converts:

> Thus she came to learn that 'sawdust' is another name for a black man who worked with the most unyielding variety of tobacco plants and that 'cow udders' were the black women who nursed the children of plantation owners [...] she heard the sacred oath taken by the black women to drink the bitter potion to abort all children forced upon them by their owners until they were called by 'the loas' of the swamp to bring forth strong

children who would grow to wield cutlasses and cut the throats of their masters. (*LHAD* 5-6)

During the war, Sebastian Cromantine, Jeannette's future husband, fights along the forces of the colonial army in return for his freedom. After the war, the couple first set sail to England and then to their motherland, Malagueta. On the eve of the voyage, Sebastian Cromantine is visited by his deceased father's ghost, which leaves him sleepless for nights. The ghost, he recounts, has a voice "from another time, deep and lonely. It had the faraway gravity of a rootless man burdened by his inability to find a resting place" (*LHAD* 9). Sebastian's description suggests that his father's soul shall not be at peace until his bones are returned to his homeland for a proper burial. Hence, he digs up his father's skull and takes it to Malagueta. He believes that the skull provides spiritual guidance, helping him to "evoke a lineage that was not defined by time, but by the spirit, by the force of all eternities and the running music of ancestral water that coursed through his blood" (*LHAD* 14). When his wife asks him what is the point of carrying the skull all the way to Africa, Sebastian contends, "'Am gon use it, it's de Magic Latern" (*LHAD* 15). Sebastian's sacred quest to return his father's bones to his homeland is also shared by the other returnees on board who "had brought the bones of their dead ones [...] During the periodic storms at sea, the rattling of the bones on the bags helped to reassure their owners that they would make it to shore" (*LHAD* 15).

Two days before they reach the shores of Kasila, tragedy strikes the returnees as the oldest passenger on board, Fatmatta the Bird-Woman, dies. Being one of the first generation of African slaves transported to America, she is actually the only returnee with an access to the precolonial history of Kasila. Fatmatta has a vision just before she breathes her last, revealing the conditions of life in Virginia, Carolina and Mississippi, where the former slaves lived before they retracted to Africa. In her vision, Fatmatta speaks to a vulture that comes to take her to the land of origin:

> "You're going home," it [the vulture] said. Her eyes met the eyes of the bird and she saw a long ancestral bridge with a lot of people crossing from one end to the other; and suddenly everything was clear to her. Cut of from the land of coalescence of men and spirits, burdened by servitude, she had merely been fulfilling a destiny circumscribed by fate, by an old animated life rhythm that went round the universe like a great flame and then she knew that she would not die in the land of leeches but that she would return, shed all signs of degradation and abuse. Because by the persistence of its look, […] the great bird had come to take her home to that land where her navel string was buried. (*LHAD* 67)

Realising that she will die before setting foot on her homeland, Fatmatta makes sure that she is given a proper burial on land as it shall secure her spiritual reintegration with her roots. The dream of returning to Mother Africa, as reflected in Fatmatta the Bird-Woman's painful vision, is a leitmotif in the novel. The slave trade was the major cause in the creation of African diasporic communities. Thus, a brief discussion of the term "diaspora" and its application in the African context is advisable at this juncture.

Broadly speaking "diaspora" means "the voluntary or forcible movement of peoples from their homelands into new regions" (Ashcroft *et al.*, *Empire*, 68-69). As such, the formation of diasporic communities is recognised as "a central historical fact of colonization" as it involved "the temporary or permanent dispersion and settlement of millions of Europeans over the entire world" (69). In his article "Diasporas in Modern Societies: Myths of Homeland and Return," William Safran introduces six principles in order to reach a definition of this highly elusive term. For Safran, the concept of diaspora is to be applied to expatriate minority communities whose members share several of the following characteristics:

> 1) they or their ancestors have been dispersed from a specific original "centre" to two or more "peripheral" or foreign regions; 2) they retain a collective memory, vision or myth about their original homeland [...] 3) they believe they are not – and perhaps cannot be – fully accepted by their host society and therefore feel partly alienated and insulated from it; 4) they regard their ancestral homelands as their true, ideal home and a place to which they or their descendants would (or should) eventually return – when conditions are appropriate; 5) they believe that they should, collectively, be committed to the maintenance or restoration of their original homeland and its safety and prosperity; and 6) they continue to relate personally or vicariously, to that homeland in one way or another, and their ethnocommunal consciousness and solidarity are importantly defined by the existence of such a relationship. (x)

As Safran's principles suggest, the notion of home assumes utopian proportions in the diasporic imagination as it metaphorically stands for the ultimate destination in diasporic communities' search for cultural roots. In the context of African diaspora, the dream of returning home signifies an exodus from the despicable experience of slavery. In "Cultural Identity and Diaspora," Stuart Hall explains the symbolic connotation of home as Mother Africa in literature and visual arts as follows,

> Africa is the name of the missing term, the great aporia, which lies at the centre of our cultural identity and gives it a meaning which, until recently, it lacked. No one who looks at these textural images now, in the light of the history of transportation,

> slavery and migration, can fail to understand how the rift of separation, the 'loss of Identity,' [...] only begins to be healed when these forgotten connections are once more set in place. Such texts restore an imaginary fullness or plentitude, to set against the broken rubric of our past. They are resources of resistance and identity, with which to confront the fragmented and pathological ways in which that experience has been reconstructed within the dominant regimes of cinematic and visual representation of the West. (224-225)

The diasporic community's desire to return to the land of origin, therefore, presupposes an essentialist model of reconnection with their indigenous culture, yet the actual experience of diasporic community entails contingency, indeterminacy and conflict.

Accordingly, Cheney-Coker distances himself from what may seem to be an essentialist view of indigenous culture through his portrayal of the initial contact between the returnees and the local community of Kasila. With the arrival of the returnees, Kasila turns into an active site of cultural interaction. Sebastian Cromantine, as the leader of the returnees, speaks to the local King and tells him how they have gained their freedom in return for their part in the war. He also recounts how they, "inspired by the primordial light of their forefathers," resolved to return to Kasila and the disillusionment they felt when they are not granted enough land to cultivate for their families (*LHAD* 69). Sebastian's request to buy land for the returnees is rejected by the King, who reproaches him with a remark reflecting centuries old indigenous wisdom: "here, no one owns anything, not even the stones" (*LHAD* 70). Thus, the returnees' ambition to possess the land, a clear expression of their westernised mind, is negated by the king's reply. The cultural distance between the two communities is further reinforced when the king declares that the newcomers may stay and have all the land they need, provided that they respect the laws and the men keep off local women (*LHAD*

70). The integration of the local people and settlers entails a more painful and turbulent process than expected by the latter as distrust and prejudice against harmonious co-existence with the Other plagues all layers of both communities, as shall be discussed in detail below.

After a short period of peace, the tension between the two communities resurfaces when a plague that has been killing the settlers spreads to the neighbouring local people. They pillage the settlement founded by the pioneers, thinking that the sweet potato given to them by Jeanette Cromantine is responsible for the death of their children. Nothing is left from the settlement except for the smell of the burned bodies. The surviving group of pioneers retreat to the forest's vulva as a hideout from the indigenous people of Kasila. Hence, the dream of utopian life in the promised land ends with disillusionment for the first wave of returnees. It is only after the arrival of the second wave of liberated slaves led by Thomas Bookerman that Malagueta is revived. Historically, it is the second group of liberated slaves that secured the existence of Sierra Leone. Mary L. Clifford notes, the pioneer settlers "never would have survived as a distinct group had they not been joined in 1792 by over a thousand freed slaves" (110). Like Sebastian Cromantine, Bookerman is also an ex-combatant who has fought in the colonial war. They come to Malagueta with the prospect of unlimited land and building new and better homes for their families. They are more organised and determined than the pioneer settlers. They plan and build the city and institute a form of administration. Soon Malagueta becomes a popular destination for traders and investors and attracts new breeds of settlers from different parts of the world. The population of the town becomes increasingly heterogeneous. The people in the town speak a hybrid language that every day receives "new words as more and more of them [new settlers] appear from all parts of the world with their accounts of wars, famine, kidnappings and revolts" (*LHAD* 191).

The difficulties encountered by diasporic communities in the process of identity formation are presented through the marriage between a returnee, Gustavius Martins and a local woman, Isatu Dambolla. Gustavius has been transported to the New World by the slave traders after spending his childhood in Malagueta. Although time, suffering and the war have worked havoc in his memory, they have not completely erased all the memories of his country from his heart. Gustavius finds in Isatu's indigenous blood "the resources of a heritage to which he [has] lost all claim to knowledge [...]" (*LHAD* 188). It is not only Gustavius that Isatu helps with her knowledge of the terrain. When the returnees seek refuge in the forest after the pillage of their settlement by the locals, Isatu, also known as "a child of nature," assures their survival in the wilderness by teaching them to make tools, preserving food and building dwellings (*LHAD* 107). Her marriage with Gustavius, on the other hand, has made Isatu "aware of things that would otherwise have escaped her: the equal role of women in the building of a community; the importance of believing in individual efforts for the good of the community" (*LHAD* 199). However, the initial optimism engendered by the harmonious union of the couple soon gives way to disillusionment with the advent of their families' acts of mutual exclusion fuelled by ethnic essentialism. Isatu's father, following the cultural codes of his tribal community, does not consent to his daughter's marriage with one of "what he called the Oporto, the white/black people" and threatens "to expel all the settlers from Malagueta, if she went ahead with her decision" (*LHAD* 94). Similarly, Isatu, despite her efforts that have assured their survival in the forest, is never "fully accepted by anyone [among the returnees], except for the Cromantines" (*LHAD* 187).

The couple's infertility motivates both communities' criticism against the marriage between a former slave and a local woman. Isatu, who has suffered from repeated miscarriages, complains to Gustavius that "all dem women are saying am a bad woman 'cause all the pikin die before they born, and dey say ah kill 'em" (*LHAD* 190). The wives of the settlers even come to "regard her as a witch" (*LHAD* 192). Treated as an outsider, Isatu resolves to visit Mobida the diviner to seek a cure for her barrenness. After questioning her husband's bond with the land, Mobida concludes that Isatu is not blessed with a child she has put a lot of distance between herself and her parents by marrying a foreigner. The couple thus leaves for Isatu's hometown, Bolanda to seek reconciliation with her parents in order to conceive a child. Sawida Dambolla, Isatu's mother, welcomes the couple with an injunction of spiritual cleansing which concurs with Mobida's verdict on the cultural impurity of the couple: "we will have to wash you and your husband" (*LHAD* 198). When she suspects that Gustavius does not seem to understand the significance of her words, she plunges into a long speech about the cultural divide between the settler and the local African community;

> They have a dubious notion of freedom so that man is perceived as living in a world where he is independent of nature. Space is a thing they have not learnt how to deal with, because they are pulling down everything: trees, groves, shrines; insulting the souls of the dead. Rites that help us into adulthood mean nothing to them, the spiritual is suspect, and very little thought is given to the relationship between what we bring into this world and what we take with us to our graves. Or for that matter to the little things that are much more important than the big ones in our lives. (*LHAD* 192)

The virulence of ethnic animosities between the two communities is nowhere more evident than in Sawida's speech. For Isatu's mother, the returnees are not their descendants forced to move to the New World by the slave trade, but the Westernised "Others." They are contaminated by the Western way of life and thought and have lost their respect for local customs. Sawida, therefore, concludes that the couple is to be cleansed of all the impurities that Gustavius contracted in his years in exile and with which he contaminated Isatu by marrying her.

Magical realism's functional role in reconciling dichotomies and oppositions becomes increasingly evident in Cheney-Coker's depiction of the cultural purification of the couple since it requires their initiation with the world of spirits. The role of the dead in Sierra Leonean culture is revealed early in the novel. It is during Fatmatta's burial that the leader of the returnees, Sebastian Cromantine, has a revelation that "death was not so much a question of going back in time but a revelation of things to come, because this world was merely an extension of the past and death was like a mirror into the future" (*LHAD* 70). The idea of the dead as the guide of the living is evoked again when Sawida suggests that Gustavius is to reconcile with the ghost of Isatu's father, Santigue Dambolla. Before he drops dead next to the banana grove where people throw their garbage, Santigue Dambolla goes to a diviner and learns about Isatu's unfortunate fate. For Sawida, it is the news he cannot be a grandfather that has brought him to death before his time. After his death, his ghost can freely walk among the living. Soon the household realises his presence. They leave the doors open and put food on the table in the dining room so that he can come and go as he pleases. Gustavius Martins is the only one who cannot see the dead man moving about the house. It is again regarded as a consequence of his being forcibly uprooted from his homeland: "[y]ears of being in the wasteland of America had stripped him [Gustavius] of the power to make contact with the dead" (*LHAD* 202). In order to re-establish his contact with the dead, Sawida instructs Gustavius to choose some of the dead man's belongings and keep them as a token of reconciliation. Gustavius chooses "the sword of Mobido of Timbuctoo, the porcelain jug with the voluptuous woman and one of the white-laced gowns that he could wear on his castaway body" (*LHAD* 202). The dispute between the two men ends with Sawida's emphatic reassurance that Gustavius is now part of the family: "welcome home son" (*LHAD* 202).

It is only after his reconciliation with Isatu's dead father that the members of the local community start to treat Gustavius Martins respectfully. Gustavius' acceptance in the larger community paves the way for the first stage of the couple's cultural cleansing. Next, they need to re-establish their bond with the African soil. The couple stay in Bolanda and work with Santigue's fellowmen and women to restore the long-neglected land to productivity. Their work in the fields is furthered by a community of spirit;

> [...] the couple from Malagueta became farmers in the translucent world, surrounded by the ghosts of the founders of that town, who had achieved permanence among the trees and the fields, and who made the burden of the transformation easy for the Martinses. Six months later, when the dry clouds had sucked up the rain, they looked at the field and were content with their labours. They had restored the trees to good health, planted three varieties of rice, got the cows milking again, and had the potatoes, yams and corn ready for the harvest. (*LHAD* 203)

Brenda Cooper, in her reading of the scene, suggests that the return to the land "is redolent with essentialist connotations of the biological and natural cycle of things with which they had to be in harmony before being able to participate in the human natural cycle of reproduction" (*LHAD* 131). In this light, the restoration of the land to productivity can be seen as a symbolic rendition of the return of Isatu's reproductive power. However, there is yet another ritual that the couple has to go through before they can be blessed with a child that they have long yearned for: a ritual of spiritual cleansing performed by two enigmatic dwarfs.

The dwarfs, sent by Santigue's ghost, appear in the town unexpectedly and set their camp under a large baobab tree. They announce to the crowd gathering around them that they have supernatural powers as "they had discovered the herbs that could prolong life, shorten the forms of people, and allow them to be in several places at the same time" (*LHAD* 205). They choose Gustavius and Isatu to take part in their performance, claiming that although being "tainted by the garbage of [their] union" they are pure at heart (*LHAD* 132). The garbage refers to the cultural impurity of their union, and it is attributed to the fact that Gustavius, being away from the African soil for such a long time, "had lost the power to understand the origins of man" (*LHAD* 132). They offer to cleanse the couple by washing them "with the sap of the leaves of the grove where the foetuses of [Gustavius'] wife have been trapped for years" (*LHAD* 206). Cheney-Coker describes the ritual scene vividly:

> A week later, Gustavius and Isatu Martins stood naked in front of a boiling cauldron, inhaling the pungency of leaves and roots which the dwarfs had gone to the forest to find. Spirals of smoke rose from the pot, and the senses of the man and the woman were filled with a vapour that made them innocent and childlike in the baptism of their second coming. When they were beginning to feel their feet moving into the territory of their regeneration, the dwarfs touched them with the tails of horses soaked in the cauldron. The voices of the dwarfs spoke as if in a dream, and the woman felt the encrustation of the dirt and garbage that years of marriage to a man without the roots of the forest had imposed on her, while the man felt the garbage of the world across the sea of blood rubbing off his body, so that they were one again, cleansed of all impurities, and could touch each other with their feathery hands which had been anointed, and with their bodies which had been repossessed by new seeds, so that the fecundity of the woman could respond to the male power of the husband. (*LHAD* 206)

The couple is thus cleansed from the impurities inflicted upon them by the experience of slavery. Nine months after the ritual, Isatu gives birth to a boy. She names him Garbage, as a reminder of the place where her father was found dead, "so that he will not forget his roots" (*LHAD* 208). The strange name Isatu gives to her son can also be regarded an implication of his parents' mixed cultural heritage. As he grows up, Garbage becomes a mediator between the Western and Indigenous cultures. He receives a Western education and becomes a national poet, but he never loses his contact with his cultural roots. He is also the only one to talk to Sulaiman the Nubian, whose apparition shall return to Malagueta one hundred and fifty years later. Garbage, in other words, becomes a pertinent example of Cheney-Coker's idea of hybrid postcolonial identity. The first phase of Malaguetan history is thus sealed by the birth of a Creole child, symbolising the new hybrid identity, a fusion of the settlers and the local people. In the remainder of the novel, Cheney-Coker focuses on the events of the recent past of the country: the domination of British Colonialism in the region, the invasion of the Arabs, the anti-colonial uprisings and the ensuing independence and finally the failure of the post-independence government to stay away from the ideological order of colonialism.

While the settlers grapple with the problems of cohabitation with the indigenous people, the threat of colonialism draws closer as a group of English colonisers led by Captain Hammerstone embark on the shores of Malagueta. As his name suggests, Hammerstone is a representative of ruthless brutality of colonisation. Having obtained a commission from the Colonial Office, he is instructed to build a fort, protect new traders and put down any rebellion or uprising by the founders of the town. In order to convey the impact of colonialism in the history of Malagueta/Sierra Leone, Cheney-Coker first draws attention to the proto-utopian quality of life in the country before the colonial intrusion. Peace and prudence reign in the town. Unlike the colonists for whom the idea of profit serves as the only reason for fighting a war, the Malaguetans try hard to avoid bloodshed. As the omniscient narrator notes, "ever since they had built the new Malagueta, they [the Malaguetans] had by some unwritten rule banned the use of guns except for the hunting game" (*LHAD* 156). Later in the novel, it is revealed rather humorously that "the greatest crime that was ever committed in the first years of the founding of the town was that of a woman pouring hot water on her husband because he had fallen in love with his mother-in-law who was only three years older than he was" (*LHAD* 209). Before taking action against Captain Hammerstone and his men, the Malaguetans hold meetings to discuss the best method of dealing with the presence of the foreigners and of the possibility of mobilising enough men to draw them out of Malagueta. The meetings where men and women can freely express their ideas contradicts with the well-established binary opposition between the coloniser and the colonised in Western historiography where the former is constructed as the champion of civilisation and the latter as the uncivilised masses. Some settlers are reluctant to fight, arguing that the idea that "sent them sailing to Malagueta precluded the shedding of blood" (*LHAD* 164). When Captain Hammerstone prevents a funeral procession from passing by the garrison, the attitude of most reluctant members of the community changes from favouring peaceful coexistence to outright hostility. The armed action against the colonisers is justified as Gustavius Martins advocates that it cannot be regarded as a war but "as a legitimate act of expelling a pest" (*LHAD* 217).

In an attempt to demonstrate the superiority of the British Empire, Hammerstone introduces himself to the settlers as "a representative of a king who already controlled a large portion of the world between the islands of the Nordic tribes and the ancestral grounds of the aborigines of Australia, and with a vast trade in sugar, cotton, spices and gemstones" (*LHAD* 158). The captain justifies the presence of the colonial powers in the country simply by referring to their economic and military might. Contrary to his expectation, Hammerstone's words evoke hostility and hatred among the settlers as his very personage brings back the horrible memories of slavery. Thomas Bookerman's reply to the arrogant captain reflects the settlers' determination not to allow the colonisers to blow out their torch of freedom:

> You done come like a tief 'mongst us, and you gon tell us how you gon steal our land, how you gon build factories, and take our women and chillum for your bed and workshop. Ain't never known any king be good to black people. We all come here 'cause de king done lie to us; tell us fight for him and he gon give us land, gon give us respect and we gon be safe. And we done believe him, but he gives us land ain't fit for man or animal. People dying there 'cause ain't no thin you kin do wid dat land: marshes, swamps, thorns, thistles, and it's cold. So we come here and make dis place real nice, and we got a little happiness, and our women ain't afraid no more people gon be taking their chillum. Now you want to live here, but why you don't stay where you come from? Because we ain't gon be letting you do nothing to us now we free. We is our own men now, dem chains no longer round our necks and we ain't gon let you, you hear, Mr King. (*LHAD* 159)

Through his portrayal of the colonial expansion in Malagueta/Sierra Leone, Cheney-Coker lays bare the hegemonic strategies the British Empire employed in order to subjugate the indigenous people. Captain Hammerstone and his men pay their first visit to the clergy in the town, a group of nuns known as the twelve virgins. He promises to provide them with books, paper and ink necessary for the religious education they conduct in the church. Cheney-Coker registers the benefits of the visit almost with the astute observation of a historian: "The visit itself afforded the captain the important first link he had tried to make with the people of Malagueta. Through the exegesis of the church, he felt he could establish contact with a wide section of the community, so that he and his men would not have to go around explaining why they thought they could bring progress to the place" (*LHAD* 165). In addition to the clergy, the colonisers also exploit the poor by providing them with portions of sugar, flour and cooking oil in return for their labour. Captain Hammerstone recruits a group of natives for the construction of the garrison. The natives do not have any sympathy for the Malaguetans or the white men; they accept the job simply because they are driven by "the voracity of hunger" (*LHAD* 166). It is again amongst the poor that the captain organises an army of mercenaries that shall eventually defeat the resistance group led by Thomas Bookerman, paving the way for the establishment of colonial rule in the country.

Nonetheless, it is not the victory that the colonisers have won on the battleground, but the local community's obeisance to white imperial power that deprives the anti-colonial resistance in Malagueta/Sierra Leone. Historian John R. Cartwright observes that the Creoles, the dominant class in the country, modelled their lifestyle on that of their former masters as they valued "literacy in English, Christianity, and a marked attachment to English social values and to England as a spiritual home" (qtd. in Clarke 130). The gradual invasion of the Malaguetan society by shallow westernisation thus finds direct and forceful expression in the novel. In order to assimilate the local culture, the colonial administration systematically attacks the beliefs of the indigenous community. They are particularly concerned with the traditional practices that help the local people communicate with their ancestors. Thus, the first thing the colonial administration bans is "the practice of leaving food by the graveside of their beloved" on the ground that it is not "healthy" (*LHAD* 167). It is later followed by another ban on the visits paid to diviners and seers (*LHAD* 240). The colonisers restore the habits of bourgeoisie lifestyle in place of the traditional cultural practices. Parties where the local Creole community mixes with the colonisers become an important part of Malagueta's social life. They help instil in the people of Malagueta the notion of class consciousness since only the wealthy minority can attend the parties and other social gatherings organised by the colonisers. It is first through Isatu's naïve point of view that Cheney-Coker reveals the class divisions taking root in the country: "One day, she wasn't sure when, they were going to give up all façade of unity and start fighting each other, because they were already beginning to talk of the poor and the 'aristocrats' among them and developed serious notions of class" (*LHAD* 191).

With the rise of the aristocracy, the pride and self-confidence of the early settlers in their indigenous culture starts to give way to a communal inferiority complex since the people of Malagueta now see themselves as "men and women without the fine graces, refined speeches and manners which not so long ago they laughed at when practised by their spurious masters" (*LHAD* 214). They seek European validation by mimicking their lifestyle and cultural practices. Thomas Bookerman views with contempt the beginnings of the rise of an oligarchy: "men who only yesterday were shopkeepers with bad teeth and could barely read now ordered evening jackets in black Venetians and hopsacks; women who only yesterday were content to wear hand-me-downs and keep clean houses had taken to buying gold and parading in silk and brocade at church services" (*LHAD* 213). The mimicry of European masters has serious repercussions on the political history of the country. The new class of aristocrats prevent their sons from fighting on the side of the anti-colonists. While some of them even shake the hands of the soldiers or send gifts to Captain Hammerstone as if they were freeing them from tyranny, others become business allies with the colonisers, encouraging a truce so that they can continue prospering. Hence, the dream of communal unity that the founders of the country have established starts to dissolve. The disillusionment caused by the disintegration of the communal ties is reflected in Thomas Bookerman's decision to end the armed struggle and leave Malagueta for a while: "Finding himself surrounded by only those men resolved not to give up [...] Thomas Bookerman realised the hoped-for uprising would not materialise" (*LHAD* 235).

It is towards the end of the war between Captain Hammerstone and the anti-colonists that Sulaiman the Nubian, now known as Alusine Dunbar, returns to the town one hundred and fifty years after his death. He has grown invincible, for he has "conquered the last mystery of how to be alive in the same place where he [died] over a hundred years before" (*LHAD* 289). Yet, his unearthly power has not prepared him for the radical transformation that Malagueta has undergone in his absence. "The destruction has started," Alusine Dunbar laments as he discovers that all the familiar landmarks of the old town have been destroyed by the new administrators who try to stamp their rule on the town (*LHAD* 289). He goes through the town seven times until he finally finds the house of the gold merchant N'jai, where he lodged centuries ago. Ironically, it is an ancient baobab tree that helps the old magician to locate N'jai's house.

Before he arrives in town, Alusine Dunbar haunts Garbage in his dreams, instilling in him a deep thirst for knowledge and history. As his passion for history turns into an obsession, Garbage starts to wander in the streets of the town seeking the traces of the old settlers. On one of his solitary wanderings, he finds the owner of the voice that has been talking to him in an abandoned apothecary. Expecting the arrival of his young disciple, the old seer introduces himself, "[m]y name is Sulaiman the Nubian, but the sands of the desert erased that from the memory of this town a long time ago. Like the town itself, the meaning of that name belonged to a past harmattan which will not be repeated, so I changed it a long time ago to Alusine Dunbar, a name with which I hope to see the future of this town" (*LHAD* 287). Alusine Dunbar is also concerned with the eradication of the link between the old and the new generations of Malaguetans: "I am afraid for your generation because you are going to see such changes here that nothing would be left of the memory of Fatmatta the Bird-Woman" (*LHAD* 295). He, then, prophesises that "[o]ne age is about to end in Malagueta, a new reign without honour but with embellishment of falsehood […] is about to begin" (*LHAD* 304).

This premonition is not the only reason why he has returned to Malagueta, though. "I had seen the leopards," he confides in Garbage, "going for the goats and I had to come before they ate all of them" (*LHAD* 288). As his simple metaphor suggests, Alusine Dunbar has returned to rescue the people of Malagueta from the tyranny of colonialism.

Alusine Dunbar's clairvoyance proves to be true with the arrival of new colonising powers in two waves. First the English colonial reinforcement arrives in ships full of surveyors and soldiers and then the Arab traders who establish a coalition with the British, exploiting the diamond mines of the country. In the absence of a strong national opposition, Malagueta becomes "a town stamped with the permanence of English laws, [...] the blacks were themselves the messengers of the metaphysical transition – darkness to light, neo-paganism to classicism – the encyclopaedic mind of the English would be admired by the best sons and daughters of the town" (*LHAD* 259). Cheney-Coker is careful to note that the process of cultural assimilation that has begun with the original settlers' initial mimicking of the colonisers' luxurious lifestyle continues through the next generations,

> Some of the grandchildren of the original founders of the town were indeed drawn into all kinds of marriages with the new rulers. They were so fascinated with the prospect of being accepted into the houses of the English that they went to the Notary Public and changed their names from African to Christian so that the pronunciation would not break the jaw of the English when they met at parties. To the strings of music played by a black band that had been trained to play 'classical music' they forced their unclassical bodies to respond to the torturous strains of the baptism from 'native' to 'civilised.' (*LHAD* 325)

However, the colonial administrators are never satisfied and continue to impose new discriminatory laws against the people of Malagueta, insulting their racial and cultural background. For instance, when they open a new club house with a "beautiful garden" "surrounded by a one-foot-thick stone wall with a heavy iron gate at the entrance," they hang an inscription on its door, reading "Africans and dogs are not allowed" (*LHAD* 300).

The attitude of the public towards the colonial administration and the rising aristocracy start to change as there appear a number of riots and uprisings throughout the country: "A rising tide of resentment against the colonial regime and its local supporters was finding expressions in a boycott of stores, pressures on local workers to go on strike and an occasional spate of unexplained fires in various parts of Malagueta" (*LHAD* 368). Using the internal strife in the country as an excuse, the colonial administrators invite "the leaders of the people from the surrounding towns, which were now part of Malagueta, to sign a treaty which barred the great-grandchildren of the founders of Malagueta from ever owning land outside the area that Thomas Bookerman had painstakingly laid out" (*LHAD* 369). However, the atmosphere of social unrest remains in the country. Convinced that Malagueta is now ungovernable, the colonial administration starts to withdraw from the country, appointing a transitional government consisting of Ali Baba and his forty ministers. General Masimiara becomes the head of the army.

When Malagueta finally achieves independence after centuries of slavery and colonialism, the indigenous politicians prove to be far more vicious than the colonisers. "The encyclopaedic pillaging and theft that would grip Malagueta," the omniscient narrator bemoans, "began on the day Ali Baba and the forty ministers took over the reins of Malagueta" (*LHAD* 381). The first indigenous government is overthrown by General Misimiara, who becomes the head of the military government with Colonel Lookdown Okongo. Later, the trade union leader Saku Maru is invited to restore civil government in the country. Yet, his reign is also tainted with corruption and political tyranny, which motivates General Misimiara to stage a second coup. However, he is captivated and sentenced to death. It is at this darkest hour of the country that Alusine Dunbar comes back to Malagueta on a flying carpet. Using his supernatural powers, he unleashes a harmattan, a dust-laden wind, and cleanses Malagueta of the strains of dictatorship:

> President Sanka Maru walked to a window, pushed the curtains aside and saw a magic carpet flying in the air, not knowing that it had come a long way and that its arrival had been predicted by an albino afraid of light. Mesmerised by the occurrence, Sanka Maru thought he was seeing things when an old man lowered himself from the carpet, waved to him, and disappeared under a tree. (*LHAD* 395)

In her reading of the scene, Brenda Cooper draws attention to magical realism's role as a cultural corrective discourse: "This is what magical realism is all about – a genuine outrage against modern politicians motivates the novel which employs devices that are supernatural to make the point boldly and memorably" (142). The novel ends with the frozen tableau of public disgrace of those who plunder the nation's wealth and sources for personal gains.

Cheney-Coker's magical realist account of Sierra Leonean history in *The Last Harmattan of Alusine Dunbar* offers insightful information on the long and painful process of nation building with all its accompanying difficulties and problems. The history of Sierra Leone begins with a settlement established by a group of former slaves who return to their homeland from a slave plantation in America. Cheney-Coker does not treat diasporic community's aspirations to return to the land of origin in keeping with the conventional ethnic and nationalistic imaginings. He demonstrates that the utopian dream of homecoming is entangled with a series of cultural and social problems. Yet, in Sierra Leone, national consolidation requires more than communal integrity. The process of cultural integration between the returnees and the local community is interfered with by the colonial invasion. Perhaps more importantly, when the Malaguetans eventually declare their independence, they come to the bitter realisation that their indigenous politicians are not better than their old masters.

The subtlety of Cheney-Coker's magical realist design lies in his ability to blend the history of the country with its cultural repertoire, including such supernatural elements as seers, magicians sceptres and ghosts. Yet, the existence of the supernatural does not lead the novel to slip into a sense of escapism. Magical realism provides Cheney-Coker with the necessary textual space to reinterpret Sierra Leonean history from an indigenous perspective. It is through two magical characters, embodiments of Sierra Leonean cultural traditions, that Cheney-Coker lays bare the misconduct of the colonial administration as well as the tyrannical rule of the indigenous government. In explaining the role of Sulaiman the Nubian in the novel, Pietro Deandrea argues, "[t]he Creoles developed from the intermarriages of settler Africans from a number of ethnic groups and knew very little about their ancestors. Sulaiman's role in the novel is therefore akin to efforts made by the Creoles to fill this gap by tracing their own cultural genealogy [...]" (40). In other words, Sulaiman rewrites the country's history with his premonition that he has revealed at the beginning of the novel. Similarly, Fatmatta the Bird-Woman, the other key magical realist character in the novel, proves to be a textual agent of anti-colonial discourse. While her life in the slave plantations uncovers the ways in which slavery seeks to exploit the female body, her haunting sceptre protects the Malaguetan community against the colonisers. It can therefore be concluded that *The Last Harmattan Alusine Dunbar* presents a pertinent example of magical realism's ability to negotiate with the complex identity of the postcolonial subject and generate anti-colonial discourse by blending the real/the historical and the fantastic within the same textual body.

Conclusion

After a series of uncertain beginnings in the early twentieth century, magical realism seems to have finally arrived at its destination. Reified in syllabuses and bestowed a canon of its own, the mode has found a proper articulation both in academia and literary circles. It is now regarded as an acclaimed literary phenomenon on a global scale. However, in order to reach its current position, magical realism had to go through a series of trails of theoretical definition and appropriation as well as an effort to distance itself from its sister genre, the fantastic. Historically speaking, it was particularly after the proliferation of postcolonial literatures in the 1980s and the 1990s that magical realism achieved its current status as a major literary mode in world literature. The appropriation of magical realism into different cultural contexts made it difficult to formulate a set definition for the term. Although critics seem to agree upon the fact that the oxymoron suggests a combination of the real and the fantastic, their opinions with regard to the meaning of the resultant hybrid textual space differ to a great extent.

There are basically two theoretical approaches aimed at resolving the problem of definition. The first approach simply brings together the key theoretical texts written by the prominent practitioners and scholars of the mode in the form of a compendium. The other approach offers a list of generic characteristics drawn from the textual analysis of certain magical realist novels. Both approaches have made valuable contributions to the studies on magical realism, yet they also have certain drawbacks. While the former approach fails to establish analogies between the different theories of magical realism in a historical context, the latter generates a reductive way of viewing magical realism as it ignores the initial phase of the mode in its art-historical context.

Aiming to explore the function of magical realism in the novelistic representation of history and national identities in Anglophone postcolonial literature, this study has covered the history and development of the term "magical realism" from its inception to the present and identified the defining characteristics of the mode by establishing analogies between its appropriation in different cultural and historical contexts. Accordingly, the first and second chapters have surveyed the theoretical development of magical realism in order to identify the characteristics of the mode that make its wide dissemination and appropriation in different cultural contexts possible. In the light of the conclusions drawn from the first part of the study, the third and fourth chapters have attempted to delineate the place of magical realism in postcolonial Anglophone fiction through a textual analysis of the four novels selected from the two major postcolonial locations, India and Africa. This chapter attempts to summarise the fundamental findings and conclusions drawn from the study and emphasises the weight, originality and contribution of the research.

The survey and analyses of the bulk of the theoretical work on magical realism have shown that the term has undergone dramatic shifts throughout its long history. Yet, it is still possible to discern certain shared concerns and patterns of thought in its theoretical development. In the course of research, it has become increasingly evident that magical realism appeared as a dominant narrative mode in different locations following a period of cultural crisis. Initially Franz Roh and then Massimo Bontempelli formulated their theories of magical realism in the aftermath of the Great War. Similarly, the appearance of magical realist works of fiction in Latin America and former colonies coincided with the end of colonial hegemony. In other words, magical realism has been symptomatic of cultural crisis. Magic realist artists and magical realist writers attempted to heal the wounds caused by the Great War or a trauma experienced immediately after the collapse of the institutionalised colonial administration by incorporating the formal and thematic possibilities of magical realism into their works.

The idea of cultural healing, however, is not the sole factor that helps link the pictorial origin of the term with its later appropriation into literature. As its very name suggests, magical realism offers a new and an innovative way of representing reality, yet the experimentalism inherent in the mode is always and necessarily anchored in phenomenal reality. Much of the theoretical effort in defining magical realism has been devoted to the techniques of espousing the real and the fantastic within a single textual body and the thematic possibilities such a combination can bring forward. As has been noted time and again throughout this study, it is particularly this unceasing process of (re)definition and (re)appropriation of the concept that provides magical realism with its creative energies.

The critical genealogy of magical realism presented in the first chapter has helped formulate one of the principle arguments of the present study: magical realism is an outcome of a long and diverse tradition with certain recurrent themes and shared artistic concerns. It is a literary mode that has been distinguished from its inception by three defining characteristics. First, magical realism is an innovative narrative mode, seeking new ways of presenting and interpreting empirical reality through artistic experimentation. Second, the experimental fervour inherent in the mode does not lead the artist to lose his/her touch with social and historical realities of the time. Third, magical realism is a profoundly flexible narrative mode, easily adaptable to different theoretical and cultural contexts. These three defining characteristics have stayed with the mode throughout its historical development. Therefore, the main thrust of this study has been centred on the findings presented in chapter 1 as they provide an interpretive grid necessary for the analysis of the selected novels.

It was with the emergence of postcolonial studies seeking a cultural reconciliation between the coloniser and the colonised that magical realism found a proper theoretical formulation. Contrary to the essentialist view of magical realism as an authentic expression of Latin America, the critics of the new paradigm focused on the textual possibilities of the mode that enable postcolonial writers to negotiate with the complex composite identity of the postcolonial subject and thereby generate an anti-colonial discourse. Consequently, a new critical vocabulary emerged to define magical realism in the works of influential postcolonial critics. Homi Bhabha's "third space," Suzanne Baker's "dual spatiality" and Brenda Cooper's "fertile interstices" are all aimed at describing the narrative possibilities provided by magical realism. The sense of ambiguity and change prevalent in their formulations in fact reflect the futility of the theoretical efforts to pin down this highly elusive concept that draws its creative power from its constant appropriation into new theoretical and cultural contexts.

Chapters 3 and 4 have incorporated the conclusions drawn from the theoretical discussions on magical realism in the foregoing sections in analysing the four novels selected for this study. The discussion conducted in these chapters is centred on the question of how the novelists have exploited the third space provided by magical realism in their representation of history and nation. Being the fruits of magical realist writers' desire to revisit their history as well as their enthusiasm for reinventing that past, the four novels provide symptomatic instantiations of the relationship between history, nation and narration. The four novelists critically return to a wide range of historical moments and open successful and thought-provoking dialogues with their national past. Hence, the novels in question should be seen as revisionist attempts espoused with the narrative possibilities of magical realism rather than mere fictionalisations of history to authenticate its representation. The socio-political history is presented side by side with the indigenous cultural repertoire, including myths, legends and beliefs in supernatural entities, such as seers, magicians and ghosts. The equilibrium between the two narrative planes, the fantastic and the historical, is mediated through the narrators that relate their stories in a matter-of-fact style.

First and foremost, the analysis of the four novels has demonstrated magical realism's capacity to negotiate the issues of cultural diversity, hybridity and nation formation as well as its ability to respond to stylistic variations inherent in postcolonial literatures. The four novels considered here explore a multitude of thematic possibilities and are products of different artistic tendencies and writing techniques. In the Indian subcontinent, Salman Rushdie and Shashi Tharoor wrote their novels within the convergence of postcolonialism and postmodernism in the 1980s. Both writers' creative power lies in their critique of the official accounts of Indian history through a vigorous combination of postmodern writing techniques and magical realism. Whilst they make visible those facts obscured by Western historiography by calling upon ancient myths and legends of the nation, they also show that they are fully aware of the manipulative power of historiography and draw attention to its status as a narrative construct. The novels in question provide insights into the role magical realism played in the transformation the Indian English novel underwent in the 1980s.

The novels selected from Anglophone African literature, Ben Okri's *The Famished Road* and Syl Cheney-Coker's *The Last Harmattan of Alusine Dunbar* do not share the postmodernist experimentation of their Indian counterparts, but they are both profoundly concerned with hybrid cultural identity. These two African novelists reinvigorate myths, cultural traditions and beliefs in order to depict the painful process of national consolidation in the aftermath of political independence. In *The Famished Road* Ben Okri revives the ancient myth of the *abiku* in order to portray the contemporary political history of Nigeria. Unlike the other three novelists treated here, Cheney-Coker employs magical realism in relating the history of a fictional country, Malagueta, which metaphorically stands for his home country, Sierra Leone. Consequently, the stylistic distance between the four novelists has helped to validate one of the theoretical contentions of this study: magical realism is a flexible narrative mode capable of responding to a variety of stylistic and thematic inclinations in different literary traditions.

As the conclusions drawn from this survey have demonstrated, magical realism does not necessarily rise out of particular societies where scientific and magical views of the world coexist. It is a narrative mode that draws its creative energies from a blending of binaries as manifested in its oxymoronic name. The successful incorporation of magical realism into the four novels and the transformation they led to in the history of the Indian and African English literatures have concurred with the findings presented as hypotheses in the early part of the study. While Rushdie's magical realist *magnum opus* paved the way for a new wave of writers dubbed the post-Rushdie generation, including Shashi Tharoor himself, Ben Okri and Syl Cheney-Coker's experimentation with the mode help them to find their individual literary voices, distancing them from the preceding literary tradition and its dominant writers. Perhaps the most important influence of magical realism on postcolonial writing has been its role in the transformation of the novel from being a mere imitation of the Western mimetic tradition to an active dialogic discourse of decolonisation, giving voice to silent or silenced communities. Given the wide dissemination of magical realism and its growing popularity in the current literary scene, the present study can only be regarded as an accessible introduction to major critical concerns and issues related to magical realism. Yet, it is hoped that the historical survey presented shall provide a critical medium for the exploration of magical realism in different literary traditions.

WORKS CITED

ABRAMS, M. H. and Geoffrey G. Harpham. *A Glossary of Literary Terms.* 9th ed. Boston: Wadsworth Cengage, 2009.

ACHEBE, Chinua. "The Novelist as Teacher." (1965). *Hopes and Impediments: Selected Essays.* Doubleday: London, 1989. 40-46.

___. "An Image of Africa: Racism in Conrad's *Heart of Darkness.*" (1975) *Hopes and Impediments: Selected Essays.* Doubleday: London, 1989. 1-20.

___. *Things Fall Apart.* (1958) Johannesburg: Heinemann, 1996.

ADENIJI, Abiodun. "The Spirit-child as a Metaphor for Disruption and Cohesion in Nigerian Literature: A Case Study of Fagunwa, Tutuola, Achebe, Soyinka, Clark-Bekederemo and Okri." *Literature, Language and National Consciousness.* Eds. T. A. Ezeigbo and K. King-Aribisala. Lagos: U. of Lagos P. 193-206.

ALLENDE, Isabel. "Writing As an Act of Hope." *Paths of Resistance: The Art and Craft of the Political Novel.* Ed. William Zinsser. Boston: Houghton Mifflin, 1989. 41-63.

ANDERSON, Benedict. *Imagined Communities: Reflections on the Origin and Spread of Nationalism.* New York: Verso, 1983.

ARISTOTLE, *Poetics.* Trans. John Warrington. New York: Everyman's Library, 1963.

ASHCROFT, Bill. *Post-colonial Transformation.* London: Routledge, 2001.

ASHCROFT, Bill, Gareth Griffiths, and Helen Tiffin, Eds. *The Empire Writes Back: Theory and Practice in PostColonial Literatures.* London: Routledge, 1989.

___. Eds. *Key Concepts in Postcolonial Studies.* London: Routledge, 1998.

___. Eds. *The Post-colonial Studies Reader.* London: Routledge, 1995.

BAKER, Suzanne. "Binarism and Duality: Magic Realism and Postcolonialism." *SPAN: Journal of the South Pacific Association for Commonwealth Literature and Language Studies.* 36.1 (1993). 82-87.

___. "Magic Realism as a Postcolonial Strategy: *The Kadaitcha Sung.*" *SPAN: Journal of the South Pacific Association for Commonwealth Literature and Language.* 32 (1991). 55-63.

BAKHTIN, Mikhail M. "Discourse in the Novel." (1935) *The Dialogic Imagination.* Ed. Michael Holquist. Trans. Caryl Emerson and Michael Holquist. Austin: U. of Texas P., 1981. 259-422.

___. "Epic and Novel: Towards a Methodology for the Study of the Novel." (1941) *The Dialogic Imagination.* Ed. Michael Holquist. Trans. Caryl Emerson and Michael Holquist. Austin: U. of Texas P., 1981. 3-40.

___. "From the Prehistory of Novelistic Discourse." (1940) *The Dialogic Imagination.* Ed. Michael Holquist. Trans. Caryl Emerson and Michael Holquist. Austin: U. of Texas P., 1981. 41-83.

___. *Problems of Dostoevsky's Poetics.* Ed. and Trans. Caryl Emerson. Minneapolis: Minnesota UP, 1984.

BALL, John Clement. "Pessoptimism: Satire and the Menippean Grotesque in Rushdie's *Midnight's Children.*" *Salman Rushdie.* Ed. Harold Bloom. Philedephia: Yale UP, 2003. 209-232.

BARKER, Francis, Peter Hulme and Margaret Iversen. "Introduction." *Colonial Discourse and Postcolonial Theory.* Manchester: Manchester UP, 1994.

BARRY, Peter. *Beginning Theory: An Introduction to Literary and Cultural Theory.* Manchester: Manchester UP, 1995.

BARTHES, Roland. *S/Z.* Trans. Richard Miller. New York: Hill and Wang, 1974.

BATTY, Nancy E. "The Art of Suspense: Rushdie's 1001 (Mid-)Nights." *Reading Rushdie: Perspectives on the Fiction of Salman Rushdie.* Ed. D. M Fletcher. Atlanta: Rodopi, 1994. 69-81.

BHABHA, Homi K. *The Location of Culture.* London: Routledge. 1994.

BOEHMER, Elleke. *Colonial and Postcolonial Literature: Migrant Metaphors.* Oxford: Oxford UP, 1995.

___. "Transfiguring: Colonial Body into Postcolonial Narrative." *Novel: A Forum on Fiction* (Spring 1993): 26.3, African Literature Issue. 268-277.

BOOKER, Keith M. *Critical Essays on Salman Rushdie.* New York: G.K. Hall, 1999.

BOWERS, Maggie Ann. *Magic(al) Realism.* London: Routledge, 2004.

BRENNAN, Timothy. "The National Longing for Form." *The Postcolonial Studies Reader.* Eds. Bill Ashcroft, Gareth Griffiths, and Helen Tiffin. London: Routledge, 1995. 170-175.

CARPENTIER, Alejo. "On the Marvelous Real in America." (1949) Trans. Tanya Hungtinton and Lois Parkinson Zamora. *Magical Realism: Theory, History and Community.* Eds. Lois Parkinson Zamora and Wendy B. Faris. Durham: Duke UP, 1995. 75-88.

___. "The Baroque and the Mavelous Real." (1975) Trans. Tanya Hungtinton and Luis Parkinson Zamora. *Magical Realism: Theory, History and Community.* Eds. Lois Parkinson Zamora and Wendy B. Faris. Durham: Duke UP, 1995. 89-108.

___. *The Kingdom of This World.* (1949) Trans. Harriet De Onis. New York: Farrar, Straus and Giroux, 2006.

CÉSAIRE, Aimé. *Notebook of a Return to the Native Land.* (1939) *The Collected Poetry of Aimé Césaire.* Trans. Clayton Eshleman and Annette Smith. Berkley: U. of California P., 1983.

CHAMBERLAIN, Lori. "Magicking the Real: Paradoxes of Postmodern Writing." *Postmodern Fiction*. Westport: Greenwood, 1986. 5-19.

CHANADY, Amaryll Beatrice. *Magical Realism and the Fantastic: Resolved Versus Unresolved Antinomy*. New York: Garland, 1985.

___. "The Territorialization of the Imaginary in Latin America: Self-affirmation and Resistance to Metropolitan Paradigms." *Magical Realism: Theory, History and Community*. Eds. Lois Parkinson Zamora and Wendy B. Faris. Durham: Duke UP, 1995. 125-144.

CHENEY-COKER, Syl. *The Last Harmattan of Alusine Dunbar*. London: Heinemann, 1990.

CHILDS, Peter, and R. J. Patrick Williams. *An Introduction to Post-Colonial Theory*. London: Prentice Hall, 1987.

CHING, Erik, Christina Buckley and Angelica Lozano-Alonso. "Introduction(s)" *Reframing Latin America: A Cultural Theory of Reading of the Nineteenth and Twentieth Centuries*. Eds. Erik Ching, Christina Buckley and Angelica Lozano-Alonso. Austin: U. of Texas P., 2007.

CLARKE, George Elliott. *Odysseys Home: Mapping African-Canadian Literature*. Toronto: U. of Toronto P., 2002.

CLIFFORD, Mary Louise. *The Land and People of Sierra Leone*. New York: J. B. Lippincott, 1974.

COLLINS, Larry and Dominique Lapierre. *Freedom at Midnight*. New Delhi: Vikas, 1976.

COOPER, Brenda. *Magical Realism in West African Fiction: Seeing with a Third Eye*. New York: Routledge, 1998.

CRANE, Ralph J. *Inventing India: A History of India in English-Language Fiction*. London: Macmillan, 1992.

DAS, Bijay Kumar. *Postmodern Indian English Literature*. New Delhi: Atlantic, 2003.

DASH, Michael. "Marvellous Realism: The Way out of Négritude." *The Post-colonial Studies Reader.* Eds. Bill Ashcroft, Gareth Griffiths, and Helen Tiffin. London: Routledge, 1995. 199-201.

DAVIS, Angela. *Women, Race and Class.* New York: Random House, 1981.

DESANI, G.V. *All About H. Hatterr.* 1948. New Delhi: Penguin, 1998.

DESHPANDE, C. R. *Transmission of the Mahabharata Tradition: Vyasa and Vyasids.* Simla: Indian Institute of Advanced Study, 1979.

DEANDREA, Pietro. *Fertile Crossings: Metamorphoses of Genre in Anglophone West African Literature.* Amsterdam: Rodopi, 2002.

D'HAEN, Theo L. "Postmodernisms: From Fantastic to Magic Realist." *International Postmodernism: Theory and Literary Practice.* Eds. Hans Bertens and Douwe Fokkema. Amsterdam: John Benjamins, 1997. 283-293.

DHARWADKER, Aparna and Vinay Dharwadker. "Language, Identity and Nation in Postcolonial Indian English Literature." *English Post-coloniality: Literatures from Around the World.* Ed. Radhika Mohanram and Gita Rajan. London: Greenwood, 1996. 90-106.

DOMBROSKI, Robert. "The Rise and Fall of Fascism." *The Cambridge History of Italian Literature.* Eds. Peter Brand and Lino Pertile. Cambridge: Cambridge UP, 1996. 493-497

DURIX, Jean-Pierre. *Mimesis, Genres, and Post-Colonial Discourse: Deconstructing Magic Realism.* New York: St. Martin's, 1998.

___. "Salman Rushdie." *Conversations with Salman Rushdie.* Ed. Michael R. Reder. Jackson: UP of Mississippi, 2000. 8-17.

DUTT, Kailash Chunder. "A Journal of Forty-Eight Hours of the Year 1945." *Selections from 'Bengaliana.* Comp. and ed. Alex Tickell. Nottingham: Trent, 2005. 149-159.

DUTT, Shoshee Chunder, *The Republic of Orissa: A Page from the Annals of the Twentieth Century.* 1845. Rpt. ed. Subhendu Mund. *Sateertha Bulletin.* Spring, 1995. 12-16.

ECHEVARRÍA, Roberto González. *Alejo Carpentier: The Pilgrim at Home.* London: Cornell UP, 1977.

ELLIOTT, J. E. "What's 'Post' in Post-Colonial Theory?" *Borderlands: Negotiating Boundaries* in *Postcolonial Writing.* Ed. Monika Reif Hülser. Amsterdam: Rodopi, 1999. 43-56

FANON, Frantz. *The Wretched of the Earth.* (1961) Trans. Constance Farrington. Suffolk: Penguin, 1963.

___. *Black Skin, White Masks.* (1952) Trans. Charles Lam Markmann. London: Pluto, 2008.

FARIS, Wendy B. *Ordinary Enchantments: Magical Realism and the Remystification of Narrative.* Nashville: Vanderbilt UP, 2004.

___. "The Question of the Other: Cultural Critiques of Magical Realism." *Janus Head* 5.2 (2002): 101-119.

___. "Scheherazade's Children: Magical Realism and Postmodern Fiction." *Magical Realism: Theory, History, Community.* Eds. Lois Parkinson Zamora and Wendy B. Faris. Durham: Duke UP, 1995. 163-190.

FLORES, Ángel. "Magical Realism in Spanish American Literature." *Magical Realism: Theory, History and Community.* Eds. Lois Parkinson Zamora and Wendy B. Faris. Durham: Duke UP, 1995. 109-117.

FRANCO, JEAN. *An Introduction to Spanish-American Literature.* London: Cambridge UP, 1969.

GANDHI, Leela. *Postcolonial Theory: A Critical Introduction.* New York: Columbia UP, 1998.

GIKANDI, Simon. "Chinua Achebe." *Encyclopedia of African Literature.* Ed. Simon Gikandi. London: Routledge, 2005. 9-13.

___. "Colonialism, Neocolonialism and Postcolonialism." *Encyclopedia of African Literature.* Ed. Simon Gikandi. London: Routledge, 2005. 169-176.

GONZÁLEZ, Aníbal. "Literary Criticism in Spanish America." *The Cambridge History of Latin American Literature: The Twentieth Century. Vol. II.* Ed. Roberto González Echevarría and Enrique Pupo-Walker. Cambridge: Cambridge UP, 1996.

GOPAL, Priyamvada. *The Indian English Novel: Nation, History, and Narration.* New York: Oxford UP, 2009.

GORRA, Michael Edward. *After Empire: Scott, Naipaul, Rushdie.* Chicago: U. of Chicago P., 1997.

GUENTHER, Irene. "Magic Realism, New Objectivity, and the Arts during the Weimar Republic." *Magical Realism: Theory, History and Community.* Eds. Lois Parkinson Zamora and Wendy B. Faris. Durham: Duke UP, 1995. 33-73.

HALL, Stuart. "Cultural Identity and Diaspora." *Identity, Community, Culture, Difference.* Ed. Jonathon Rutherford. London: Lawrence & Wishart, 1990. 222-237.

HART, Steven M. "Magical Realism: Style and Substance." *A Companion to Magical Realism.* Eds. Stephen Hart and Wen-chin Ouyang. Woodbridge: Tamesis, 2005. 1-13.

HAYASHIDA, Nelson O. *Dreams in the African Church.* Amsterdam: Rodopi, 1999.

HAWLEY, John C. "Ben Okri's Spirit-Child: *Abiku* Migration and Postmodernity." *Research in African Literatures* 26.1 (1995): 30-39.

HEGERFELDT, Anne C. *Lies that Tell the Truth: Magic Realism Seen through Contemporary Fiction from Britain.* Amsterdam: Rodopi, 2005.

HUTCHEON, Linda. "The Pastime of Past Time: Fiction, History, Historiographic Metafiction." *Postmodern Genres*. Ed. Marjorie Pweloff. Norman: U. Of Oklahoma P, 1989. 54-75.

___. *Poetics of Postmodernism: History, Theory, Fiction*. New York: Routledge, 1988.

IMBERT, Enrique Anderson. *El Realismo mágico y otros ensayos*. Caracas: Monte Avila, 1975.

IRELE, Abiola. "Négritude: Ideology and Literature." *Philosophy from Africa: A Text with Readings*. Ed. P. H. Coetzee and A. P. J. Roux. Cape Town: Oxford UP, 2002.

ISER, Wolfgang. *The Implied Reader: Patterns of Communication in Prose Fiction from Bunyan to Beckett*. Baltimore: Johns Hopkins UP, 1974.

JAMESON, Fredrick. "On Magic Realism in Film." *Critical Inquiry* 12.2 (1986): 301-325.

JEWELL, Keala. "Massimo Bontempelli." *Encyclopaedia of Italian Literary Studies*. Vol. 1. Ed. Gaetana Marrone. London: Routledge, 2007.

KAFKA, Franz. *Metamorphosis. The Penguin Complete Short Stories of Franz Kafka*. Trasns. Willa and Edwin Muir. Ed. Nahum N. Glatzer. Harmondsworth: Penguin, 1954.

KANAGANAYAKAM, Chelva. *Configurations of Exile*: South Asian Writers and Their World. Toronto: Tsar, 1995. 96-110.

KERMODE, Frank. *The Sense of an Ending; Studies in the Theory of Fiction*. New York: Oxford UP, 1967.

KING, Bruce. *The Internationalization of English Literature*. Oxford: Oxford UP, 2004.

KRISTEVA, Julia. *Desire in Language: A Semiotic Approach to Literature and Art*. Trans. Thomas Gora, Alice Jardine and Leon S. Roudiez. Ed. Leon S. Roudiez. New York: Columbia UP, 1980.

LATHER, Patti. *Getting Smart: Feminist Research and Pedagogy With/In the Postmodern*. New York: Routledge, 1991.

LAUTRÉMONT, C. De. *The Songs of Maldoror* (*Les Chants de Maldoror*). Trans. G. Wernham. New York: New Directions, 1943.

LEAL, Luis. "Magical Realism in Spanish American Literature." Trans. Wendy B. Faris. *Magical Realism: Theory, History and Community*. Eds. Lois Parkinson Zamora and Wendy B. Faris. Durham: Duke UP, 1995. 119-124.

LIM, David C., ed. *The Infinite Longing for Home: Desire and the Nation in Selected Writings of Ben Okri and K. S. Maniam*. New York: Rodopi, 2004.

LIMAN, Abubakar. "Postcolonial Discourse: The Case of Ben Okri's *Famished Road. Currents in African Literature and the English Language* 1.1 (1977): 63-79.

LOTHSPEICH, Pamela. "*The Mahabharata's* Imprint on Contemporary Literature and Film." *Culture in a Globalised India*. Eds. K. Moti Gokulsing and Wimal Dissanayake. New York: Routledge, 2009.

The Mahabharata. Trans. Chakravarthi V. Narasimhan. New York: Colombia UP, 1998.

MÁRQUEZ, Gabriel García. *One Hundred Years of Solitude*. Trans. Gregory Rabassa. New York: Harper & Row, 1970.

___. "Conversation with Plinio Apuleyo Mendoza: Writing, Inspiration and Magic Realism." 23 Sept. 2009. <http://www.ranadasgupta.com/printer_friendly.asp?pagetype=N&id=52>

McGRATH, Kevin. *The Sanskrit Hero: Karṇa in Epic Mahābhārata*. Leiden: Brill, 2004.

McLEOD, John. *Beginning Postcolonialism*. Manchester: Manchester UP, 2000.

MEHROTRA, Arvind Krishna. "Introduction." *A History of Indian Literature in English.* Ed. Arvind Krishna Mehrotra. London: Hurst, 2003. 1-27.

MENTON, Seymour. *Magic Realism Rediscovered 1918-1981.* Philadelphia: The Art Alliance, 1983.

___. "Magical Realism: An Annotated International Chronology of the Term." *Essays in Honor of Frank Dauster.* Eds. Kristen F. Nigro and Sandra M.Cypress. Newark: Juan de la Cuestra, 1995. 125-155.

METCALF, Barbara D., and Thomas R. Metcalf. *A Concise History of India.* Edinburgh: Cambridge UP, 2001.

MISHRA, Vijay, and Bob Hodge "What is Post(-)colonialism?" Ed. Patrick Williams and Laura Christman. *Colonial and Post-Colonial Theory: A Reader.* New York: Harvester Wheatsheaf: 1993. 276-290.

MOH, Felicia Oka. *Ben Okri: An Introduction to His Early Fiction.* Nigeria: Fourth Dimension, 2001.

MONTROSE, Louis A. "Professing the Renaissance: The Poetics and Politics of Culture." *The New Historicism.* Ed. H. Aram Veeser. London: Routledge, 1989. 15-36.

MPHAHLELE, Ezekiel. *Voices in the Whirlwind and Other Essays.* London: MacMillan, 1972.

MUKHERJEE, Meenakshi. "The Beginnings of the Indian Novel." *A History of Indian Literature in English.* Ed. Arvind Krishna Mehrotra. London: Hurst, 2003. 92-102.

NANAVATI, U. M. and Prafulla C. Kar. "Introduction." *Rethinking Indian English Literature.* Eds. U. M. Nanavati and Prafulla C. Kar. New Delhi: Pencraft, 2000.

NANDY, Ashis. *The Intimate Enemy: Loss and Recovery of Self under Colonialism.* New Delhi: Oxford UP, 1983.

NEHRU, Jawaharlal. Speech delivered in the Constituent Assembly, New Delhi, August 14, 1947, on the eve of the attainment of Independence. Modern History Sourcebook <http://www.fordham.edu/halsall/mod/1947nehru1.html> 21 Aug., 2009.

NICHOLS, Prescott S. "Cesaire's Native Land and the Third World." *Twentieth Century Literature* 18.3 (1972). 156-166.

"Nobel Prize." <http://nobelprizes.com/nobel/literature/> 23 Jan. 2009.

OGOT, Bethwell A. "Kenya Under the British, 1895 to 1963." *Zamani: A Survey of East African History*. Eds. B. A. Ogot and J. A. Kieran. Nairobi: East African Publishing House, 1968. 255-290.

OGUDE, James. "East African Literature in English." *Encyclopedia of African Literature*. Ed. Simon Gikandi. London: Routledge, 2005. 220-227.

OKRI, Ben. *Birds of Heaven*. London: Phoenix, 1996.

___. *The Famished Road*. New York: Anchor, 1993.

OLIVA, Renato. "Redreaming the World: Okri's Shamanic Realism." *Coterminous Worlds: Magical Realism and Contemporary Postcolonial Literature in English*. Amsterdam: Radopi, 1999. 171-196.

OMAN, John Campbell. *The Great Indian Epics: The Stories of The Ramayana and The Mahabharata*. New Delhi: Asian Educational Service, 1994.

ONEGA, Suzan. "A Knack of Yarns: The Narrativization of History and the End of History." *Telling Histories: Narrativizing History, Historicizing Literature*. Ed. Suzan Onega. Amsterdam: Radopi, 1995. 7-18.

OUYANG, Wen-chin. "Magical Realism and Beyond: Ideology of Fantasy." *A Companion to Magical Realism*. Ed. Stephen Hart and Wen-chin Ouyang. Woodbridge: Tamesis, 2005, 13-20.

PALMER, Eustace. "Re-lighting Sierra Leonean History: A Comparative Study of the Re-interpretation of Aspects of Sierra Leonean History by Syl Cheney-Coker and Yema Lucilda Hunter." *New Perspectives on Sierra Leone Krio.* Eds. Mac Dixon-Fyle and Gibril Cole. New York: Peter Lang, 2006.

PARRY, Benita. *Postcolonial Studies: A Materialist Critique.* New York: Routledge, 2005.

PRICE, David W. *History Made, History Imagined: Contemporary Literature, Poiesis, and The Past.* Chicago: U. of Illinois P., 1999.

QUAYSON, Ato. "Magical Realism and the African Novel." *The Cambridge Companion to the African Novel.* Ed. F. Abiola Irele. Cambridge: Cambridge UP, 2009. 159-176.

RAO, A. Sudhakar. *Myth and History in Contemporary Indian Novel in English.* New Delhi: Atlantic, 2000.

REDER, Michael. "Rewriting History and Identity: The Reinvention of Myth, Epic, and Allegory in Salman Rushdie's *Midnight's Children.*" *Critical Essays on Salman Rushdie.* Ed. M. Keith Booker. New York: G. K. Hall, 1999. 225-254.

REEDS, Kenneth. "Magical Realism: A Problem of Definition." *Neophilologus* 90 (2006): 175-196.

REISS, Timothy. J. "Négritude." "Nationalism and Post-nationalism." *Encyclopedia of African Literature.* Ed. Simon Gikandi. London: Routledge, 2005. 506-509.

REYNOLDS, Margaret, and Jonathan Noakes. *Midnight's Children, Shame, The Satanic Verses: The Essential Guide to Contemporary Literature.* London: Vintage, 2003.

RICHARDS, David. "Framing Identities." *A Concise Companion to Postcolonial Literature.* Ed. Sherly Chew and David Richards. Oxford: Wiley-Blackwell, 2010. 9-28.

ROBB, Peter. *A History of India*. New York: Palgrave, 2002.

ROH, Franz. "Magic Realism: Post Expressionism." Trans. Wendy B. Faris. *Magical Realism: Theory, History and Community*. Eds. Lois Parkinson Zamora and Wendy B. Faris. Durham: Duke UP, 1995, 16-31.

RUSHDIE, Salman. "Commonwealth Literature Does not Exist." *Imaginary Homelands: Essays and Criticism 1981-1991*. London: Granta, 1991. 63-70.

___. "Dynasty." *Imaginary Homelands: Essays and Criticism 1981-1991*. London: Granta, 1991. 47-52.

___. "Errata or Unreliable Narration in *Midnight's Children*." *Imaginary Homelands: Essays and Criticism 1981-1991*. London: Granta, 1991. 22-25.

___. "Gabriel García Márquez." *Imaginary Homelands: Essays and Criticism 1981-1991*. London: Granta, 1991. 299-307.

___. "Imaginary Homelands." *Imaginary Homelands: Essays and Criticism 1981-1991*. London: Granta, 1991. 9-21.

___. "In God We Trust" *Imaginary Homelands: Essays and Criticism 1981-1991*. London: Granta, 1991, 376-392.

___. "In Good Faith." *Imaginary Homelands: Essays and Criticism 1981-1991*. London: Granta, 1991. 393-414

___. "Introduction." *Imaginary Homelands: Essays and Criticism 1981-1991*. London: Granta, 1991. 1-6

___. *Midnight's Children*. New York: Knopf, 1981.

___. "The Assassination of Indira Gandhi." *Imaginary Homelands: Essays and Criticism 1981-1991*. London: Granta, 1991. 41-46.

___. "The Riddle of Midnight." *Imaginary Homelands: Essays and Criticism 1981-1991*. London: Granta, 1991. 26-33.

SAFRAN, William. "Diasporas in Modern Societies: Myths of Homeland and Return." *Diaspora* 1.1(1993): 83-99

SAID, Edward. *Orientalism*. 1978. London: Penguin, 1995.

SALAT, M. F. "Making the Past Present: Shashi Tharoor's *The Great Indian Novel*." *Contemporary Indian Fiction in English*. Ed. Avadhesh K. S. Singh. New Delhi: Creative, 1993. 125-134.

SCHROEDER, Shannin. *Rediscovering Magical Realism in Americas*. London: Praeger, 2004.

SHARMA, Meenakshi. "Narrating India: Strategies of Narrativisation and Historiography in Shashi Tharoor's *The Great Indian Novel* and Vikram Seth's *A Suitable Boy*." *Writing in a Postcolonial Space*. Ed. Surya Nath Pandey. New Delhi: Atlantic, 1999. 125-140.

SIMPKINS, Scott. "Sources of Magical Realism/Supplements to Realism in Contemporary Latin American Literature." *Magical Realism: Theory, History and Community*. Eds. Lois Parkinson Zamora and Wendy B. Faris. Durham: Duke UP, 1995. 145-159.

SHAH, Nila. *Novel as History: Salman Rushdie, Shashi Tharoor, Rohinton Mistry, Vikram Seth, Mukul Kesavan*. New Delhi: Creative, 2003.

SINGH, K. S. "*The Mahabharata*: An anthropological Perspective." Ed. K. S. Singh. *The Mahabharata in the Tribal and Folk Traditions of India*. New Delhi: Indian Institute of Advanced Study, 1993. 1-9.

SINGH, K. H. Kunjo, *Humanism and Nationalism in Tagore's Novels*. Delhi: Nice, 2002. 26-39.

SLEMON, Steven. "Modernism's Last Post." *Past the Last Post: Theorizing Post-Colonialism and Post-Modernism*. Hemel Hempstead: Harvester Wheatsheaf, 1991. 1-11

___. "Magic Realism as Postcolonial Discourse." *Magical Realism: Theory, History, Community.* Eds. Lois Parkinson Zamora and Wendy B. Faris. Durham: Duke UP, 1995. 407-427

SOMMER, Doris. "Irresistible Romance: The Foundational Fictions of Latin America." *Nation and Narration.* Ed. Homi K. Bhabha. London: Routledge, 1990. 71-98.

SOYINKA, Wole. *Art, Dialogue, and Outrage: Essays on Literature and Culture.* New York: Pantheon, 1994

SPINDLER, William. "Magical Realism: A Typology." *Forum for Modern Language Studies.* 29.1 (1993): 76-85.

THAROOR, Shashi. *Bookless in Baghdad and Other Writings about Reading.* New Delhi: Penguin, 2005.

___. *India: From Midnight to the Millennium and Beyond.* New Delhi: Penguin, 1997.

___. *The Great Indian Novel.* Delhi: Penguin, 1989.

___. "Of Novels and Nations: A Diverse Life in a Diverse World." *Harvard International Review* (Fall 2002): 78-81.

TODOROV, Tzvetan. *The Fantastic: A Structural Approach to a Literary Genre.* Trans. Richard Howard. Ithaca: Cornell UP, 1975.

WALDER, Dennis. *PostColonial Literatures in English. History, Language, Theory.* Oxford: Blackwell, 1998.

WALTER, Roland. *Magical Realism in Contemporary Chicano Fiction.* Frankfurt: Vervuert, 1993.

WARNES, Christopher. "Naturalizing the Supernatural: Faith, Irreverence and Magical Realism." *Literature Compass* 2 (2005): 1-16.

WHITE, Hyden. *Tropics of Discourse: Essays in Cultural Criticism.* Baltimore: Johns Hopkins UP, 1979. 90-99.

WIEMANN, Dirk. *Genres of Modernity Contemporary Indian Novels in English.* Amsterdam: Rodopi, 2008.

WILKINSON, Jane. Ed. *Talking With African Writers.* London: James Currey, 1992.

WILLIAMS, Adebayo. "Nationalism and Post-nationalism." *Encyclopedia of African Literature.* Ed. Simon Gikandi. London: Routledge, 2005. 493-500.

WITT, Mary Ann Frese. *The Search for Modern Tragedy: Aesthetic Fascism in Italy and France.* New York: Cornell UP, 2001.

YOUNG, Robert C. *Postcolonialism: A Historical Introduction.* Oxford: Blackwell, 2001.

ZAMORA, Lois Parkinson, and Wendy B. Faris. "Introduction: Daiquiri Birds and Flaubertian Parrot(ie)s." *Magical Realism: Theory, History, Community.* Eds. Lois Parkinson Zamora and Wendy B. Faris. Durham: Duke UP, 1995. 1-11.

STUDIES IN ENGLISH LITERATURES

Edited by Koray Melikoğlu

ISSN 1614-4651

1   Özden Sözalan
    The Staged Encounter
    Contemporary Feminism and Women's Drama
    2nd, revised edition
    ISBN 3-89821-367-6

2   Paul Fox (ed.)
    Decadences
    Morality and Aesthetics in British Literature
    2nd, revised and expanded edition
    ISBN 3-89821-573-3

3   Daniel M. Shea
    James Joyce and the Mythology of Modernism
    ISBN 3-89821-574-1

4   Paul Fox and Koray Melikoğlu (eds.)
    Formal Investigations
    Aesthetic Style in Late-Victorian and Edwardian Detective Fiction
    2nd, revised and expanded edition
    ISBN 978-3-89821-593-0

5   David Ellis
    Writing Home
    Black Writing in Britain Since the War
    ISBN 978-3-89821-591-6

6   Wei H. Kao
    The Formation of an Irish Literary Canon in the Mid-Twentieth Century
    ISBN 978-3-89821-545-9

7   Bianca Del Villano
    Ghostly Alterities
    Spectrality and Contemporary Literatures in English
    2nd, revised editon
    ISBN 978-3-89821-714-9

8   Melanie Ann Hanson
    Decapitation and Disgorgement
    The Female Body's Text in Early Modern English Drama and Poetry
    ISBN 978-3-89821-605-5

9   Shafquat Towheed (ed.)
    New Readings in the Literature of British India, c.1780-1947
    ISBN 978-3-89821-673-9

10 Paola Baseotto
    "Disdeining life, desiring leaue to die"
    Spenser and the Psychology of Despair
    ISBN 978-3-89821-567-1

11 *Annie Gagiano*
    Dealing with Evils
    Essays on Writing from Africa
    2nd, revised and expanded edition
    ISBN 978-3-89821-867-2

12 *Thomas F. Halloran*
    James Joyce: Developing Irish Identity
    A Study of the Development of Postcolonial Irish Identity in the Novels of James Joyce
    ISBN 978-3-89821-571-8

13 *Pablo Armellino*
    Ob-scene Spaces in Australian Narrative
    An Account of the Socio-topographic Construction of Space in Australian Literature
    ISBN 978-3-89821-873-3

14 *Lance Weldy*
    Seeking a Felicitous Space on the Frontier
    The Progression of the Modern American Woman in O. E. Rölvaag, Laura Ingalls Wilder, and Willa Cather
    ISBN 978-3-89821-535-0

15 *Rana Tekcan*
    The Biographer and the Subject
    A Study on Biographical Distance
    ISBN 978-3-89821-995-2

16 *Paola Brusasco*
    Writing Within/Without/About Sri Lanka
    Discourses of Cartography, History and Translation in Selected Works by Michael Ondaatje and Carl Muller
    ISBN 978-3-8382-0075-0

17 *Zeynep Z. Atayurt*
    Excess and Embodiment in Contemporary Women's Writing
    ISBN 978-3-89821-978-5

18 *Gianluca Delfino*
    Time, History, and Philosophy in the Works of Wilson Harris
    ISBN 978-3-8382-0265-5

19 *Taner Can*
    Magical Realism in Postcolonial British Fiction: History, Nation, and Narration
    ISBN 978-3-8382-0724-7

Sie haben die Wahl:
Bestellen Sie die Schriftenreihe
Studies in English Literatures
einzeln oder im **Abonnement**

per E-Mail: vertrieb@ibidem-verlag.de | per Fax (0511/262 2201)
als Brief (***ibidem***-Verlag | Leuschnerstr. 40 | 30457 Hannover)

Bestellformular

☐ Ich abonniere die Schriftenreihe *Studies in English Literatures* ab Band # ____

☐ Ich bestelle die folgenden Bände der Schriftenreihe *Studies in English Literatures*
____; ____; ____; ____; ____; ____; ____; ____; ____; ____

Lieferanschrift:

Vorname, Name ....

Anschrift ....

E-Mail .... | Tel.: ....

Datum .... | Unterschrift ....

Ihre Abonnement-Vorteile im Überblick:
- Sie erhalten jedes Buch der Schriftenreihe pünktlich zum Erscheinungstermin – immer aktuell, ohne weitere Bestellung durch Sie.
- Das Abonnement ist jederzeit kündbar.
- Die Lieferung ist innerhalb Deutschlands versandkostenfrei.
- Bei Nichtgefallen können Sie jedes Buch innerhalb von 14 Tagen an uns zurücksenden.

ibidem-Verlag

Melchiorstr. 15

D-70439 Stuttgart

info@ibidem-verlag.de

www.ibidem-verlag.de
www.ibidem.eu
www.edition-noema.de
www.autorenbetreuung.de